D1116758

THE REVOLT OF
THE TENANTRY

THE REVOLT OF
THE TENANTRY:

The Transformation
of Local Government
in Ireland, 1872–1886

William L. Feingold

with a Foreword by Emmet Larkin

NORTHEASTERN UNIVERSITY PRESS   BOSTON

Designer: Janna Olson

Northeastern University Press
Copyright © 1984 by Carolyn Feingold

Library of Congress Cataloging in Publication Data

Feingold, William L., 1932–1981.
The revolt of the tenantry.

Revision of thesis (Ph.D. — University of Chicago, 1974)
presented under title: The Irish boards of poor law
guardians, 1872-86.
Bibliography: p.
Includes index.
1. Local government — Ireland — History — 19th century.
2. Peasant uprisings — Ireland — History — 19th century.
3. Peasantry — Ireland — Political activity — History —
19th century. I. Title.
JS4327.F45   1984   352.0415   84-4080
ISBN 0-930350-55-3 (alk. paper)

Composed in Janson by Eastern Typesetting Co., South Windsor,
Connecticut. Printed and bound by the Maple Press, York, Pennsyl-
vania. The paper is Warren's #66 Antique, an acid-free sheet.

MANUFACTURED IN THE UNITED STATES OF AMERICA
89 88 87 86 85 84   5   4   3   2   1

Publication of this book was made possible in part by a grant from
The American Irish Foundation.

❦❦ Contents

List of Tables

List of Illustrations

Foreword

MY GOOD FRIEND William L. Feingold died on Thanksgiving Day, 1981, after an extended illness, at the age of forty-nine. Shortly before his death, he asked me if I would assume the responsibility for the editing and publication of his recently completed manuscript. The manuscript was the revised and rewritten version of his doctoral dissertation, "The Irish Boards of Poor Law Guardians, 1872–1886: A Revolution of Local Government," submitted to the Department of History at the University of Chicago in 1974. Because of the great care with which the manuscript was revised, and the very high quality of the presentation, my task in editing this manuscript has been minimal. Indeed, my efforts have been largely confined to amending a number of passages in the text in the interests of greater clarity or smoothness. The manuscript, I am happy to say, is therefore very much the author's, which is only as it should be.

As the reader of this book will soon discover, William Feingold's death was a tragic loss to Irish historical scholarship. Not only was he a very fine scholar, as both the research and methodology in this volume attest to, but he was also deeply concerned about the art and science of history. Feingold understood that the art of history was more than good writing or felicitous phrasing. He understood that it involved architecture as well as structure, plot as well as narrative, and that the conceptualization of a problem demanded not only the ability to ask the right questions of the evidence, but the ingenuity to devise the means that would allow those questions to be answered in terms of that evidence. More than most historians, Feingold also appreciated that the art and science of a historical presentation are intimately bound up with each other, and that history without a satisfactory human dimension can only be a dessicating expe-

rience. There is, therefore, a nice mix of narrative and analysis, personalities and social forces, evidence and ideas, accident and will in this volume,
which combine to give the reader an unusually rich, rewarding, and sat-
isfying historical experience.

In his writing, however, William Feingold was not only an articulate
man, but a humble one. So much so, in fact, that perhaps even a discerning
student reading the epilogue to this volume might not fully appreciate the
originality and significance of his contribution to the understanding of
modern Irish history. In part, his originality lies in the fact that he was
the first professional historian ever to write a book about Irish local government in the nineteenth century, and in doing so he has set such a
standard and model for future Irish historians that this volume is certain
to become a classic in the genre. Feingold did not merely define the di-
mensions of Irish local government for future Irish scholars, however; he
has also reperiodized it for them, and all those conventional views on the
subject that have been propagated in the general histories for more than
half a century will now have to be fundamentally revised. A fresh assess-
ment, in fact, will have to be made of the various aspects of local government in the municipalities, poor law guardian boards, and grand juries
both in themselves and in relation to each other; that chronological wa-
tershed in Irish local government, the County Councils Act of 1898, will
have to be basically reconsidered in terms of its being a significant divide.
In a word, those who choose to take up where Feingold was forced to leave
off not only will find that they have had a large part of their work cut out
for them, but, in a very large measure, also will find that he has defined
the field for them in both space and time.

But Feingold's originality is not to be measured simply in terms of his
having been the first in the field. Through his study of local government
he has made an important contribution to our understanding of the social
and political dynamics of modern Irish history, and most particularly to
the shaping of the Irish nation-state. Perhaps this, more than anything
else, is what will give his work its enduring significance. Why the Irish
nation-state, in a century certainly not propitious to the survival of representative democracies, has remained so remarkably stable is a question
as important as it is intriguing. Feingold's answer would appear to be
twofold. First, the institutions of representative government in Ireland
have been in place longer, and at a more critical political level, than has
been generally appreciated. Second, the Irish social revolution, in which
the political and social power of the landlords as a class was broken by

their tenants in the 1880s, took place at a time and in a context that strengthened rather than impaired the vital national consensus on which the ongoing political stability of the Irish representative democracy would come to rest.

To Feingold, the establishment of the boards of guardians in the Irish Poor Relief Act of 1838 was a crucial event in the history of Irish representative institutions. From that date, all but the smallest of the tenant farming class acquired the right to vote as ratepayers for poor law guardians, and the more substantial among that class also gained the right, if elected, to sit as poor law guardians. In spite of all the various devices conceived to weight the system in favor of the interests of the landed classes, therefore, the tenants then had the means, if they had the will, to oust the landlords from power at the boards of guardians. For forty years the tenants were satisfied to serve their apprentice and journeyman stages at the boards of guardians, and in that period they learned the techniques necessary for exercising political power. They became adept at handling not only the mysteries of parliamentary procedure and Roberts' rules of order, but also the problems of administration and the exercise of authority. When, in the late 1870s and early 1880s, the tenants decided to try their hand at becoming masters of the boards, they had already acquired the experience that allowed them within a relatively short period to effect a revolution in the control of the boards everywhere in Ireland except Ulster.

When one also realizes that the total number of guardians who were Roman Catholics was about equal to the number of Roman Catholic priests in Ireland in 1880, and that they were as evenly distributed, except in Ulster, as was the clergy, the political and social significance of this rural elite becomes readily apparent. The emergence of these local worthies as a group would make it possible in time to structure grass-roots political associations that were not entirely dominated by the clergy, and that would make those who aspired to leadership at the national level more responsive to the concerns expressed at the grass-roots level. The real point of all this, of course, is that the period between the collapse of the Repeal Association in the 1840s and the rise of the Home Rule movement in the 1870s was not a political wasteland strewn with frustrated and lost opportunities, but rather a period in which an emergent rural elite of strong Roman Catholic farmers was making its contribution to the shaping of an indigenous Irish political system that would itself emerge—and with a vengeance—full-grown, in the 1880s.

The politicization of this rural elite, however, only raises the question of why they chose to revolt when they did, which is really another way of asking why that social upheaval, the land war of 1879–81, occurred when it did. Indeed, the causes of the land war, which has come to be viewed by many historians as the critical episode in the shaping of the Irish nation-state, have become a favorite subject of academic debate in the last decade. The "traditional" explanation that the real cause of the land war was the severe agricultural depression of 1877–79, which resulted in the Irish tenant farmers' taking action in order to protect themselves from a repetition of those disasters that had occurred thirty years earlier in the Great Famine—namely, mass starvation, eviction, and emigration— has given way to the argument of "rising expectations." This argument maintains that the cause of the land war was really to be found in the unprecedented prosperity enjoyed by the Irish tenant farmers in the decade prior to the onset of the agricultural depression of 1877–79; they refused to accept a reduction in their incomes or their standard of living, and attempted to shift their losses to the landlords by demanding a substantial reduction in rent. More recently, however, the argument for "rising expectations" has itself been challenged by those historians and social scientists who prefer to argue for a "mobilization thesis." They maintain that the real cause of the land war was in the emergence of a new political elite, which was itself the product of a basic change in the Irish social structure after the Famine.

Though Feingold was among the first of those who argued most persuasively for the "mobilization thesis," he argued it with a very significant difference. To Feingold, the land war of 1879–81 was only one of several critical episodes in the transfer of power from the landlords to the tenants as a class. That process had actually begun in the early 1870s, long before the beginning of the land war, and was not really completed until 1886, when the land war had been over for some five years. The social revolution, which took place in Ireland in the 1880s, therefore, was of longer duration and of greater complexity than has been generally realized; but it was a real social revolution, in which the nationalization of the boards of guardians was only its outward and visible political sign. The real power of the landlords as a class had depended on the social deference accorded them by their tenants, and by 1886 that deference—outside Ulster—was a thing of the past.

After 1886 the economic and social signs of the power and influence of this newly emerged tenant elite were unmistakable. The inability of the

landlords, for example, to stand up to the "Plan of Campaign" ot 1886–
87, in which they surrendered yet another twenty percent of their rent to
the tenants, was proof positive that their will as well as their power as a
class had been broken, and that the formal ownership of the means of
production must inevitably fall to the tenants in time. Indeed, the fact that
the tenants as a class did not generally take advantage of the Land Purchase
Acts of the late 1880s and early 1890s was yet another indication that they
knew they had won, and that the land they occupied must eventually
become theirs, and on their terms. Finally, the fact that no such social
revolution took place in Protestant Ulster merely emphasized the profound
social change that had taken place in the other three provinces. Partition,
therefore, became inevitable, and the only question of any real importance
in regard to it was of its extent. That the new nation-state would be
essentially Roman Catholic and confessional, and that it would be run in
the interests of the larger farmers as a class, was also inevitable. Indeed,
the social revolution of the 1880s was consolidated with such energy and
firmness by this new rural elite that they have remained the dominant
social, economic, and political class in Ireland almost to the present day.
For his anatomy of the boards of guardians, therefore, and especially for
his explanation of the how and why of this social revolution, Irish historians will long be in the debt of William Feingold.

The author of this book, however, has left historians of Irish history
with yet another legacy that will perhaps prove even more exciting than
his very significant contribution to knowledge. As he explained in his
epilogue, he has perhaps raised more questions than he has answered in
this book, and he has therefore left us all with a great deal to think about
and to accomplish. In concluding this foreword, therefore, and by way of
example, I should like to address myself to just two of those many questions. The first has to do with the persistence of landlord representation
in boards of guardian offices after 1886 in the three provinces of the south
and west long after the social revolution was over; the second has to do
with the role of the Roman Catholic clergy in helping to effect this social
revolution in those three provinces. In regard to the first, Feingold was
undoubtedly quite correct in pointing out that the crucial distinction is
not to be found merely in the *number* of board offices retained by the
landlords after 1886, but in the *kind* of landlord who managed to survive
in those board offices in the south and west. Telling effect is given to this
point by what happened in Ulster, where the aristocratic magnificos actually increased their representation as against the lesser gentry, thereby

endorsing with even greater emphasis the system that had been all but swept away in the south and west. Feingold was also correct when he argued that the landlords in the south and west were now board officers largely because of their standing as individuals in the community, and not, as formerly, because of the social deference accorded them as a class. What he could have further emphasized, perhaps, was that the elective and appointive modes that required the return of guardians to the boards in equal numbers in terms of those modes biased the system in favor of the landlords' being returned to board offices. The absenteeism of the appointed, or ex-officio, group weakened the landlord interest at the boards, but in the course of time the landlords must have encouraged the return of ex-officios who would be able to attend; that, in addition to pressure from the tenants, would have tended to prevent the ex-officio guardians, magnificos who had a greater tendency to be absentees, from taking up their positions at the boards. Furthermore, in any area where there was a substantial Protestant strong farmer class, such as Carlow, Queens, or Kildare Counties, the elected element among the guardians would be correspondingly weakened, and the ability of the landlords to sustain themselves in the board offices would be strengthened. In other words, the limited representative nature of the system created a strong political disposition in favor of the landlords as a class, and the triumph of the tenants was not only all the more remarkable, therefore, but all the more significant.

Finally, because so little work has been done on the political role of the Roman Catholic clergy at the local level in the period between 1850 and 1880, Feingold was not able to say very much about their influence in regard to the nomination and election of guardians. He did point out, however, that there appeared to be a correlation between the very pronounced area in Tipperary where the boards were all radicalized early (that is, all three board officers were tenants), and the fact that this area fell within the spiritual jurisdiction of the archbishop of Cashel, T. W. Croke, who had very decided Land League and Nationalist sympathies. I would be prepared to go even further, and maintain that the three areas with the most pronounced disposition towards radicalism early on (that is, north Munster, including Tipperary, Limerick, and east Clare; western Connaught, including Mayo and west Galway; and north Leinster, including Meath, Westmeath, Kings, and Longford) were all areas where the clergy had long been highly politicized and were prone to assume a very active role in both national and local politics between 1850 and 1880. Moreover, these were all areas in which the very considerable influence of

Paul Cullen, the archbishop of Dublin, was minimal, at least as far as politics were concerned, among those bishops who exercised spiritual jurisdiction in those areas. But whatever may be determined about the political role of the clergy at the local level in those areas, it was Feingold who has provided us with the basic framework in time and space that will allow for its historical examination.

In conclusion, I should like to take this opportunity not only to take my last leave of my good friend William Feingold, but also to pay my respects to his wife, Carolyn, whose patience in the preparation of this book for publication has been exceeded only by her understanding.

EMMET LARKIN

The University of Chicago
July, 1983

Preface

THIS BOOK FOCUSES upon two areas of historical inquiry that have not received the attention they deserve from scholars. The first is local government in nineteenth-century Ireland, a subject that frequently concerned contemporaries and generated a massive amount of parliamentary legislation and inquiry, but which for some reason has been treated only rarely in the historical literature. The second is Irish local politics in the nineteenth century, particularly the politics associated with the numerous movements of popular protest that emerged during the century. To be sure, historians have become aware of the importance of local influences on the shape and substance of these movements and in the past decade have begun to scrutinize these influences much more closely than had earlier generations of scholars, who tended to focus on the more dramatic events and personalities at the summit of the movements. Nevertheless, much more work needs to be done before we can begin to understand the causes and mechanics of popular protest as it was practiced in nineteenth-century Ireland.

This volume does not pretend to constitute a comprehensive investigation into either of these subjects. Although its generalizations are intended to apply to all of Ireland, or regions of it. only a relatively narrow period, the years 1872–86, is covered; only one branch of local government, the Irish poor law administration, is treated in depth; and the discussion of popular agitation is confined essentially to the single topic of local government control and matters related to it.

Nevertheless, the events and issues discussed within these boundaries were so closely tied to the broader questions that shaped the Irish political and social milieu in the second half of the nineteenth century that it is

possible to extract from them insights into many of the more general political and social developments of the age. The years 1872–86 were a pivotal
period in the politicization of the Irish masses. They were the years when
the issues of land reform and Irish national independence converged to
form the basis of the two most successful movements of popular protest
of the century: the Land League and the Home Rule movement. Central
to the land reform issue was the long-enduring struggle between the landlord class and the tenantry for control of the soil. The national struggle
was directed against British rule.

When applied at the local level, however, these two issues become one,
for the simple reason that at that level the most immediate manifestation
of British rule was in the local government structure that administered
Parliament's laws, and control of that structure was traditionally the preserve of the landlord class. Thus, it was possible for tenant partisans to
argue cogently that the landlord was both rack-renter and colonial despot,
occupying seats in government that rightfully belonged to the native,
meaning tenant, class. Indeed, the local nationalist partisans did make that
argument, and during that period attempted to oust landlords from their
seats in local government wherever such ejection was possible. That possibility existed, of course, only in those local bodies with an elected
membership.

And that is where the poor law administration came into the picture.
For, among the various boards and agencies that constituted the Irish local
administration in the nineteenth century, only two—the municipal and
town authorities and the boards of guardians, which administered the poor
law—contained elected elements; and of these two, only the boards of
guardians operated in the rural districts, where landlord power was most
keenly felt and vigorously challenged.

The inevitable confrontation between landlords and tenants for control
of the boards, which was inherent in these conditions, forms the central
theme of this study. Its central objectives are to discover how power was
exercised in Irish local government and who exercised it, in what ways
the power relationships changed as a result of the struggle, and what
connections existed between the official local politics and partisan politics
outside the boards.

In the research and writing of this book I received invaluable assistance
from many people and organizations to whom I now offer thanks. Emmet
Larkin, my mentor while I was a student at the University of Chicago,

first guided me into this fruitful field of study and provided valuable commentary and criticism for the doctoral dissertation on which this book is based. He and my other two readers, William H. McNeill and Charles Gray, must be credited for the thoroughness and conscientiousness they brought to their task. Two long-time friends and colleagues, Samuel D. Clark and James S. Donnelly, devoted hours of intensive discussion with me over points of evidence and interpretation, and copyedited a portion of the manuscript. Their comments helped lend focus to a seemingly chaotic mass of data.

Assistance for specific portions of the study was given by Maurice O'Connell, who supplied data for the Tralee election analysis that would have been impossible to obtain through published sources, and Sile Daly of Dublin, granddaughter of James Daly, who, with her family in Castlebar, provided insights into the character of their fiery Land League ancestor. My travails in Dublin were eased considerably by the always congenial and helpful staffs of the National Library, Trinity College Library, University College—Dublin Library, State Paper Office, and General Valuation Office. The last in particular amiably put up with my proddings almost daily over the course of a year.

I am deeply indebted to the Ford Foundation for providing a fellowship which made the initial overseas research possible; to the American Council of Learned Societies for a grant-in-aid to do follow-up research; and to Richard D. Winchell, president of Bellevue College, for providing assistance for the typing of the final manuscript. And a special vote of thanks is reserved for my wife, Carolyn, who deferred her own career aspirations to give me time for research and writing, and whose support in so many intangible ways has kept me on course over the years.

Bellevue, Nebraska   W. F.
June 10, 1981

◈◈ Introduction

For more than eighty years in the history of Ireland—the period between the Irish Poor Relief Act of 1838 and its dissolution in the early years of the Free State—the initials "P.L.G." affixed after an Irishman's name signified for both the holder and his peers a certain mark of achievement. The reason for this was that the title for which the initials stood, Poor Law Guardian, was, for the first sixty years of the period—before the so-called County Councils Act of 1898 created the more distinguished "C.C."— the only public title to which most rural Irish countrymen could aspire. The countryman could, if he lived in a town, possibly win election to the town council or town commission and gain the right to use the "T.C." when fixing his name to correspondence or public documents. Or, if he was well-connected, financially independent, and knowledgeable in the ways of high-level politics, he might contest a parliamentary constituency and become one of the hundred Irishmen sporting the distinguished "M.P." The "J.P." (Justice of the Peace), "H.S." (High Sheriff), and "D.L." (Deputy Lieutenant) were also possibilities, but only if he owned property, held a noble or gentle title, or had connections among the property-owning classes. These offices of county government were the preserve of the wealthy and well-born. But for the simple Irish farmer or shopkeeper who lived outside the town or city and who wished to make a name for himself in public affairs, only one reasonable opportunity existed in the nineteenth century—to win election to the local board of guardians.

The boards of guardians are most familiar to students of Irish history as the bodies that administered the Irish Poor Relief Act of 1838, the well-known "Irish poor law," which introduced the unfamiliar and despised "workhouse test" principle to Irish poor relief practices. Imported from

England (where the principle had been implemented, with some success, as the "new poor law" of 1834), the law required that able-bodied paupers seeking relief be made to enter a workhouse to "test" the sincerity of their claims of inability to gain subsistence through wage-paying labor. The workhouse experience—made deliberately confining, laborious, and humiliating—became for many Irishmen and their families the only alternative to starvation, and that alternative became for the Irish people yet another grievance against the British government. The boards of guardians were established as part of the poor law administration, one board for each of the 130 newly established poor law unions, and were granted the power to levy and expend taxes for the construction and maintenance of the workhouse system.

In recent years additional light has been thrown upon the administrative aspects of the boards of guardians' operations. Yet the body of research is even here relatively small. T. P. O'Neill's article in *The Great Famine* and Cecil Woodham-Smith's *Great Hunger* both discuss boards of guardians' activities during the famine period. R. B. McDowell's *Irish Administration, 1801–1914* traces the development of the boards from their original role as purely relief-giving bodies to their ultimate role as bodies responsible for the local administration of every new program relating to health and welfare enacted by Parliament during the last half of the nineteenth century. However, in all the works mentioned, the boards are only an incidental part of a larger study devoted to other events and developments. Of all secondary studies to date, only Sir George Nicholls's *History of the Irish Poor Law* covers the boards of guardians in depth, and that study, published in 1856 as a justification of Nicholls's role in creating the Irish poor law, is of little value to historians wishing to know about the boards after their initiation during the Great Famine.

Virtually nothing has been written about the other great role the boards fulfilled in the nineteenth century—their role as local representative institutions. Perhaps because they have always been thought of as administrative bodies, and because it has always been assumed that representative government did not come to the Irish localities until the creation of the elective county councils in 1898, the fact that poor law guardians were elected to their offices appears to have escaped the notice of scholars. It is true that the boards were not purely representative. Half their membership (before 1847, three-fourths) were elected by the ratepayers of the unions under a liberal franchise; the other half (before 1847, one-fourth) were appointed from among the union's justices of the peace sitting as ex-officio members. This arrangement, however, makes the boards an even more desirable subject for political study, because the recruitment provisions insured that the elected guardians and the ex-officios would represent the two great social classes who in Ireland were involved in continual conflict throughout the last half of the nineteenth century—the tenant-occupiers and the landlords.

The dispute between the two groups was not purely economic. Land tenure was, to be sure, one of the leading issues. The Irish system of land tenure before the great reforms of 1881–1903 was entirely biased towards the landlords. Tenants had no permanent legal claim to their holdings, and many could be evicted at will by the landlords. They could not sell their right to occupancy to other tenants; therefore, any improvements they made in their holdings reverted to the landlord upon vacancy. Rents were fixed by the landlord at rates that were unjustly high (so the tenants believed). The evils of the system were brought home to the tenantry with devastating force during and after the Great Famine of 1847, when the smaller tenants, unable to pay their rents, were evicted by the millions and left to perish in roadside ditches or migrate to the towns or to America, where they entered the ranks of the landless proletariat. Immediately after the Famine, tenant organizations devoted to land reform began to spring up in many localities, and by the early 1850s the Tenant-Right movement had begun to make its force felt in parliamentary politics. The landlords, of course, were on the other side.

But there was a second great issue that absorbed the attention of the Irish people throughout the last three-quarters of the century and which eventually became part of the landlord-tenant struggle. This was the issue of Irish national independence, which found its focus in the Act of Union of 1800. The Act of Union abolished the ancient Irish Parliament and transferred the government of Ireland to the British Parliament acting through its Irish administration. Ireland was granted representation in Parliament, but the 100 Irish members were only a small, ineffectual minority, completely outnumbered by the 558 British representatives. With the Act of Union the British had hoped to absorb a troublesome and rebellious legislature into a larger body, where they would be powerless to assert their will against British policy.

Beginning with Daniel O'Connell in the 1830s, Irish discontent with the act began to appear for the first time on a large scale. O'Connell's vast movement for Catholic emancipation in the 1820s had been built upon the shoulders of the Catholic peasants in conjunction with the Catholic priesthood. In the next decade he used essentially the same power base to establish a movement for repeal of the Act of Union, which had the effect of identifying Catholic rights with Irish national rights. O'Connell was challenged by Young Ireland, a movement of intellectuals who found O'Connell's constitutional methods too moderate and his emphasis on Catholicism too confining. For the Young Irelanders the distinction between Irish patriotism and West Britonism was founded not on religion but on race. The struggle between Britain and Ireland was a struggle between Gaels and Anglo-Saxons, not Catholics and Protestants. The Young Ireland movement ended in 1848 in an aborted uprising, but not before they had provided Irish nationalism with a cultural dimension; in the late 1850s the Irish Republican Brotherhood used their ideas to found the Fenian movement, dedicated to the creation of an Irish republic.

These issues—religion, nationalism, and property rights—were not intrinsically interdependent issues; nevertheless, the structure of Irish society made it inevitable that they would eventually be identified as variations of a single question. Most of the landlords of Ireland were members of the class known as the "Protestant Ascendancy," descendants of the English invaders who had confiscated Irish land and virtually enserfed its population. Not only were they the principal landowners in the country, they were also mostly Protestant and mostly of Anglo-Saxon stock. The tenantry, on the other hand, were the tillers of the soil but not the owners, and outside the Protestant plantation region in Ulster they were mostly Catholic and Gaelic. It did not require too great a mental adjustment for tenants to begin to recognize a community of interests on all the issues, and in a sense the history of nineteenth-century Ireland might be viewed as the evolution of this common identification. When in 1879 Michael Davitt, John Devoy, and Charles Stewart Parnell proposed that a movement be founded to fight for both land reform and Irish self-government, the Irish tenantry, having been exposed to a half-century of opposition to landlords on both questions, easily made the connection and followed the three leaders into battle.

It will be seen, therefore, that the existence of two groups of men confined within a single boardroom, one representing the Irish tenantry, the other the landlords, was potentially explosive. The great social and political conflicts were bound eventually to find their way into the proceedings of the guardians with untold consequences for the relationship between the two elements. Because the boards, moreover, possessed legal powers to raise and expend funds, to issue contracts, and to choose their own leaders, it was inevitable that the dispute over issues would eventually become a struggle for power. It is in this connection that a study of the boards of guardians is most profitable. The boards of guardians afford the researcher a unique opportunity to study the political conflicts of nineteenth-century Ireland under somewhat controlled conditions. There were boards of guardians in every part of the country, all operating under the same legal conditions, all meeting regularly in weekly sessions, the proceedings of most, many of which have survived, being recorded in minute books or press reports. The contestants on both sides were numerically matched, and recruitment was the same for all boards of guardians. Starting from this point of constitutional uniformity, it may be possible to isolate differences and identify similarities in the politics of different boards at given points and over time, and to draw from these observations conclusions about the character of local politics in Ireland. Much work has been done on the national movements of the time, but little is known about the patterns of local political activity. I hope that the present study will shed some light on this neglected aspect of Irish history.

The chronological limits of the study (1872–86) are not intended as the strict limits of the local government revolution that will be described. As with most broad political developments, the revolution had its origins in earlier developments and may have continued on in some places after the major thrust had ended in most other places. The difficulty in obtaining information about boards of guardians in obscure parts of the country makes it impossible to fix definite limits, or, for that matter, to make generalizations about local politics, even during the period under survey, that would apply to every locality. The opening date, 1872, was settled on because the Local Government Act of that year, which converted the poor law administration from a relief institution to a recognized branch of local government, happened to coincide with incidents on two boards of guardians that appeared to foreshadow the struggle to come. The terminating date, 1886, was chosen for methodological reasons which will be explained in the text, but it was probably also the last year of any major conflict between the elected and ex-officio guardians. The reader may have noticed that these years coincide roughly with the Home Rule movement, which began in 1870 and developed, first under Isaac Butt, then under Parnell, into an effective organization which almost brought about the realization of a separate Irish parliament in the abortive Home Rule bill of 1886. This is not just coincidence, for the Home Rule struggle played a central role in the revolution in local government. But a second major event that occurred during these years—the land war of 1879–81—also played its part, and it will be one of my objectives to assess the influence of each movement on the revolution in local government. My major objectives will be to demonstrate that the revolution occurred and describe its course, to explain why it was possible and why it occurred, and to understand its significance in terms of changing power relationships in Irish society.

As a footnote, it should also be explained that the term adopted in the text to describe the tenants' assault on the poor law boards, board "nationalization," was taken from the contemporary press. *Nationalization* today connotes socialism, or the bringing of institutions under central government control. To Irish nationalists of the nineteenth century it had an almost opposite meaning: a localization of control in the hands of nationalist partisans. I apologize for any confusion that might arise from this usage, but it seems more appropriate to use the language of the people themselves, than to risk sacrificing authenticity to expediency by artificially imposing a more neutral term.

THE REVOLT OF
THE TENANTRY

Prologue:
The Fortnight of the Prophet

ON SATURDAY, May 18, 1872, the guardians of the Roscommon poor law union convened in the workhouse boardroom to conduct the weekly business meeting. Twenty-three guardians were present—about three times the number who normally attended.[1] Fifteen were elected guardians; the remaining eight were ex-officios. Lord Crofton,[2] the chairman of the board, presided, making his first appearance at the board since his reelection seven weeks earlier as chairman for the second consecutive year. The board's two other officers—Vice-Chairman B. W. Bagot, J.P., an ex-officio member, and Deputy Vice-Chairman John Shiel, an elected member—were also present. Lord Crofton sounded the gavel and convened the meeting.

The first matters taken up by the board concerned routine business: a letter from the Poor Law Commissioners advising the guardians of a change in auditors; a letter from the registrar general saying that his inspector had found the door of the workhouse strong closet difficult to open and close; some tenders for the supply of turf with prices varying from 1s to 1s 2d per box; a question from one of the members as to why the Roscommon union should not follow the example of the Boyle union and purchase Irish coal rather than English coal, since the former was cheaper; and a notification from the union clerk that £320 of the poor rate remained uncollected. The guardians accomplished this business speedily and turned to the next question—a proposed resolution in support of Home Rule.

The board had been given notice of the resolution two weeks earlier by its proponent, Alexander O'Connor Eccles, who held an elected seat on the board. The resolution read:

> That believing that the best interests not only of Ireland but of the United
> Kingdom are involved in a speedy settlement of the question of Home Rule

3

for Ireland, in accordance with the wishes of her people . . . we consider that it is all important at the present juncture that the popular will should be unmistakably and unanimously expressed, and that the Boards of Guardians, the principal representative bodies at present in the country, are the best and most efficacious medium through which the national wish can be conveyed, we hereby record it as the opinion of the board, representing the feelings and wishes of the inhabitants of the Roscommon union, that it is right and just that the people of Ireland should have sole and supreme control in the management of her internal affairs.[3]

Eccles raised his hand to move the resolution, but Lord Crofton intervened, noting that the next order of business was a motion in favor of Home Rule and begging the board to permit him a few words on the subject. "I don't often inflict a speech on you," he told the members, "nor shall I do so today. It is my opinion—and one that is, I believe, shared by many in the room—that being assembled for the *sole* purpose of transacting business connected with the poor relief, nothing is more out of place or inopportune than the discussion of political subjects [hear, hear]." He continued, "I remember last year, on the occasion of my election as chairman, being struck by the remark of a gentleman present, that every guardian on entering this room, ought to hang up his politics with his hat. I think it is much to be regretted that this good advice has not been more closely followed, and that now the hat and the politics have parted company—the hat hangs peacefully on the wall—the politics accompany the would-be politician to the table [hear]." Then, addressing himself to the question at hand: "On the merits or the demerits of the question I do not propose to enter. I care not whether the subject be Home Rule or Foreign Rule—whether the questions advanced emanate from Whig or Tory—I take my stand solely on the ground that a board room is not a fit place to discuss and ventilate subjects of a political nature. On these grounds," he concluded, "I refuse to receive the proposed or any similar motion, but not wishing to take the entire responsibility on myself, I intend to poll the board whether or not they wish to receive Mr. Eccles' motion. Further I wish to say, that in the event of a majority against me, I will immediately place my resignation in your hands [applause]."

The chairman's speech apparently took the members by surprise. Eccles rose to his feet, begging for time to reply, but the chairman refused, saying that any other business beyond a poll of the board was out of order. Within moments the entire board room was in disarray, some members pleading with Lord Crofton to permit Eccles to be heard, others pleading with

Eccles to retire. But the chairman refused to yield, and Eccles finally agreed to the poll, remarking, "This is the first time any board of guardians has been forced to choose between Home Rule and its Chairman." In the poll the board chose Home Rule, but the margin was not convincing. Twelve of the guardians voted to receive the motion; eleven voted not to receive; all eight ex-officios had voted in the negative.[4]

Lord Crofton rose, submitted his resignation and left the room, muttering that he thought he had been elected chairman of a board of guardians, not "a Board of Politicians." The initiative then fell to B. W. Bagot, the vice-chairman, who was next in succession for the chair. Bagot voiced his dissatisfaction with what had happened and warned the members to hesitate before they placed the board in a position they might later regret. However, his position on the resolution was the same as Lord Crofton's. There was an organization in town, he noted, which went by the "high-sounding" and "euphonious" title of the Roscommon Home Rule Association, "at whose meetings gentlemen who loved political debating could air their elocution to their heart's content." Why then, he asked, was there a need to disturb the harmony of the board of guardians, and what, after all, was the opinion of such a "hole in the corner" meeting worth, or what influence "could it be supposed by any sensible man to exercise?" With the question unanswered, he also tendered his resignation and departed, leaving John Shiel, the deputy vice-chairman, to deal with the perplexing situation. Shiel, who had voted against the introduction of the resolution, had nothing to add, and he simply declared the meeting adjourned and took his leave. The remaining ex-officios and their supporters followed closely behind.

The remaining members, who were all now Home Rulers, held a brief conference in which they decided that the meeting was not adjourned, since Shiel did not have the legal power to adjourn a meeting without a show of hands, and they proceeded to elect a new chairman. The man they chose, Thomas A. P. Mapother, was a justice of the peace but not an ex-officio member. He was one of the few magistrates in Ireland to hold an elected seat on a board of guardians. A landowner and a member of an old Catholic family in Roscommon, Mapother had been an active advocate of tenants' rights during the 1850s and 1860s, when all other landowners in the region had opposed them. His own tenants' rents were fixed at a level below Griffith's valuation, which made him an anomaly among Irish landlords.[5] As Mapother took over the chair, the significance of the event gripped the members in the room. "The day's proceedings are extraordinary," one of them observed, "when we have the pleasure of seeing as our Chairman a Catholic magistrate and a member of the Home Rule Association." "It would appear," added a second, "as if the finger of providence was guiding our proceedings." A third chimed in gleefully, "And he is the only right blood to be in it—a descendant of the old Kings of Ireland!"[6]

During the two weeks following the eventful meeting, the nationalists' coup became the subject of great controversy in the Roscommon union. Opposition to Eccles's action was voiced not by conservatives alone but also by other nationalists, and the controversy raged in the two Roscommon newspapers, the *Roscommon Journal* and the *Roscommon Weekly Messenger*. The publisher of the *Messenger* was none other than Eccles himself; the publisher of the *Journal*, William Tully, was also a nationalist and a member of the Roscommon town council. The rival publishers had been instrumental in founding the Roscommon Home Rule Association only six weeks earlier, and both were members of its executive committee.[7] But the two men held completely different views about the nature of politics and what was proper and improper action for the nationalists to take. A few days after Lord Crofton's resignation, Colonel Edward Chichester, an ex-officio who had been present at the meeting, wrote Eccles a letter, which Eccles published in the *Messenger*, charging Eccles with conjuring up the entire incident to glorify his own position among the nationalists on the board and in the Home Rule Association. Indeed, he depicted the association as Eccles's own creature, a "Temple of Idolatry in which you [Eccles] personate the Golden calf." The Home Rule resolution, he charged, was not an expression of the desires of all Roscommon nationalists, for many of those who voted for it did so in response to "pressures" placed on them by Eccles; and many, he added, "complain in private of their bondage." The nationalist victory, he added further, was not a victory of substance but one of fortuitous circumstances—"a piece of undeserved luck" arising from the "impulsive disgust of our Chairman at finding himself . . . the unwilling President of a political meeting." He concluded with an appeal to the nationalists not to place Eccles in the "Chair of Moses," but rather to "leave business men and friendly men to transact business in a friendly manner."[8]

Tully agreed with Colonel Chichester about the inadvisability of Eccles's resolution, but for quite different reasons. His concern was not for the disruption created at the board, but for the impression that others outside the nationalist organization might gain about the Home Rule movement from the defiant activities of the nationalist guardians. He had expressed this concern even before the meeting, in an editorial written two weeks earlier, after Eccles had given the board notice of his motion. After pointing out that the Home Rule resolution had never been presented to the association for consideration, Tully wrote: "The time will come to pour into Parliament petition after petition—when our best men have come to the front (and but few of them have taken their places as yet)—then will be the time for every effort to be made, and we must not be too scrupulously nice." He warned, "But that time has not come yet. We do not see the point in flaunting in the face of everyone an opinion on which many avowedly have not as yet made up their minds, and many of whom may yet be with us if not irritated by needless offensive action just now."[9]

In holding this opinion Tully was not alone among the Roscommon nationalists. A few of the association's members—at least a majority of them if Tully is to be believed—held Tully's evolutionary views on the question. The remainder, however, supported Eccles's more militant and activist position, which advocated immediate action not just against the ex-officios but against "landlordism" in all of its trappings. One activist guardian even went so far as to suggest at the May 18 meeting that landholdings of over 1,000 acres be "split up" into smaller holdings and distributed among the rent-paying tenants of Ireland. Such "radical" suggestions as these Tully considered to be absurd and therefore positively dangerous to the cause of Home Rule. In commenting in the *Journal* on this suggestion Tully observed that "one gentleman, who expressed a preference for radicalism, which happily has nothing to do with Home Rule, and which is, in fact, somewhat antagonistic to it, wanted 1,000 acre farms split up into smaller ones, but he did not seem to see how the same rule applied to his own case as a 100-acre farmer."[10]

Cautious as he was, Tully found little cause for celebration in the events of May 18. The unnecessary humiliation of the ex-officios, he believed, agreeing with Colonel Chichester, had been the product not of any sincere feelings on the part of the nationalists about Home Rule, but of the self-seeking character of one man—Alexander Eccles. Tracing the events leading up to the meeting, he pointed out to his readers that Eccles's giving notice of a motion on May 4 had been unauthorized and done without the knowledge and consent of the executive committee of the association; that Eccles had had ample opportunity to consult the committee at a meeting they had held only two days earlier; and therefore that Eccles must bear the sole responsibility for an action which, as time would tell, would prove damaging to the prospects of the association. And in another column on the same page of the *Journal*, he described the events of May 18 and Eccles's part in them in language that revealed his agreement with Chichester's view of Eccles as a man with messianic pretensions.

> Chairman, Vice-Chairman, and Deputy Vice-Chairman fled in dismay before the inspired Prophet and his devoted band of followers. They numbered eleven, and he was the twelfth, and as narrated of Peter in the Acts:
>
> 14 He stood up before the eleven, and lifted up his voice and said, ye men of Roscommon, hearken to my voice.
> 42 And fear came upon every soul and many wonders and signs were done.
> 44 And all that believed were together and had all things in common.
> 45 And sold their possessions and goods and parted them to all men (yes, even hundred acre farms) as every man has need. [11]

Eccles, not one to be publicly criticized without responding, defended his position, pointing out in the next edition of his own paper that he had called a public meeting prior to the board meeting of May 18 to "seek affirmation directly from the people" and had been given a unanimous vote of confidence. He closed with a denunciation of Tully as a creature of the landlord class, and of Colonel Chichester as a "Cawtholic" pretender. [12] And at the next meeting of the association's executive committee he brought charges against Tully as a man who "has done all in his power to injure the Home Rule movement," demanding in consequence that Tully be removed from the executive committee. Tully, present at the meeting, levelled a similar countercharge and urged that the same action be taken against Eccles. [13] In the end, the quarrel was mediated and neither man was forced to resign. But the fundamental division over tactics continued to exist and to sap the strength of the nationalist organization for seventeen months more, when Tully, in November 1873, finally admitted that a "reconsideration" of his former position on political activities of the boards of guardians was in order. [14]

While the nationalists aired their private grievances and personal antagonisms, the ex-officios busily organized their own forces for a counterattack upon the board offices. The day following Lord Crofton's resignation, Colonel Chichester wrote a letter to the Local Government Board describing the events of the meeting and asking that the board order a new election of board officers. A letter from the Local Government Board ordering an "immediate" election was read at the following meeting of the guardians (May 25), and an election was called for the following week (June 1).[15] During the two-week interval, the ex-officios set out to rally support from conservative members who had not attended the earlier meeting. Their efforts met with success: three additional ex-officios and four conservative elected guardians attended the June 1 meeting, some of them such infrequent attenders that their entry into the board room caused Mapother to remark that the room that day was "ornamented by the presence of some guardians who have not shown themselves here within my experience before." The new additions raised the conservatives' strength to fifteen, which was more than they needed to recapture the offices. Colonel Chichester, the new candidate for chairman (Lord Crofton had refused to reconsider his resignation), was elected by a margin of five votes, one of the nationalists having defected at the last moment to the conservative side. John Shiel was raised to the vice-chairmanship (Bagot had also refused to reconsider), and another ex-officio, Henry Smyth, J.P., was elected deputy vice-chairman.[16]

This ended for the time being the bid of the Roscommon nationalists for control of the board of guardians. The struggle had been fought throughout by both sides on political principles—the right of Ireland to self-government, and the right of guardians to discuss political subjects. But at the very end of the election meeting, after Colonel Chichester had been installed as chairman, B. W. Bagot, the ex-vice-chairman, submitted a resolution barring political discussions at all future board meetings, which he prefaced with a statement that revealed another dimension of the conflict having nothing to do with politics but a great deal to do with the social differences of the contestants:

> This new doctrine [that the boards of guardians are representative bodies] is setting class against class; it contrasts the ex-officio guardians with the elected guardians, and attempts to shew that the interests of the former are opposed to those of the latter. The Legislature in its wisdom had appointed the ex-officio guardians, who are generally gentlemen of education and intelligence in the Union and owners of four-fifths or three-fourths of the property in the country, and pay more than half the rates. They are appointed by Act of Parliament, and although the elected guardians could not claim this title, yet
> A man was a man for a' that,
> and in this room every guardian gets credit only in proportion as his personal character and education give weight to his words.[17]

As soon as Bagot finished, Eccles rose to his feet to challenge his remarks, but Bagot quickly withdrew his motion barring political discussion, and the chairman ruled Eccles out of order. Eccles tried again to be heard, but Chichester, now with a majority at his back, sounded the gavel and adjourned the meeting.

1

Poor Law Politics and "Landlordism" in the 1870s

LANDLORDISM was the term used by political agitators in Ireland during the last quarter of the nineteenth century to describe the framework of aristocratic privilege and landlord ascendancy that governed Irish social and economic relationships prior to the land war and the legal reforms that war set in motion. In its most commonly applied form landlordism was, for the tenants, the symbol and expression of social injustice resting on a land tenure system that permitted the exaction of high rents without providing security of tenure. To many, such as Michael Davitt who employed the opprobrious term more advantageously than anyone, it meant "the menace of eviction, the dark, dread shadow which almost always loomed over three or four hundred thousand households." It meant also for Davitt the tyranny of foreign rule, which supported the land system with laws enforced by coercion.[1] Used in its broadest context, therefore, landlordism applied to the whole complex of privileges—social, economic, and political—that enabled the Irish landowner to monopolize the institutions of government, the benches of justice, the manor houses, the hunting grounds, and all other symbols of class ascendancy.

When applied politically in a local context, landlordism signified the aristocratic domination of the institutions of local government. Supported by appointment procedures, which were hedged round with property qualifications, legal strictures, and numerous informal safeguards, the aristocracy before 1880 monopolized or dictated the composition of virtually all public offices in Ireland except for the few parliamentary constituencies and the elective seats on municipal corporations. They or their sons filled most of the important administrative posts in the national government, most of the commissions of the peace and seats on grand juries, and most of the higher county offices—the lieutenancies, deputy-lieutenancies, and high sheriffs' posts. They had virtual power of appointment, either as the legal appointing authority or through their great influence among those who did the appointing, in all offices of any consequence. The seats on grand juries and baronial presentment sessions and the magistracies in the counties, therefore, which were not occupied personally by the aristocracy and gentry, were almost always filled by small landowners, by their land agents, or more rarely, by tenants whom they considered trustworthy. This political monopoly, which in rural Ireland was essentially complete, was considered by the tenantry to be simply the fruit of landlordism.

In the midst of this framework of aristocratic domination, however, there was one local government institution extending into rural Ireland in which the power of the great landowners was limited. This was the poor law administration, represented in the Irish localities by the boards of guardians. The boards had been created in 1838 as the administrative arm of the Irish poor law, which had introduced the first poor relief system to Ireland. Patterned with only minor modifications on the English "new poor law" of 1834, the Irish poor law contained the principle of the work-house test, which in England had been devised to discourage idlers and loafers from applying for the dole. Although the workhouse test was some-what more feasible in England, where industrialization and economic expansion provided at least seasonal employment for most of those seeking it, in economically backward Ireland it was disastrous. No sooner had the Poor Law Commissioners announced their "preparedness" in 1845, than famine struck. Families held out as long as they could, and then found their way into the workhouses, which soon became filled to capacity, while the helpless boards of guardians turned away pathetic hordes to die in roadside ditches. Because there was less agricultural production there was less income, and therefore little money for poor rates, so the boards turned out many of those who had been fortunate enough to find refuge in the work-house, and thousands of others perished. It would be foolish to hold the Irish poor law responsible for the million deaths that occurred during the Great Famine of the forties; still, the Famine was proof enough of the folly as well as the insensitivity of Parliament, in trying to apply the workhouse test in a country such as Ireland.[2]

The Great Famine had a beneficial effect on the boards of guardians in one respect: by confronting them with a condition of continual crisis so soon after their establishment, it forced them to learn the ways and means of administration much more quickly than they might have done otherwise. They emerged from the Famine as an efficient, well-coordinated administrative network, to which Parliament subsequently assigned numerous functions not directly related to poor relief, and often far afield from it. In 1848 they were given the responsibility of assisting evicted tenants to emigrate; the Medical Charities Act of 1851 charged them with administering the local dispensaries; and other acts made them responsible for such duties as apprenticing workhouse boys to the navy and merchant marine, placing illegitimate and orphaned children with foster parents, inspecting sanitary conditions in the union and arranging for the construction of water lines and sewers, inspecting sanitary conditions in bakehouses and workshops, providing lists of names of persons eligible for jury duty and for the parliamentary franchise, and such other diverse functions as dog catching and cattle inspection and vaccination.[3]

Many of these assignments required additional staff, and additional staff meant higher expenditures. Such projects as sewer construction and water inspection required subcontracting, which further increased expenditures. In 1870, the boards of guardians were responsible for the disbursal of £668,202, which was about £200,000 more than ten years earlier and £300,000 *less* than ten years subsequently.[4] But the assignment of contracts and the hiring of personnel also meant an increase in the amount of patronage at the disposal of the guardians. By 1870, therefore, the boards of guardians were generally recognized as not only administrators of relief, but as a full-fledged local government institution sharing local administration with the grand juries in the countryside and with the municipal and town authorities in the urban areas. The 1872 Local Government Act, which converted the Poor Law Commission into the Local Government Board and assigned it the responsibility for overseeing all local government in Ireland, merely confirmed legally what had already become a fact.

The manner in which the boards of guardians were structured made it difficult for landowners to exercise the same kind of influence they exercised over the membership of other local government authorities. The county authorities—the grand juries, presentment sessions, and commissions of the peace—were all appointive. Appointment to the grand juries, which were the principal fiscal authorities of the county, required ownership of land worth at least £50, which immediately excluded tenants. Grand jury appointments were made, moreover, by the high sheriff who consulted with the local gentry, so that even qualifying landowners had to pass an informal barrier. Presentment sessions did not require property ownership, but the members were picked by the grand jury from lists made up of the hundred highest cesspayers in the barony, and every justice of the peace in the county had the right to sit at will as a voting member of the presentment sessions. Even so, these sessions carried much less power than the grand juries. Their function was to draw up proposals for local projects to be presented to the grand juries for approval and funding. Only the grand juries could tax. Property qualifications also were unnecessary for seats on the Commission of the Peace. But since appointments were made by the Privy Council after nominations by the county lieutenant and lord lieutenant of Ireland, seats on the Commission of the Peace were virtually assured for the local gentry or their nominees.[5]

Each board of guardians, however, contained an elected element subject to modest landholding requirements—ownership not being one of the requirements—and elected by the ratepayers under a wide franchise that covered all but the laboring, artisan, and subsistence farmer classes. Landowners, in addition to being granted the franchise, were given separate representation on the boards in the form of an ex-officio element composed of justices of the peace. These special privileges, and others that will be mentioned shortly, undoubtedly provided the landowners with an advantage over the tenantry in influencing the proceedings of the boards, but there was still the elected element which, legally, at least, was beyond the power of the landowners to control, except as voters. But elections notwithstanding, the landowners—or, as they were called at the time, the "landed interest"—controlled the membership of the boards of guardians in the 1870s every bit as thoroughly as they controlled the county and dominated the national offices. This situation had not been anticipated by the founders of the Irish poor law, who had incorporated the elected element as it had been incorporated in the English system precisely because it guaranteed a voice for the ratepayers. And to insure further against landowners' control of the boards' proceedings, there were certain limitations on the ex-officio membership, which had not been included in the English law. The founders had sought to achieve a system in which the tenants' and landowners' power would balance each other and theoretically, through continual contact between the two groups, teach them tolerance and cooperation. But in creating the boards of guardians and making their adjustments, the founders had operated on the basis of their experience in England, where landlords did not exercise as much social and economic influence over their tenants as Irish landlords did. Consequently, the safeguards they devised proved in practice as unrealistic with regard to the political balance as the workhouse test had been with regard to relief prohibition. This should become clearer with an examination of the board membership provisions and of the actual state of affairs of board politics during the 1870s.

Unions, Electoral Divisions, and Rating

The basic administrative unit of the poor law was the poor law union, which had come into existence under the Irish Poor Relief Act of 1838. Ireland was originally divided into 130 unions. These areas were further subdivided into electoral divisions, a term unknown in the English administration, consisting of several townlands. The original number of electoral divisions was 2,049, but this was increased in 1848 to 3,438. At the same time, with a view to improved management, the number of unions was increased to 163.[6] The Irish unions were much larger than the British, of which there were more than 600 in England and Wales. The difference was due to Ireland's poorer condition, which necessitated larger unions to distribute the tax burden broadly. The Poor Law Commission, which had been granted wide powers in laying out the details of the administration, had attempted, when determining sizes of unions, to strike a balance between the need for a broad tax base and the need for accessibility to the workhouse. Since population and topographical conditions varied widely in different parts of the country, union sizes also varied. Where population density was high, as in the cities and larger towns, the unions tended to be smaller; where the population was thinly dispersed, as in most parts of Connaught, the unions were larger. But as a rule, the Commission drew the borders so that the furthest point in any union was no more than twenty miles from the central market town which contained the workhouse. The names of all unions were derived from the workhouse towns.[7]

The electoral divisions, which averaged a little over twenty per union, were originally established with the philanthropic aim of reducing evictions and keeping down the poor rates. Each division was charged with the maintenance of the destitute who had resided in it before going into the workhouse. It was believed that this would induce the ratepayers to provide employment rather than force the poor into the workhouse, where they would inflate the divisional rates. In practice, however, divisional rating had the opposite effect. The landlords soon discovered that evicted tenants, hoping to avoid internment in the workhouse, would wander into the local towns in search of employment. Many managed to survive in the towns for a time, then ended up in the workhouse anyway—but as charges on the town rather than rural divisional rates. Thus divisional rating actually had the effect of reducing the burden in the rural divisions.[8] The town dwellers preferred the English method of *union rating*, by which the entire union was chargeable for all of the union's poor. But except for a few minor modifications introduced in 1876, divisional rating remained the standard, much to the annoyance of the ratepayers in the towns as well as the boards of guardians, whose proceedings were often interrupted by haggling and disputing between the rural and town representatives over questions of chargeability.

The electoral divisions also functioned as the basic unit for board representation. Every division was entitled to at least one representative on the board of guardians. Practically all of the rural divisions had only one; divisions covering towns sometimes had two, three, or four, depending on the town's population. Because the number of divisions varied from union to union, the sizes of the boards also varied. The tiny unions of Corofin and Scariff in County Clare, for example, had, respectively, nine and eight elected guardians in total, whereas the larger, more densely populated unions of Enniskillen (Fermanagh) and Cork city had forty-five and fifty.[9] However, the vast majority of boards fell into the range of eighteen to thirty elected guardians, and the average for the administration as a whole was about twenty-five. Of these, about five or six at the most represented town divisions; the remainder represented divisions made up of farms and villages. Except for the unions covering the larger cities—Dublin North, Dublin South, Cork, Waterford, Wexford, and Belfast—the boards of guardians were a rurally dominated institution.

The "poor rate," which was a tax introduced by the act of 1838, was levied in equal parts on both the owners and the occupiers of holdings in the union. Rates were geared to the annual valuation of the holding. Valuations of all holdings in Ireland were originally fixed by the Poor Law Commission, but these were later revised by a commission headed by Richard Griffith (hence "Griffith's valuation") who conducted a comprehensive boundary and valuation survey during the 1850s. The ratepayer who owned and occupied his holding was responsible for both portions of the poor rate. Initially these terms applied to all landholders in the union, but an 1843 law exempted occupiers of properties valued at under £4 and made their rates chargeable to the owner. As a result of this change, landowners paid about five-eighths of the poor rates in Ireland.[10] This was considerably more favorable to the tenantry than was the county cess,[11] which was borne entirely by the occupiers. However, as will soon be shown, the change in chargeability was made with compensations to the landlords in influence over the boards of guardians' proceedings.

The central authority to whom the boards of guardians were responsible was the Poor Law Commission, a board made up of three administrative and two medical officers. The system was originally controlled by the English commissioners, but the pressures of the Great Famine induced Parliament to create in 1847 a separate Irish commission, which was responsible to Parliament through the chief secretary for Ireland, usually a member of the cabinet. In 1872 this body was merged into the Local Government Board, which became responsible for all of local government in Ireland. The chief secretary was made the president of the board, but because the chief secretary's appointment was political, and therefore subject to change, the routine administration was conducted by the highest-ranking civil service appointee, the vice-president, and his assistant, the secretary. The board was equipped with a staff of regional local government inspectors and auditors, who oversaw the activities of the boards of guardians in their districts. The central board's responsibility was generally to see that the local boards complied with the law, and to report annually to Parliament on the state of local government in Ireland. Because the powers and responsibilities of the local boards were defined by law, the central board judiciously refrained from interfering in the boards' activities unless flagrant violations of the law or disruptive practices made it necessary for them to do so. Minor administrative problems or differences that arose in the boards of guardians were normally handled informally by the able, tactful, and usually respected regional inspectors.

Where there were clear indications of law violation or serious disruption, the Local Government Board was empowered to take action against the responsible officials. The chairman, who presided over a board meeting at which relief was granted in excess of fixed guidelines or was granted to persons legally ineligible for relief, was personally liable for the amount granted in excess of the legal provision. In more serious cases, where the entire board was found to be consistently derelict in its duties, the Local Government Board could, at its own discretion, temporarily dismiss the board and substitute appointed vice-guardians (usually two) who were paid handsomely for their services out of the union rates. Such occasions arose only infrequently, and usually involved failure of the boards to agree upon the rate to be struck, or their failure to levy sufficient taxation to cover expenses. Board dismissals were common during the Great Famine but

extremely rare afterwards, until the 1880s, when political hostilities, resulting at times in complete immobilization of some boards, made it necessary for the Local Government Board on five occasions between 1879
and 1882 to exercise this power.[12] It was an effective device, the mere
mention of which was normally sufficient to bring derelict boards into
line.

The Boards of Guardians: Voting and Elections

Board membership, as has been mentioned, was composed of an elected
element and an appointed ex-officio element. The size of the elected element was determined by the number of electoral divisions and populations
of the divisions; the ex-officio element was equal in size to the elected
element except in a few unions on the west coast where boards were unable
to find a sufficient number of persons qualified to fill all ex-officio seats.
A prescribed balance was not fixed in the English poor law, which entitled
every justice of the peace in the union to an ex-officio seat. This stipulation
had been incorporated in the Irish law specifically to avoid a preponderance
of the ex-officios on the boards. Before going into the specific reasons for
the inclusion of this provision in Ireland, it might be better to set the
context with a brief discussion of the provisions pertaining to board
membership.

The inclusion of a representative element had been the first consideration of the poor law's founders when outlining the composition of board
membership. Such an element had been included in the English poor law,
and it was considered necessary for the same reasons to include it in the
Irish law: since the poor rate was a new tax to be imposed on top of existing
taxes, it was thought essential to gain the ratepayers' compliance by granting them a voice over its expenditure. This conclusion also found support
in contemporary thought dominated by political economists, who viewed
the world in terms of a continuum of productiveness in which rewards
and penalties were distributed in proportion to relative contributions in
capital or labor. Applied to political situations, where influence was the
principal commodity, only a brief adjustment was required to convert the
economic formula into a politico-economic formula that based the reward (influence) on the amount of the investment (taxes). Or, as George
Nicholls, the English Poor Law Commissioner who drew up the Irish poor
law, put it:

The raising and disbursing of a poor rate involves nothing political, but it is to be regarded rather in the light of mutual assurance, in which the community joins for the purpose of being protected against the effects of pauperism, and each member contributing in proportion to his means, and each having an interest according to the amount of his contributions. If, therefore, the amount contributed be the measure of each ratepayer's interest, it ought in justice also, *within certain convenient limitations*, to be the measure of his influence. [Italics added][13]

The phrase "within certain convenient limitations" was a necessary addition to cover a number of exclusions and privileges incorporated for political reasons in violation of the principle of contribution and reward as stated by Nicholls. Excluded from the voting franchise, though under the original act compelled to pay rates, were occupiers of holdings valued at under £4. No reason was given for their exclusion, but it was probably the result of the prejudices of Parliament against the poorer classes, whom they considered dangerous, idle, and untrustworthy, and whom they omitted from the other franchises granted in the 1830s under the reform bill of 1832 and the poor law amendment act (the "new poor law") of 1834. Other variations concerned special privileges for landowners.

In accordance with the dictates of the contribution-reward principle, voting in poor law elections was conducted by a complicated system of multiple and cumulative votes which biased the elections in favor of larger landowners and occupiers. Since the owners and occupiers of holdings shared equally the rate burden on the holding, each was entitled to equal votes in the poor law elections. Every ratepayer rated at over £4 was entitled to at least one vote, but vote entitlement increased for owners and occupiers of higher-valued properties. This was done according to a six-stage scale as follows:

Valuation	Vote Entitlement
£4–19	1 vote
£20–49	2 votes
£50–99	3 votes
£100–149	4 votes
£150–199	5 votes
over £200	6 votes

Six votes was the maximum that any individual ratepayer could achieve in the role of an occupier or owner. But the votes for both roles and for different properties could be accumulated, so that the occupier who owned

his holding could achieve as many as twelve votes, and the occupier or
owner who held more than one property in the union could cumulate the
votes to which he was eligible for each property. Special further provision
was made for "beneficent landholders." These were occupiers who, usually
because they held their deeds in perpetuity at a fixed rent, paid less rent
than the values of their properties warranted. Standing for all practical
purposes half-way between landowners and occupiers, these beneficent
landholders (who were a small minority of the population) were entitled
to additional votes (up to six) for that portion of their valuation that exceeded the nominal rent, treating the difference as though it were rent
received. Thus, for example, an occupier who paid £30 annual rent on a
property valued at £50, would be entitled to five votes—three for being in
the fifty–to–ninety-nine pound landholding category, and two for the
twenty-pound difference between his rent and his valuation (the vote entitlement on £20 valuation being two votes). The law, however, set a limit
of eighteen votes as the maximum number any single ratepayer in the
union could achieve.[14]

The most important of the special privileges for landowners was the
provision in the law for voting by proxy, a privilege that was extended to
owners but not occupiers. Like the exclusion of under-£4 occupiers, the
provision reflected the class prejudices of the Parliament that enacted it.
The inclusion of a proxy vote could be justified on practical and theoretical
grounds, but there was no logical reason why it should be extended to one
class of voters and not the other. Nevertheless, George Nicholls attempted
such a justification in the report he submitted with the poor law bill,
offering the argument that "the occupier is always present, and may vote
in person," but that the landowner, who was often away from the union,
"would be unprotected without his power of voting by proxy."[15] The
accuracy of his assumption that occupiers would always be present could
certainly be questioned, as well as his failure to concede that occupiers
who happened to be absent were, by his own contribution-reward principle, equally entitled to protection. The truth of the matter was that
Nicholls and Parliament were suspicious of the Irish tenantry and fearful
that their experiment in local representative government in Ireland might
get out of hand, so they made a concession to the Irish Conservatives in
Parliament, who had been clamoring for the one-sided proxy vote.

There was also a theoretical justification for the one-sided proxy which
was found in David Ricardo's dictum, repeated by Nicholls in his report,
that "the rate is levied upon property, and thus in fact becomes a portion

of the rent, which would be increased by the amount of the rate, if this were not levied for poor law purposes; so that in reality it is the landlord, the permanent owner of the property, who bears the final burthen of the rate and not the tenant or temporary occupier." "It seems convenient with justice," Nicholls therefore concluded, "that every facility should be afforded to the owner by protecting his interest with his vote."[16]

Vote recording in Irish poor law elections was accomplished by a unique method involving open voting papers. On the assigned day each year (by law March 25 or the day most convenient to it), a "returning officer" toured the electoral divisions dropping off at the homes of eligible voters ballots known as "voting papers," containing the names of the candidates contesting the representation of the division. The electors marked the papers, signed their names, and returned the papers to the officer, who returned on the following day. The officer then returned to his office and counted the votes, within the sight, as the law provided, of any enfranchised ratepayers who wished to observe. Throughout this time, the papers were left open, providing ample opportunity for interested parties, either before or after the papers were counted, to discover which candidates each voter preferred. The opening that this method offered to would-be intimidators often proved irresistible; thus electoral intimidation was a common feature of poor law elections. Parliament in the 1840s considered for a time abandoning the open voting paper system and substituting the open ballot, which was used in parliamentary elections and after 1835 in municipal elections in Ireland. Under this method voters were required to go to a central polling place to record their votes. After investigating the question, however, Parliament decided to retain the voting papers, since many members of Parliament felt that under the open ballot system "intimidation and undue influence of another kind might . . . be as effectually practised, and in a more turbulent manner, when the electors proceeded to the polling places to record their votes."[17] As with so many other features of the Irish poor law, considerations of expediency and law and order were behind the open voting paper system.

The cumulative vote, the proxy vote, and the open voting papers were the principal provisions of the law relating to guardians' elections. The first apportioned influence by wealth; the second by landownership; and the third, inadvertently, by ability to coerce, which meant, in the 1870s, also landownership. Two final provisions in the qualifications for membership in the two board elements also weighted the administration in favor of wealth and landownership. First, elected guardians were required to meet a property qualification somewhat higher than that required for the franchise. The qualifications for each union were fixed by the Local Government Board, but the law set a maximum qualification at £30. The average qualification during the 1870s and 1880s was about £20. In some prosperous localities and in the cities it reached the full £30, while in districts where holdings were of small average value, the Local Government Board sometimes found it necessary to fix it as low as £8 or £6 to secure popular representation. While these qualifications did not limit board membership to the wealthy, they did exclude the classes at the bottom of the electorate—the small farmers and shopkeepers, almost all artisans, and all laborers. Clergymen were excluded from board membership by law. Subsistence farmers, cottiers, laborers, and most artisans were excluded by the £4 qualification from the franchise as well. As a rule, the candidate for a poor law guardianship had by law to be, if not a landowner, a professional man, prosperous businessman, or "comfortable" farmer, at least a man of some visible and stable means of income. These, of course, were legal qualifications which did not necessarily have any bearing on political qualifications.

Second, all ex-officios were required to be invested to preside on the judicial benches of the county or counties in which the union was situated. Originally the ex-officios were limited in number to one-third of the elected guardians, but an 1847 act increased their proportion to a level of equality with the elected guardians. Ex-officios' appointments were made as follows: If the number of qualifying magistrates in the union was greater than the number required as ex-officios, the available seats went to the magistrates with the highest land valuations. No exceptions were made and no substitutions allowed. Formal appointment was not even required, since these magistrates were designated to their office by the act that created the office. If the number of qualifying magistrates was smaller than the number required, the guardians were then allowed to make up the difference from non-resident magistrates presiding in the county. This recourse was not often resorted to because most unions outside the sparsely populated regions along the west coast had many more than the required number of magistrates. In some west coast unions, however—such as Belmullet, Newport, and Westport in Mayo and Dingle in Kerry—the scarcity of magistrates was so severe that the boards were unable to fill the ex-officio seats even by including justices in the county. The board of the Dingle union had only nine ex-officios, although its elected membership was twenty-two.[18]

The original decision to carry the ex-officio element over from the English poor law had been based largely on political considerations. As with all the provisions in the Irish act, Nicholls had a ready theoretical explanation for the inclusion of separate representation for the landowners. This was derived from the basic principle of political economy that held that owners of the land had a permanent interest in it, while tenants' interests were only temporary. The complete organization of a board of guardians, therefore, seemed to Nicholls to require "some union" of the two kinds of interests.[19] Such abstract argumentation could not have carried much weight with the hard-nosed politicians in Parliament. More convincing might have been a second argument made by Nicholls based on administrative considerations. The elected guardians, he argued, were by definition discontinuous holders of their offices, and "their proceedings might be changeable, and perhaps even contradictory, and confusion might arise through the opposite views of successive boards." The ex-officios, as permanent appointees, would, in this respect, serve as a "corrective."

But at bottom, neither political theory nor the desire for continuity was the true motivation. The ex-officios had been included for the same reason that they had been included in the English boards, which was that to exclude them would be to risk the resistance of the landowners to payment of the rates and compliance with the law, and thus jeopardize the success of the entire system. This consideration was particularly relevant in Ireland, where the landowners were all-powerful. Nicholls may have thought it in poor taste to bring up the question in an official report to Parliament, but one of the M.P.'s who participated in the deliberations, Lord Clements, was not so reticent in expressing the idea, which must have been in the minds of all of his colleagues. In a pamphlet that he published at the time of the poor law debates he wrote:

> To throw the administration exclusively into the hands of the tenantry, and to exclude the gentry, either from principle or in practice,—when the gentry are possessed of such immense power for good or for evil as in Ireland, and where their interests are so directly concerned,—would be contrary to every principle of sound policy, and would immediately raise up a natural spirit of distrust, and hostility, on the part of the class who have the means of giving effect to their feelings, and whom it is of the most vital consequence to influence favourably and to conciliate. The institution of *ex-officio* guardians therefore is most useful.[20]

Utility was a most convincing argument, though only one of several that pointed inevitably to the inclusion of an ex-officio membership.

Because most members of Parliament agreed about the need for an ex-officio membership, the provision ordering their creation passed without much difficulty. Some serious questions were raised, however, about how the ex-officios were to be selected and how strong their membership on the boards should be. That they should be justices of the peace was universally accepted by those who supported the bill. All the great landed proprietors in Ireland were magistrates, so the designation of magistrates as ex-officios would embrace the aristocracy, gentry, and the rest of the powerful class about whom Lord Clements had been so concerned. As to the question of *which* magistrates should be designated, some, including Nicholls, favored elections conducted among the owners; this would enable the owners to choose the more efficient and conscientious of the justices for the ex-officio seats. But Parliament, reluctant to introduce a procedure that might exclude the largest, most powerful owners, assigned the seats to the highest-rated justices, thus ensuring the domination of the ex-officio element by the aristocracy and higher gentry.[21]

An inherent danger in the admission of an ex-officio membership made up of magistrates was the real possibility that the magistrates might outweigh the elected guardians during the boards' proceedings. "Should this occur," wrote Nicholls, who anticipated the problem, "the elective character of the board would of course be destroyed," which would "detract from the popular character of the governing body, and lower it in the confidence of the people." Nicholls advised, therefore, that the number of ex-officios be limited to one-third of the elected membership. No fixed proportion had been included in the English poor law, but Nicholls believed that it was justified in Ireland, because the larger size of the Irish unions and the larger number of justices per square mile in Ireland made it more likely that the ex-officios would dominate the Irish boards unless some limitation were placed upon them.[22] The majority of Parliament agreed on the need for a numerical limitation, but considered the degree of limitation a matter for negotiation. The figure Parliament finally settled on after succumbing somewhat to pressure from the Irish landowning members was one-third. In other words, ex-officios were to be one-third of the elected guardians, or one-fourth of the entire board. And this was the ratio written into the Irish Poor Relief Act.

The expansion of the ex-officio representation to a level of equality with the elected guardians did not occur until nine years later, when it was included as a corollary to a revision of the rating procedures. During the opening years of the act's operation, strong opposition to payment of the rates had come from the small farmers and cottiers, who had been suffering under the burden of agricultural distress that prevailed at the time through-out the British Isles. The imposition of the new rate had been met by mass protest meetings and, particularly in the West, by violent gatherings called "poor law riots." To placate the more overburdened of the tenantry, in 1843 Parliament (in an act entitled "An Act to Make Further Provision for the Destitute Poor in Ireland") exempted occupiers of properties valued at under £4 from paying poor rates, stipulating that their portion of the rates were to be paid by the owners of their holdings. In order to compensate the owners for this additional imposition, Parliament in 1847 repealed the one-third ex-officio limitation, but added the further provision that the number of ex-officios "shall in no case exceed the number of elected guard-ians."[23] This arrangement remained in effect for the rest of the century, until the county councils act of 1898 abolished altogether the ex-officio element.

One can judge from these membership provisions that the board com-position and selection procedures had been designed to bring order and stability to the system through a balance of interests. The cumulative voting procedure grew out of the need for a system that would incorporate both a broad ratepayer base and special privileges for larger and more influential ratepayers. Thus the interests of the large classes of small farm-ers and landowners were matched in the sliding scale of vote entitlement by proportionally higher grants of influence for the smaller classes of pros-perous farmers and landowners. Again, the one-sided proxy vote was an attempt to offset the advantage held by occupiers over absentee landowners in the ability to vote in poor law elections. The fact that the provision in effect penalized absentee occupiers was considered inconsequential by a Parliament prejudiced toward landowners and concerned about the high costs that might be incurred if all ratepayers were granted the right to vote in absentia. Finally, the division of the boards into elected and ex-officio members was an attempt to balance the influence of the landowners and occupiers not—as under the cumulative vote—in their roles as ratepayers, but in their roles as separate social classes. In fixing the proportions Par-liament attempted to arrive at a ratio that would offset the greater influence of the magistrates by numerical advantages for the elected members. Thus the poor law was established by the manipulation of bodies and votes, as though they were entries on a ledger sheet.

As improbable as the contribution-reward principle might seem in ret-rospect when applied to Irish politics, George Nicholls, the chief architect of the system, had high hopes for its success. Discussing, at the end of his second report to Parliament, the superb balance that the poor law had achieved, he predicted that the distinction between elected guardian and ex-officio would eventually cease to exist in the minds of the Irish people, as continual contact between the two groups and the need to make the system work created an attitude of mutual dependence and cooperation:

> Each individual member will feel that his influence depends upon the opinion that his colleagues entertain of him; and hence will arise an interchange of good offices, and a cultivation of good will, beginning with the boards of guardians, and extending throughout the entire union, and eventually, it may be hoped throughout the country; and thus the union system may become the means of healing dissentions, and reconciling jarring interests in Ireland.[24]

An optimistic picture indeed, though one perhaps more apropos of England than Ireland. For in manipulating their entries on the ledger sheet, Parliament had failed to take into account the real factors that governed Irish politics and permitted the landowners to hold their ascendant position. These were not votes and numbers of persons, but social custom and class prejudice supported on the landlords' side by sophisticated organization and great power to intimidate. The tenants' position, on the other hand, was exemplified by disorganization, political backwardness, and an attitude of helplessness.

Class and Power: The Board Managers in the 1870s

Nicholls's hopes for a balanced administration in which guardians were recognized for their personal merits rather than class status did not come to pass. As events developed, the ex-officios garnered for themselves the lion's share of actual power on the boards while contributing little to board management in the practical sense, while the elected guardians did most of the work but gained little influence. This situation is readily revealed by an examination of the power structure on the boards in the 1870s, and by an analysis of guardians' attendance during the same period.

First, the power structure: An important measure of the ex-officios' influence on the boards was their success in securing control of the board officer positions. Control of the offices was essential to control of the boards' proceedings. This was because of the central role the officers played in directing the proceedings, and also—more importantly—because of the acknowledged informal power one needed to obtain an office. Boards of guardians' officerships were not organized on the principle of a division of labor as officerships are in most administrative organizations. Normally, official functions are distributed among several officers, such as a chairman to preside over meetings, a secretary to take minutes and handle correspondence, and a treasurer to keep the accounts. Secretarial functions on boards of guardians were performed by the union clerk, a salaried official who was not a member of the board. Union accounts were kept by a local bank appointed by the Local Government Board. The official responsible for seeing to the proper performance of these functions, and actually the only board officer at any given moment, was the chairman, who presided at the meeting at which questions about the performances were raised. It was he who could be fined by the Local Government Board for costs incurred by the ratepayers as a result of his dereliction of duties.

Because it was essential that a properly authorized, duly elected officer be present at board meetings, the law provided for the election of three officers: a chairman-of-the-board, who had right to the chair when he was present, and two substitute chairmen—the vice-chairman and deputy vice-chairman—who presided in that order when other officers were absent. If all three chairmen happened to be absent on a given day, the board could elect an acting chairman from among the members present. As presiding officer the chairman performed a number of routine functions, such as examining and putting his signature to the account books, minute book, and workhouse records; fixing the agenda for the meeting; accepting or ruling on motions made before the board; and in some cases, depending on the custom of the individual board, revising the lists of eligible relief recipients for the coming week based on information given him by the relieving officer or board members.

Thus, the chairman possessed a number of powers. Because he was responsible for fixing the agenda he could arrange the order of business so as to give priority to some measures and to neglect others. As presiding officer, if he disliked a motion he could allot it scant discussion time or rule it out of order. If he desired to obstruct a motion and thought he could summon the support of a majority of the board, he could ask for counter-motions or admit weakening amendments. There was a limit to how far he could go in obstruction, because a "two-weeks notice" rule compelled him to receive motions about whose introduction the board had been notified in writing two weeks earlier. However, the two-weeks notice rule ultimately operated in the chairman's favor, since by it he gained sufficient time to negotiate privately with uncommitted members, or to rally to the second meeting his supporters who were absent from the meeting at which the notice of motion was given. Therefore, in a contest between the chairman and a rank-and-file member over the introduction of a motion, the chairman usually held the superior position.

Much more important than these official powers, however, were the informal powers in terms of influence and prestige of which the chairman's election to his office was emblematic. Because the offices were elective, and because they were not limited to either ex-officios or elected guardians, the achievement of an office reflected the confidence and respect of the corporate membership of the board. If, as was often the case in the 1870s, the officer happened to be a member of a party or faction on the board, his election also signified the preponderance of his party within the membership. And if—translating the foregoing into social terms—he happened to be an ex-officio member, his election became symbolic of the respect, or at least the deference, of the tenant-occupiers on the board toward the landowning class. But there was also another factor. Because the stratification of the three offices dictated the order of succession to the chair, it also apportioned prestige accordingly. The offices represented therefore a hierarchy of power and status among the officeholders and board members.

Administrative hierarchy can be determined in a number of ways. It can be determined by social status, with the higher offices going to persons of higher social standing. It can be determined by administrative merit, with offices being apportioned according to proven ability or seniority. Or it can be based on political considerations such as party service or political contributions, as exemplified in big-city machines and high-level governmental policy-making appointments. In all three cases the positions within the hierarchy represent varying degrees of status or achievement within the framework of the system. So it was with the boards of guardians in the 1870s, for they doled out their offices in accordance with hierarchical standards, and an examination of the officeholders of the day reveals that the hierarchy was determined socially and by the standards of landed society.

It would be impossible to document this circumstance for the entire forty years between the passing of the poor law and the end of the 1870s. The first problem is the great number of guardians involved. There were 390 officers (3 officers each on 130 boards) each year for the first nine years of the poor law, and 489 (3 officers each on 163 boards) each year thereafter, though not all these officers changed every year. Officer turnover was fairly low, and it differed from office to office. During the ten-year period 1867–77 the changes in the various offices were 26 percent of chairmen, 59 percent of vice-chairmen, and 81 percent of deputy vice-chairmen.[25] Assuming that these percentages were representative of the entire forty-year period, the number of men who held offices during that time would have been 779 chairmen, 927 vice-chairmen, and 1,117 deputy vice-chairmen, or a total of 2,823. Many of these, particularly in the chairmanships, were titled nobles who succeeded their fathers in the office, and because these men were referred to only by their titles, the problem of distinguishing father from son complicates the problem of computing officer turnover.

A second difficulty arises in attempting to identify the social status of the earlier officeholders. Nobles are easy enough to identify by their titles, but other officers, gentry included, are referred to in *Thom's Directory*[26]— the only existing source for boards of guardians' officers' names—only by their given names. Because social status was determined at the time largely by one's relation to the land—that is to say, whether one owned or rented his land and, if he were a landowner, how much land he owned—it is necessary to know for each officer whether he was tenant or owner and what his land valuation or acreage was. The difficulty is that individual landholdings were not compiled until 1876, when Parliament published a report on all landowners in Ireland holding one acre or more of land. This publication, known informally and referred to hereafter as the Domesday Book,[27] is the only useful guide to landowners in the nineteenth century, but the further in time that one moves from its publication date, the less likely one is to find his subject or the correct size of his subject's holdings.

Tenants can be identified in two ways: one negatively, through their failure to appear in the Domesday Book; the other positively, through the listings in the valuation manuscripts, which luckily survive and are stored in the archives of the General Valuation Office.[28] Because *Thom's Directory* gives the addresses of board officers, it is an easy matter to locate an officer in the appropriate valuation manuscript, and these manuscripts list both the tenant and the immediate lessor of the holding. But the manuscripts are compiled by lot numbers within the various townlands, so that holdings occupied by one person in different townlands, unions, or counties of Ireland can be collated only with great difficulty. Therefore, the identification of an officer as a tenant on one holding is no guarantee that he is not the owner of another holding. The only way to avoid such error is to work with the valuation records in conjunction with the Domesday Book, using the former to discover whether the individual was an occupying tenant, and the latter to see that he was not also an owner. The point to be emphasized is, however, that the Domesday Book is crucial to any accurate identification of a person's relation to the land, and its publication in 1876 makes it almost essential that studies of the obscure men who held most of the offices on boards of guardians be limited to the years immediately preceding and following its publication.

The year selected for this study of board officers is 1877. The year seems appropriate because it is near enough to the Domesday Book to ensure accuracy of data, yet also far enough from the events leading to the formation of the Land League in 1879 to exclude the possibility of those events' being reflected in the power arrangements on the boards of guardians. The rise of the Land League, as will later be shown, wrought great changes in the character of the power relationships on the boards. The year 1877, therefore, may be considered a typical year in the poor law administration at the very end of the landlords' long and exclusive domination of the institutions of local government in Ireland. Moreover, an understanding of the thoroughness of aristocratic control in so late a year as 1877 will further the appreciation of the revolutionary character of the events that followed.

The most striking feature of the board officer composition in 1877 was the degree to which the offices were occupied by landed proprietors. Of the 489 officers in all categories on all boards, 339 (69.3 percent) were landowners of varying size whose names appeared in the Domesday Book. To this figure, for our purposes, must be added ninety-one (18.6 percent) others whose names were not in the Domesday Book but who were justices of the peace listed in the magistracy lists in *Thom's Directory*. Very often sons of the gentry who did not hold land in fee but who had an interest in the family estate were given posts on the Commission of the Peace. Sometimes land agents, also without title to land, were so rewarded for their services. Although neither of these classes would appear in the Domesday Book because neither owned land, they were so closely tied to the landed interest that to count them as tenant-occupiers along with farmers and shopkeepers would be to distort the data, giving the tenantry the appearance of having more representation than they actually had. Although it is true that some of these men sided politically with the tenantry, the vast majority of them at that time were firmly connected politically and socially with the Protestant Ascendancy and the landed interests, and the tenants regarded them as such. For our purposes, therefore, the distinction between landlord and tenant will be understood to include in the landlord class all landowners and all justices of the peace whether listed in the Domesday Book or not, and, in the tenant class, those who only occupied land and buildings and paid rent.[29] When, therefore, the non-landowning justices are added to the Domesday Book group, the total membership of the landowning officers in 1877 is 430, or 87.9 percent of all officers.

In terms of the specific offices they held, the owners were concentrated in the two higher offices (see Table 1). The owners in effect monopolized the top two offices, and held a very large majority of the deputy vice-chairmanships. The tenants were virtually excluded from the higher offices and were present only in a small minority in the lowest office. There may not have been a legal qualification for the holding of a board office, but as these proportions suggest, offices were reserved, by mutual understanding or by some other informal rule, largely for landowners, and this rule was more rigidly enforced with each step up in the hierarchy.

Concentrating now only on the landowning group, one finds a similar hierarchical pattern when estate sizes are correlated with the various offices. The Domesday Book provided, for each landowner listed, the acreage and total valuation of all lands owned, first in all of Ireland, then by county. For our purposes the valuations are much more useful than the acreage. This is because the quality of the land varied so widely from one part of Ireland to another and even within a townland, that it would be impossible to establish satisfactory equivalency ratings with which to compare landed wealth on the basis of acres owned. An estate of 1,000 acres in fertile Meath might have been worth ten times the value of the same number of acres in the mountain districts of Mayo.[30] But land valuations were established for the express purpose of rating holdings against each other for tax purposes. They bore little relation to actual land values, which in the 1870s were in many cases considerably higher than the valuations, but they do

TABLE 1

Landowner and Tenant Officers on Boards of Guardians, 1877

Office	Owners		Tenants	
	Number	Percentage	Number	Percentage
Chairmen (163)	161	98.8	2	1.2
Vice-chairmen (163)	152	93.3	11	6.7
Deputy vice-chairmen (163)	117	71.8	46	28.2
Total (489)	430	87.9	59	12.1

provide a satisfactory basis for comparing relative landed wealth, which is what we are interested in here. Therefore, for our purposes, holding sizes will be described by land valuation rather than acreage.

With the valuations listed in the Domesday Book for all holdings in Ireland, the landowners can be ranged in the various offices from the highest to the lowest in valuation and the median point found for each office. Because no valuations could be determined for the ninety-one justices who were not listed in the Domesday Book, these officers were excluded from the sample. The sample consisted therefore of 339 owners: 145 chairmen, 115 vice-chairmen, and seventy-nine deputy vice-chairmen. The median valuations of these groups were as follows:

Chairmen	£2,034
Vice-chairmen	545
Deputy vice-chairmen	203

The range of valuations within each officer group was extremely broad. The land of the lowest-valued chairman, for example—Major-General Edmund Roche of the Midleton (Cork) union—was valued at £30, while at the other end of the scale the land of the Earl Fitzwilliam, the largest landowner in Ireland (exceeding the Duke of Leinster by £28), who presided over the Shillelagh (Wicklow) union, was valued at £46,599. Similarly, land valuations of the vice-chairmen ranged from a low of £18 to a high of £10,970 (David Wilson of Balleymoney, Antrim, and the Earl of Belmore of Enniskillen, Fermanagh); and those of the deputy vice-chairmen from a low of £1 to a high of £2,584 (Richard Butler of Castlecomer, Kilkenny, and Sir F. W. Heygate, Bart., of Limavady, Londonderry). Given these wide variations, it would be impossible to make any reasonable generalization about the kinds of men who held the various offices. But the cases mentioned are extreme examples since most of the officers tended to cluster near to the median points, so that a description of the relative social positions of the median owners would help to fix the majority of officeholders in their context in Irish land-owning society.

All the officers under consideration, first of all, were landowners, but not all were landlords. The distinction depends, of course, on whether the owner had tenants. Strictly speaking, most owners, even owners of fifty or 100 acres, could be considered landlords under this definition, since most of them rented space to at least one or two farm hands. In the eyes of contemporaries, however, these men were considered independent farmers or "freeholders" rather than landlords since they worked their farms themselves and received very little income from rents. It would be difficult to say at which point a land-owning farmer became a landlord in the eyes of his neighbors. If he were a cattle grazier he might hold 300 or 400 acres and still be considered a farmer. Many graziers who rented their land occupied holdings of this size. A farm of 400 acres in the 1870s could have held a valuation of about £400 if it were situated in a fertile region like County Meath, or it could have been £100 or less in the mountainous areas of Mayo. Nationally, the ratio of acreage to valuation was about thirty-seven acres to £20 of valuation, or roughly two-to-one. Taking the median valuation of the deputy vice-chairmen, which was £203, one can say that most of the holders of that office who fell below the median mark would have owned fewer than 300 or 400 acres of land, and therefore would most likely have been freeholding farmers rather than landlords.

At the other extreme were the aristocracy and squirearchy—some of the latter were working farmers but most were definitely landlords—men who received a sizeable portion or almost all their landed income from rents. A minimum valuation for this group is even more difficult to esti- mate than was the maximum for the freeholders, since the group ranged from small squires like Ernest Knox of Killala, Co. Mayo, of the Knox-Gore family, whose valuation was £366, to the great marquesses and earls who owned thousands of acres in different parts of the country. However, a minimum thousand acres, or (using the national ratio) about £500 val- uation, would certainly include most of this group without admitting many freeholders or tenants. And if this figure is applied to the officers it can be seen that the chairmen rose well above this mark with a median land valuation of £2,034, as did also the upper half of the vice-chairman group with valuations over the median of £545. At the top were the aristocratic chairmen—men like the Duke of Leinster and the Earl Fitzwilliam, or beneath them the Marquess of Ormonde (£16,357), the Earl of Erne (£17,039), Lord Dunsandle (£11,860), as well as Sir George Hodson, Bart., and Lord Emly, whose valuations fell below the median mark for chair- men.[31] Also among the chairmen were some high-ranking gentry like Capt. E. R. King-Harman of the Roscommon-Sligo region and Evelyn P. Shirley of Carrickmacross, Co. Monaghan, whose holdings exceeded in value those of many barons and earls (£12,629 and £20,744 respectively), as well as others of less notable wealth such as the aforementioned Ernest Knox of Killala. In between the aristocrats and high gentry and the smaller free- holders stood a heterogeneous group of large freeholders and "middling" squires who were in the lower half of the vice-chairmen's and the upper half of the deputy vice-chairmen's groups. Taking the 339 officers as a whole, seventy-four (22 percent) had valuations under £200, eighty-four (25 percent) had valuations between £200 and £500, and 181 (53 percent) had valuations over £500. Thus, at least half the officers were squires and aristocrats, and not more than one-fourth of them were smaller freehold farmers; these groups were distributed among the offices with most free-holders in the lower and most squires in the higher offices.

The aristocrats were a special group among the officeholders of 1877. Sometimes landowners were given vice-chairmanships on boards whose chairmen were smaller landowners than they. This occurred in sixteen unions in 1877. But wherever titled noblemen held a board office, they invariably held the highest office. There were all together forty-five no-blemen among the officers in 1877, and all but three of them were chairmen of their respective boards; the remaining three were vice-chairmen on boards whose chairmen were noblemen of higher rank. This rigidity stemmed no doubt from the dictates of contemporary protocol: to offer a nobleman less than the highest available office would have been considered an insult and effrontery, which almost certainly would have been met by the nobleman's curt refusal. On the other hand, not all noblemen were willling or able to accept offices on boards of guardians. Some, like the Marquess of Sligo in Westport, were satisfied to leave the union in the hands of other capable and trustworthy gentlemen. In Sligo's case the surrogate was his brother, Lord John Browne, who owned no land in his own right but who lived on and managed the family estate while the Marquess spent most of his time in England.[32] The usual procedure was for guardians to offer the chairmanship to the largest landowner in the union, who was usually a nobleman, or to someone else in his family. The decision to accept or refuse then became the nobleman's, and the dictates of social etiquette were fulfilled.

As this review of board offices suggests, power relationships on the boards in the 1870s were governed by the standards and values of landed society. In spite of the lack of any official set of requirements for holding a board office, other than that the holder be a member of the board, the manner in which the offices were distributed suggests the existence of an informal set of rules based on land relationships. Office-holding was for all practical purposes restricted to landowners. When tenants were ad-mitted to office they were usually placed in the lowest and least desirable of the offices. This pattern, which characterized society and politics outside the boards, formed the basis for board politics during the years prior to the Land League.

Board Attendance and Absenteeism

To hold a public office was not necessarily to exercise it, and it was characteristic of the ex-officio guardians that they rarely did. Lord Clements in 1838, drawing on the English experience under the new poor law, foresaw the possibility of absenteeism among the members of the boards of guardians. "It is probable," he wrote, "that if the doors of the Boardroom are opened wide enough, the great majority, as in England, will rarely seek admission; and that the complaint will shortly arise, that they do not afford their attendance."[33] The first part of the prediction, that few would seek admission to the boardroom, was not borne out in practice, since politically inclined tenants, having no place else to go, turned naturally to the boards of guardians. But the second part proved to be prophetic. Absenteeism was a chronic problem for the boards from the time of their establishment. This held true for both elected and ex-officio guardians, but between the two the ex-officios were by far the worse offenders.

The problem had been created in part by the law itself, which predetermined that the ex-officios would be the largest landowners in Ireland. As it happened, and as the founders of the poor law failed to recognize, the largest landowners in Ireland were absentee landlords, the very men about whom economists and others concerned with the state of Ireland complained when citing the evils of the Irish tenurial system. The great Irish landowners were notorious for abandoning their estates for the greater part of the year and leaving their affairs in the hands of land agents and bailiffs. Their frequent absences were motivated in part by their distaste for and boredom with Irish country life, and their preference for the amusements and luxuries available to them in Dublin, London, and the continental spas and salons. But often too they were drawn to the cities on business or in the performance of their many official functions. Official duties also made demands on the time of the resident ex-officios. As magistrates they were required to spend time on the bench, attend quarter sessions, and periodically look in on the baronial presentment sessions. As members of the governing class they served also in numerous other public capacities, among others as members of town commissions, boards of fairs and markets, prison boards, lunatic asylum boards, and dispensary committees. These were in addition to their private functions as owners of

estates, hosts to visiting dignitaries, and frequent visitors to the racetrack
or hunting ground. These occupations and preoccupations made them less
available for service on the boards of guardians than were the tenant-
farmers and shopkeepers in the elected membership, who were usually in
town on market days when board meetings were held.

Although ex-officio absenteeism was a continuing problem, little attention was called to it until the end of the 1870s, when a select committee
of the House of Commons began asking questions about it.[34] The committee was established in 1878 to investigate conditions on the boards of
guardians not just of Ireland, but of the entire United Kingdom, in connection with reform legislation that was then pending in Commons. A few
of the English witnesses had called to the attention of the committee the
problem of chronic absenteeism that pervaded the ex-officio membership
of the English boards. When the Irish witnesses appeared, the committee
attempted to ascertain whether the same condition prevailed in Ireland.
One of the two Irish witnesses who were questioned on the subject was
James Daly, publisher of the *Connaught Telegraph* and an elected member
of the Castlebar board of guardians in County Mayo. Daly responded that
ex-officio attendance in Ireland was "very poor," and gave as an example
his own union in which only one ex-officio attended meetings regularly.[35]
The second witness was Benjamin Banks, secretary of the Irish Local
Government Board who, when asked whether Irish ex-officios attended
meetings regularly, answered guardedly, "I have no personal knowledge
of that; but I hear in some cases complaints that they do not; they abandon
the field, in fact. . . . Of course," he added, suggesting that he knew more
about the problem than he was willing to admit, "you must make some
allowance for their circumstances, which take them away from the union
more than the elected guardians are taken away."[36]

The committee was unable to obtain more specific information than
this, since they had not requested the Local Government Board to submit
a return of attendances. Yet even a glance at press reports of guardians'
meetings and at the few minute books that have survived confirms the
verbal evidence given to the committee. Board meetings at which six,
eight, or ten guardians were present would be found to have only one or
two names bearing the suffix "J.P.," by which ex-officio members were
characteristically identified. An analysis of the minute books of six County
Mayo unions over a ten-week period in 1877,[37] the results of which are
shown in Table 2, indicates that the average attendance of ex-officios on
the six boards was one meeting in eleven per ex-officio. Elected guardian

TABLE 2

Attendance of Ex-officio and Elected Guardians in Certain Poor Law Unions during Ten Weeks in 1877

Union	Ex-officios		Elected	
	Number on Board	Percentage of Possible Attendance	Number on Board	Percentage of Possible Attendance
Ballina	21	5	21	28
Castlebar	17	5	17	35
Claremorris	14	7	19	27
Killala	13	22	13	38
Swinford	15	5	22	25
Westport	10	10	21	27
Six Mayo unions	90	9	113	29
Naas	33	12	33	33
Limerick	46	27	46	37

Sources: Mayo unions: Minute books; Naas: *Leinster Express*; Limerick: *Limerick Reporter*; see also notes 37, 38, and 39 to this chapter.

attendance was better than one meeting in four. Similar conditions obtained in the union of Naas in County Kildare, one of the most prosperous rural unions in Ireland, whose minute books have not survived but whose meetings were reported in the *Leinster Express*. An analysis of the Naas board's meetings over the same ten-week period reveals that the average ex-officio attendance in that union was one meeting in eight, whereas the elected guardians' was about one meeting in three.[38] The attendance records of both groups were generally better in unions covering large towns and cities. The ex-officios of the Limerick union, for example, attended about one meeting in four to the elected guardians' two meetings in five.[39] But in none of the unions sampled did ex-officio attendance exceed the elected guardians', though the elected guardians' often greatly exceeded the ex-officios'.

Statistical proof of ex-officio absenteeism eventually came in 1884, when the Local Government Board submitted, at Parliament's request, a report of attendances of elected and ex-officio guardians in all unions during the year ending March 25, 1884.[40] The report is extremely useful not only for attendances but for ascertaining the numbers of ex-officio and elected guardians in each union. The total number of elected guardians that year was 3,704; the number of ex-officios was 3,503. These figures are not available elsewhere because all nineteenth-century Local Government Board records were destroyed in the Custom House fire in 1921. As for attendances, the report reveals on analysis that elected guardian attendance throughout Ireland was four times ex-officio attendance. The elected guardians registered 62,632 attendances, which represent 34 percent of the possible attendances for the group (using a fifty-week year). Ex-officios attended 15,707 times, or 9 percent of their possible attendances. Neither group's record could be considered outstanding, nevertheless, the ex-officios, attending only 9 percent of the time, were clearly the more derelict.

Using the attendance figures as a guide, one might assume—and correctly so—that the routine operations of the boards were conducted by the elected guardians. The real question is, however, which elected guardians? With the ex-officios absent most of the time, the leadership had to come from some other quarter, perhaps from a few working ex-officios or from influential members of the elected element. The question of who exercised leadership during board meetings is an important one, because if this leadership came from the tenantry, it might still be argued that the tenants, in spite of the landowners' monopoly of the board offices, possessed the real power over the local poor law administration. But another question suggests itself in this connection: If, indeed, the ex-officios attended so many fewer meetings than the elected guardians, how did they manage to maintain themselves in the board offices? They apparently did not do so by force of numbers—that is to say, by outvoting the elected guardians. The survey of board attendances in 1877 as well as the parliamentary report of 1884 showed that ex-officio attendance did increase proportionally at meetings at which board elections were held, but that the ex-officios were still a small minority at these meetings.[41] Was their election to the offices purely a product of the deference accorded them by the tenant guardians, or were there, among the elected guardians, groups of tenants connected politically with the ex-officios who supported ex-officio candidates for the offices, and who supplied the leadership when the ex-officios were absent from the board-room?

The answer is that both were true. Among the elected guardians were large numbers of tenants whose interests and attitudes bound them to landed society, and who dominated the proceedings of the boards in the name of the ex-officio party. At the same time, there were tenants not directly connected with landed society who deferred to the ex-officios in the assignment of offices and submitted to the authority of the ex-officios' representatives when the ex-officios were not present. The key figure in this relationship was the land agent, the powerful and much-despised (by the tenantry) figure who occupied a crucial position in nineteenth-century

Irish society. In a country such as Ireland, in which most of the land was owned by lords who were away from their estates for the greater part of the year, the land agent became more than a collector of rents and a manager of estates: he was the personification of his employer's authority. The agent's functions extended beyond his administrative role; in his employer's absence he managed the lord's public affairs as well. A brief but apt description of the agent's diverse surrogate powers is supplied by a contemporaneous author styling himself "A Guardian of the Poor," who wrote in 1892:

> He [the land agent] is looked upon as the representative of the landlord during the absence of the latter—this period usually varying from the entire year, to the greater part of it. As the Lord Lieutenant is to royalty, so is the Irish agent to his employer. The agent is a justice of the peace, a grand juror, and often, chairman of the Board of Guardians. And on very large and scattered estates where there are two or more agents, these are all in the beforenamed posts of authority.[42]

It was common in the 1870s to find on the boards of guardians the agents of all of the large landowners in the union holding positions as elected guardians. Usually they sat with those who worked for their employers as bailiffs and clerks as well as other friends and associates for whom they had also secured seats on the board. A newspaper account of a meeting of the Kenmare board in 1869 illustrates how this combination worked. One of the elected guardians of the board, a Tenant-Right advocate named C. Lyne, brought up a motion calling for fair rents. The motion was defeated, with Lyne's vote being the only one in its favor. A few days later, the nationalist weekly, the *Nation*, reported the event and recounted the names of those who were present that day: "Mr. Trench, agent of the Lansdowne estate; Dr. George Maybury, medical officer to the workhouse; Richard Maybury, esq., occasional law advisor to Mr. Trench; Mr. Jeremiah Shea, sub-agent to ditto; Mr. McLure, agent to Mr. O'Mahony of Dromore, etc." At the meeting, as the editor observed, "not one independent elected guardian was present . . . except Mr. C. Lyne, who was so unsparingly assailed by Mr. Trench."[43]

The concept of board packing was worked to a point of refinement in the Castlebar union in Mayo. There, each large landowner had his agent on the board, three had their bailiffs, and two had their agents' brothers. The mechanics of this interplay between direct rule by the board's ex-officio officers and indirect rule through elected guardian surrogates was described for the select committee of 1878 by James Daly. When asked about ex-officios holding offices on the boards, Daly drew up a blueprint which he said applied to most unions in Ireland: "Whoever is the largest landowner in the union is, as a rule, the Chairman; second largest is the Vice-Chairman; whoever has the most influence [with the Chairman] is Deputy Vice-Chairman." Then he continued, citing the example of his union:

> [At Castlebar] the Earl of Lucan is Chairman, Mr. Larminie, his agent, is on the board; Brian Moran, his bailiff, is the rate-collector; Counsel O'Malley, a tenant of Lucan's, is Deputy Vice-Chairman. Charles Fitzgerald, a large landowner, is Vice-Chairman, Robert Powell, Fitzgerald's agent, and his brother, Edward Powell, are elected members. Sir Roger Palmer, a first-class landlord, is not on the board, but his bailiff, Andrew Walsh, and his agent, Francis O'Donel are. Sir Robert Lynch Bloss is on the board, as well as his agent, Mr. Tardy, who is an ex-officio guardian, and his bailiff, Francis Carty.[44]

"Lord Lucan," Daly asserted in conclusion, "does not attend regularly, Bloss seldom attends, C. L. Fitzgerald attends regularly, but all agents and bailiffs are regular attenders."

What did Daly mean by "regular" attendance? That the agents and bailiffs were there all the time? A majority of the time? More than the other elected guardians? The Castlebar minute books, which have survived, provide the answer. A survey of thirty Castlebar board meetings in 1877 reveals the following: Lord Lucan (the same Lucan who led the "Charge of the Light Brigade") was indeed an irregular attender, having appeared at only one meeting in the thirty, but his agent, Alex Larminie had, along with James Daly, the best record on the board with twenty-four attendances. Fitzgerald, the vice-chairman, who had by far the best record among the ex-officios, appeared at only fourteen meetings, but between him and his agent, Robert Powell, his interests were covered on all but six occasions. Sir Roger Palmer did not qualify for an ex-officio office since his estate was situated principally in the neighboring union of Claremorris. Nevertheless, his agent and bailiff represented his interests on the board as elected members, and between them they were present on all but two occasions. Sir Robert Lynch Bloss did not appear once during the thirty weeks, but his agent and bailiff attended between them about half the meetings. Of the various agents and bailiffs only Lucan's and Palmer's attended more than half the meetings.[45] But between them and their employers they managed to represent the interests of their respective estates on a regular basis. This is what Daly may have meant by "regular" attendance.

During the sample thirty weeks there were thirteen meetings at which no ex-officio guardian and no officer was present (Charles O'Malley, the elected guardian deputy vice-chairman mentioned by Daly, was not elected until the following year). At these meetings the guardians found it necessary to elect an acting chairman. The men they chose reveal a significant pattern. Robert Powell, Fitzgerald's agent, and Alex Larminie, Lucan's agent, occupied the chair seven times and four times respectively. At the two remaining meetings neither Powell nor Larminie was present, and the board chose a third member who represented no particular estate.

Not all boards, however, were governed as Castlebar was by land agents. In the union of Westport, which bordered on Castlebar to the west, there was an insufficient number of land agents to effect this kind of rule. The land in Castlebar was divided among several wealthy landowners; in Westport, three-fourths of the land was owned by one owner—the Marquess of Sligo. His agent, Sidney Smith, was an elected member of the board but not its dominating figure, because Sligo, an absentee landlord, was fortunate enough to have a brother, Lord John Browne, who lived on the estate, managed the family's affairs in Ireland, and supervised the proceedings of the board of guardians in person as its chairman. Unlike his brother, who spent all but six or eight weeks of the year in England, Lord John, the heir presumptive to the Sligo estates (since the Marquess, though married, was childless), seemed to have a taste for country life and a deep concern for the welfare of the community. Finlay Dun, a *Times* reporter who passed through Mayo in 1880, described Lord John as a man who

> farms extensively, by precept and example, and by distributing good male animals he has contributed to the advance of agriculture in the district. Mainly under his auspices, the cottages of the tenants have been improved. People have been cajoled or threatened for converting their houses into cattle or pig pens. . . . Improvements made by tenants are paid for if they remove; but premiums for entry are discountenanced.[46]

In addition to being an improving landlord, Lord John was also a capable and attentive administrator of the board of guardians. During the same thirty-week period from which the Castlebar sample was taken he missed only four meetings. Sidney Smith, his agent, occupied the chair for three of the four remaining weeks. While he was in the boardroom, Lord John completely dominated the board's proceedings. He personally proposed many of the motions, was always consulted before decisions were taken, drew up the relief lists, and took an active part in the board's debates.[47] He was, however, a fair man who was apparently respected by most of the board's members, including nationalists and Tenant-Righters who denounced landlordism in general. Because of his conscientiousness and fairness he was indispensable to the board's operation, and in subsequent years, when ex-officios came under strong attack and were removed from their offices in many unions in Ireland, the Westport members, perhaps as a tribute to Lord John's capabilities, continued to elect him as chairman until he himself withdrew in 1886.

The Castlebar and Westport boards presented an interesting contrast in board power relations, all the more striking because of their close proximity. The political structure at Castlebar was oligarchic, power being distributed among a number of members representing different estates, whereas Westport's was autocratic. Which of the two was the more typical would be impossible to say without a good deal more research in different localities. But because land ownership was the key to power in the 1870s, it is probable that most other boards resembled Castlebar and Westport in reflecting land ownership conditions in the unions. Thus unions that, like Westport, were dominated by one principal landowner probably tended toward the autocratic structure, while unions in which the land was distributed among several large owners tended toward oligarchy. In either case, the land agent was the man who made the system work, for ex-officios like Lord John Browne were rare in Ireland, and without the presence of ex-officios at the board there was little to stand between the tenants and the board offices, except the agent and his corps of followers.

Sources of Ex-officio Power

George Nicholls had thought of the ex-officios as a "corrective" to what he believed would be a changeable, confused, and administratively naive elected membership. He also believed that the limitation of their number among the membership would prevent them from overcorrecting. "Their position as magistrates," he wrote, "their information and general character, and their large prestige as owners of property, will necessarily give them much weight; whilst the proposed limitation of their number to one-third of the elected guardians, will prevent their having an undue preponderance."[48] Although it is true that his proposed limitation was not adhered to, and that Parliament subsequently fixed the ex-officio proportion at a level equal to the elected guardians, the limitation—at whatever the precise ratio might have been—was inconsequential. Because the ex-officios rarely attended meetings, it hardly mattered whether theoretically they made up one-third, one-fourth, or one-half the entire board. Numerical limitations notwithstanding, they were still powerful enough to treat the boards as though they were their own instruments. It was therefore one of the supreme ironies of the poor law that the good that was expected to arise from the ex-officios' presence on the boards failed to materialize, but the potential evil in it was realized much more completely than any of the poor law's founders could have imagined.

The essential flaw in the founders' thinking was that they confined themselves too narrowly to the poor law administration, treating it as though it were isolated from the world outside. Influenced perhaps by the scientific orientation of the world in which they lived, they thought of the poor law as a clinical experiment being conducted under controlled conditions. If this was indeed what they believed, then they were misguided or overly optimistic, for neither in England nor in Ireland was it possible to isolate the administrative from the social roles of the participants. The essential difference between the administrations in England and Ireland—and the reason that the English ex-officios never dominated their boards to the same extent as the Irish ex-officios dominated theirs—was that the social classes represented by the two elements in England were never so far apart as the Irish classes were. In England, first of all, tenants and landlords traditionally had a good working relationship: agriculture was much more prosperous than in Ireland and land tenure was fairly secure. Moreover, between the tenants and owners there stood a sizeable class of independent occupier-owners who provided a more continuous flow from the bottom to the top of the social scale. All these classes, furthermore, had had long experience working together in an administrative context in the parish vestries, ancient local bodies staffed by both gentry and commoners. Finally, there were large areas of common interest—racial, national, and religious—which also helped to soften class differences.

None of these beneficial conditions existed in Ireland. Society was divided into two classes, one poor, the other rich; one the tillers of the soil, the other the owners; one largely Gaelic and Catholic, the other largely Anglo-Saxon and Protestant. These differences were further aggravated by historically hostile relationships between tenant and landlord and between Irish and English—hostilities that in the 1830s were only beginning to build toward an inevitable confrontation. Under this two-class arrangement, class cooperation was not likely to be achieved, particularly since the class system was maintained against the tenants' will by laws that the tenantry considered to be of foreign origin. The nature of the class system in Ireland was such that the superiority of the Ascendancy pervaded all aspects of Irish life. To expect it to be different on the boards of guardians was unrealistic. Probably, therefore, the landowners would have gained control of the boards even without any ex-officio representation. They did so, as the foregoing analysis demonstrated, without attending meetings. But to carry the point further, the simple fact that they were able to secure election for their agents and bailiffs meant that the source of their power went deeper than the simple numerical advantage they gained from having surrogates among the elected guardians; it derived from their ability to control elections in such a way as to have their nominees accepted by the ratepayers.

Considered in this light, the electoral procedures mentioned earlier—the cumulative voting system, the proxy voting privilege, and the open voting papers—provide an additional perspective, because it was through these procedures that the owners were able to control elections. Although the procedures had been designed to provide balance between the various ratepaying groups in elections, in practice they strongly favored the landowning class, at least down to the time of the Land League. The least useful from the landowners' standpoint was the one-sided proxy vote. True, it enabled them to exercise the franchise when, without it, many of them would not have been able to vote. But it provided the owners with no positive advantage over the tenants because, as Nicholls had said, most tenants were available to vote in person. The owners did find one use for the proxy that enabled them to concentrate their votes on certain selected candidates, thus providing those candidates with an advantage over opposition candidates. They did this by employing a simple tactic: a number of landowners would assign their proxy votes to one individual—usually a representative of the Conservative or Liberal party—who would then have at his disposal a large bloc of votes to manipulate between the various divisional elections. The proxy-holder would then concentrate the votes in one or two divisions where close contests were expected, leaving alone the divisions where the landlords' candidates were unopposed or where they held safe majorities without the proxies.[49]

This ploy was of limited value, however, because it only worked as long as there were enough "safe" divisions to allow for sufficient concentrations of votes in other divisions. In the 1870s the tactic benefitted the landlords because few divisions were contested. In the more than 3,000 electoral divisions in Ireland in 1876, for example, only 312 contests were held, most of these in town divisions. In 1877 and 1878 the figures were even lower—259 and 235 respectively.[50] Since none of the poor law poll books have survived, it is impossible to know how many of these contests were decided by proxy votes. One can easily recognize, however, how much less effective this use of the proxy must have been in a year such as 1884— a quiet year by 1880s standards—when 554 contests were held,[51] most of them in unions in the south of Ireland. A poor law inspector who was questioned by a House of Lords select committee in 1884 on the use of the proxy vote in Ireland testified that "the use of proxies in the Limerick union increased enormously in the early 1880s, yet the proxies made not the slightest change in the personality of the elected guardians."[52] The proxy vote, therefore, was useless to the owners in a situation in which the tenantry voted and in large numbers, and in a bloc, against a list of landlord candidates.

The second procedure, the cumulative voting system, undoubtedly placed the owner in the more advantageous position in terms of man-to-man voting strength. Once again, the absence of poll books precludes any basic analysis of how the system worked, but a few calculations will show that the landlord had the advantage. Each tenant was entitled to only the number of votes he was allotted on the vote scale. For most tenants this meant one, perhaps two votes; for some—the large cattle graziers—it might have meant the maximum of six votes, unless the grazier happened to occupy two or more large holdings, in which case he could accumulate up to six votes for each holding. But a £200 valuation (the minimum required for six votes) was exceptionally high for tenants by nineteenth-century standards. A tenant-farmer was fortunate indeed if he was able to qualify for six votes on the multiple-vote scale. The owner, on the other hand, had the same number of votes as each of his tenants plus his own votes as occupier and owner of lands that he himself occupied, until he reached the maximum of eighteen votes. Because of the ability to accumulate votes, therefore, the owner's vote carried more weight than the tenant's vote did.

From the landlord's standpoint, however, there was one serious limitation to the cumulative vote system. This was in the eighteen-vote maximum, which placed a severe handicap on owners of large estates. Without that limitation, many aristocrats and country gentlemen could have accumulated hundreds or thousands of votes—at least one for each of their tenants plus the additional votes for their own occupancies. But the maximum limited them to eighteen votes regardless of the size and number of their holdings in the union, while the tenants, normally never achieving the maximum, could cumulatively acquire the hundreds or thousands of votes to which they were entitled individually. To recognize the significance of this handicap one need only consider the practical effect it could have on an owner of the magnitude of, say, the Marquess of Sligo. Sligo's estate extended to 114,881 acres, which accounted for about two-thirds of the total acreage of the Westport union. The estate encompassed the better part of fourteen electoral divisions, and the number of tenants who paid rent to him and were eligible to vote in poor law elections came to about 1,600.[53] Clearly, if the tenants decided to vote against him in a bloc, Sligo, being limited to a paltry eighteen votes, would have been powerless to obstruct them from putting their own candidates in office in about fourteen divisions in the union. The Marquess of Sligo was an extreme example, since he was one of the largest landowners in Ireland. However, other owners differed only in degree, and when it is considered that the aristocracy and gentry owned between five-eighths and three-fourths of the land in Ireland, the slight advantage they gained in the cumulative vote system seems almost negligible compared to the disability they suffered under the maximum-vote limitation. It should be quickly added, however, that the disability was contingent on a tenant bloc vote, a condition not present in the 1870s. Therefore the cumulative voting system operated to the owners' benefit.

From the owners' standpoint the most effective voting provision by far was the open voting paper system, for it, more than any other provision, enabled them to exert powerful informal influences on the electorate through the use of intimidation. Because the voting papers were open to inspection by any ratepayers who wished to examine them, they offered inexhaustible opportunities for intimidation or reprisal, and some owners had few qualms about using these opportunities to win elections for their candidates. A few examples from the contemporary press and the parliamentary debates will illustrate the point. In 1878 the *Connaught Telegraph* received a complaint about a Mayo land agent who sent a letter to his bailiff ordering him to "go from house to house to the tenants telling them to vote for . . . [name not supplied] . . . , to put a cross opposite to his name, and return the list."[54] And in another Mayo incident a land agent, Francis O'Donel (agent to Sir Roger Palmer), sent a circular note to his employer's tenants "requesting" that they vote "for Protestant rather than Catholic guardians."[55]

In a debate before the House of Commons in the same year, several other illustrations were offered by Home Rule M.P.'s claiming to be "inundated" with complaints about landlord intimidation in poor law elections, such as one concerning a magistrate in Crossmolina, County Sligo, who took a direct hand in an act of intimidation for which he was subsequently penalized by expulsion from the Commission of the Peace. He had audaciously—and imprudently—collected the voting papers from his tenants and filled them in himself![56] But perhaps the most poignant example given in the debate was one offered by Charles Stewart Parnell, whose political star was at the time just rising. In his own union of Baltinglass (Wicklow) there was a poor law election in which, in Parnell's words, "the farmers used considerable exertions to return candidates according to their views, whilst, on the other hand, the landlords of three large properties used every possible effort to prevent their return, and to support others of their own selection. In the end, the tenants who had voted in the opposition to the landlords were deprived of cutting turf on the property, and had to go nine miles for their supply of fuel. It is a common thing to tell a tenant and his family, 'you will have cold noses this winter.' "[57]

The right of cutting turf on the landlord's property was called the "right of turbary." It was usually granted gratis by the owner to his tenants, and could be withdrawn at the owner's will. Many landlords also provided other necessities, such as manure or lime fertilizer, gratuitously or at a nominal cost. Because these services could be withdrawn, they provided an excellent point of leverage for the owners against the tenants in poor law elections. I found other examples of the refusal of the right of turbary or an increase in the charge for lime being used for this purpose, either by implication or in actual practice, and where it was employed it was usually effective.[58] The few examples that came to the attention of the press or the government were more than likely just the tip of the iceberg. Because this tactic was so effective, the popular leaders in Parliament attacked the open voting paper system more energetically than any other aspect of the electoral system. From 1873 to 1879 the Home Rule party brought in six bills, all defeated or tabled, to substitute the secret ballot for the open voting papers. The secret ballot had been installed for parliamentary elections in the ballot act of 1872, and the Home Rulers—Parnell most of all— were convinced that the change had been the principal reason for the Home Rulers' winning fifty-nine seats in the general election of 1874.

But the open voting paper system—like the proxy vote and the cumulative vote—was also, for the landlords, a dubious ally. Intimidation could be effective only as long as the tenantry allowed themselves to be intimidated. Should the time arise when the loss of the right of turbary or an increase in the price of lime, or even the prospect of eviction itself, would cease to strike terror in the hearts of the tenantry, the open voting papers would lose their effectiveness and no longer serve as a means of discipline. Intimidation, furthermore, was a double-edged weapon which could serve the other side as effectively. The fear of a moonlight raid by marauding tenants, or a boycott that would close the doors of the shops in town to blacklisted offenders could, and in later years did, inspire as much fear among the landlords as the loss of a holding or the threat of a penalty at the hands of the landlord had among the tenants.[59] In this case the open voting papers could prove to be more of a handicap than an advantage to the owners. J. H. Whyte has argued cogently in connection with parliamentary elections that Parnell and the Home Rulers overestimated the impact of the ballot act on the fortunes of the Home Rule party. His contention is that deference, rather than the power of intimidation, was the root cause of the landlords' electoral power. The reason for the Home Rulers' success in 1874 was not that the ballot act eliminated intimidation as a factor, but rather that the deferential attitudes of the tenantry had begun to be replaced by an attitude of independence that was ready, given proper leadership and organization, to be converted into a posture of defiance.[60]

The poor law elections are an excellent test of Whyte's thesis. The popular leaders never succeeded in replacing the open voting papers with the secret ballot, yet as this study will show, the papers made not the slightest difference in the long run. Once the tenantry became aroused and organized they began voting on issues and paid little heed to the threats of the landlords. But back in the 1870s, this weakness in the protection afforded by the voting papers meant that the landlords were highly vulnerable in their position at the boards of guardians. They were represented by an ex-officio element that did not—could not—attend meetings regularly, and by groups of land agents and other supporters in the elected element whose places were dependent on the ratepaying electorate. The electorate, in turn, were controlled by the landlords, but not securely, since the control was exercised through a system of voting procedures that provided the landlords with, at best, equality and, at worst, a series of potentially disastrous handicaps.

The source of the ex-officios' power, therefore, was not in the law, but in their social relationship with the tenantry—in which they held, in the

1870s, most of the advantages. They were the more powerful economically, and were supported by a political tradition entitling them to the highest posts of authority. They were, moreover, the better organized, controlling the local political machines, which they used to gain the upper hand in elections. But at bottom their social superiority was more a product of the tenants' weakness than of their own intrinsic power. The tenantry—numerically superior, the producers of the country's wealth, and the class on whom the owners were dependent for the payment of rents—nevertheless submitted to the landlords' social and political domination largely out of force of habit and a sense of helplessness and inferiority. Michael Davitt stated the case aptly when he wrote:

> There was a greater evil than economic ignorance to beat down among the tenantry of Ireland, and that was their slavish social attitude towards not alone the landlord but his agent and the whole *entourage*. It was a hateful and heartbreaking sight to see manly looking men, young and old, doffing their hats and caps and cringing in abject manner to any person connected with an estate, and before magistrates and others associated with the administration of pro-landlord laws. It was a moral malady, born of feudalism and fear, the demoralizing results of the power possessed by those who had the legal authority to carry out the dread penalty of eviction. Generations of suffering and tyranny had inflicted this slavishness of manner upon a Celtic peasantry.[61]

The true source of the landlords' political power was neither legal nor economic, but psychological—the shadow of their one-time military superiority. The future of ex-officio domination resided, therefore, not with the landlords but with the tenantry; it could continue to exist in its all-embracing form only as long as the deferential state of mind was maintained. But in the 1870s it was already in decay, because there were many among the tenant class who no longer regarded themselves as abject slaves, and who believed that they were entitled to the posts of honor and prestige in local government.

2

The Farmer-Politicians of the 1870s

Society and Politics in Post-Famine Ireland

As THE ANALYSIS in the preceding chapter has shown, the means for bringing about change in the power structure of the boards of guardians ultimately rested with the Irish tenantry. Only the tenants, as poor law electors, could bring about the necessary changes in the elected membership that had to precede any successful assault on the board offices. But the conditions on the boards merely reflected in microcosm external conditions and were produced by the same causes. The question of change on the boards, therefore, ultimately reverted to the larger question of landlord-tenant relationships, and to the tenants' capacity to alter those relationships. Considered strictly from the standpoint of population, the probability of change in the tenants' favor was good. The population of Ireland in 1881 was 5,174,836, of which 3,109,476 lived outside the parliamentary boroughs. Of the three million rural inhabitants, about 24 percent lived in rural towns of over 2,000 population; the remainder—about 40 percent of the entire population—lived in villages and on farms.[1] The landowners and their families made up less than 10 percent of the whole, and the large landowners—the aristocracy and gentry, who owned at least three-fifths of the land—were less than 1 percent.

Numbers, however, were obviously not the only factor, nor even the most important one, because without cohesive action to counter the influential and well-entrenched landed interest, any effort by the tenants to force change upon the landlords—and such efforts had been made in the nineteenth century—must ultimately result in failure or at best, as with the Land Act of 1870, partial success. The tenants had to think and act as a class, and before the Land League, they were incapable of doing so. A few of the popular leaders of the 1870s, most notably Michael Davitt and, to a lesser extent at that stage, Charles Stewart Parnell, recognized the need and had a ready solution. What was most needed, they knew, was organization—organization to bring together the diverse elements within the population, and particularly to activate the largest and most important class, the small farmers of Ireland, without whose full participation any confrontation with the landlords must eventually devolve into a mere skirmish. This was the idea Davitt tried to convey in the spring of 1879 when he told his audience at the famous Irishtown meeting: "If the tenant-farmers of Ireland will organize themselves in one body, and resolve upon a settlement which the organized determination of such a purpose would render comparatively easy, the landlords of Ireland would be compelled to sell out. . . . Instead of 'Agitate, agitate,' the cry of the present should be 'Organize, organize.' "[2]

Davitt's advice on the occasion was understood and heeded, for the Irishtown meeting turned out to be a prelude to what later in the year became the establishment of the Land League—the most powerful tenant organization in Irish history. Without detracting, however, from Davitt's achievement in creating the league, it must be pointed out that the tenants' receptivity was also a result of developments dating back over the preceding half-century—developments that rendered the tenant-farmers capable of receiving, digesting, and acting on Davitt's advice. One of the most important of those developments was the evolution of a class of local leaders, groups of politically conscious and experienced men who were influential among the tenantry, and who, when called upon, were able to bring Davitt's message to the people and then perform the organizational chores required to make the Land League viable. The role of this class—indeed the very fact of its existence—has been largely overlooked by historians, even though Parnell and the other national leaders of the day utilized it extensively and usually took its opinions into account when formulating their policies. Because these local politicians also figured prominently in the activities on and surrounding the boards of guardians, a discussion of their origins, social character, and political orientations might provide a suitable starting point for this discussion of the tenants' position with regard to the boards of guardians in the 1870s.

When in the 1830s Daniel O'Connell embarked on his drive to obtain repeal of the Act of Union, he had few social and political resources at his disposal. Although his organization, the Repeal Association, had at its height dozens of branches in the Irish localities and attendance at his "monster" meetings was estimated in the hundreds of thousands, it is far from clear that the peasants involved in these activities understood O'Connell's message, or that the entire movement was not founded largely on O'Connell's enormous but transitory personal appeal. What evidence is available about the Repeal movement in the localities—and the evidence is admittedly scanty—points, as Thomas N. Brown has noted, to a high level of participation among the inhabitants of towns, since it was there that most of the Repeal Association branches and libraries were established. But though the peasants came to the monster meetings and applauded O'Connell's remarks, their lack of receptivity to other nationalist causes both earlier and later, including the Young Ireland "rising" of 1848, and their poverty, illiteracy, and parochialism suggest that their motives for attending the meetings were based more on a desire "to see the show," than to learn about what they as Irishmen could do to promote the cause of Ireland.[3]

The pre-Famine peasants lived under social and economic conditions that were less than ideal for the growth of the national consciousness, or, for that matter, political consciousness of any kind. A backward system of roads and canals and inadequate communication facilities restricted travel and hindered the flow of ideas and information between communities. Widespread illiteracy maintained by a backward system of "hedge" schools obstructed the peasant from receiving and understanding such information as did come through and made him dependent on the advice and instruction of others more literate than he, particularly the priest and the landlord. In 1840, 72 percent of the population of the four provinces were unable to read and write, and 52 percent were unable to read *or* write. Because the town populations were always more literate than the rural, these statistics do not reflect the true extent of illiteracy among the peasants—it was almost universal. Compounding the problems of communication and also helping to maintain them was a kind of cultural xenophobia arising out of a traditional clannishness which pitted province against province, parish against parish, and family against family even within the same parish. Another factor was poverty itself, caused in part by overpopulation and a land tenure system that encouraged the division and further division of the land into tiny subsistence holdings. The need to toil arduously for the barest means of survival no doubt contributed to the maintenance of the peasants' ignorance, clannishness, and dependence. Living under these conditions, the peasant possessed neither the desire nor the ability to think of himself as a member of a political community.[4]

It might have been possible to overcome this political backwardness with the proper kind of leadership, but there were few leaders, either national or local, who were willing to take the steps necessary to involve the peasants in politics. Abstract notions of liberty and justice had little meaning for the small Irish farmer. His overriding concern was survival, and his principal grievances centered around the land tenure system, which in the nineteenth century still retained characteristics of medieval manorialism. The law provided no restrictions against eviction, and leases, in the cases where they existed, were of short duration. Therefore the landlord could evict the tenant at will, and before the Famine landlords commonly resorted to this measure when tenants fell into arrears of rent or installed improvements that added resale value to the holding. Because of the tenants' insecurity of tenure, the landlord was able to exact whatever rents the market would bear, and the tenant, to retain possession of his holding, willingly paid over what otherwise might have been his profits. The small farmer, therefore, was unable to build up savings, so that during years of poor harvests his rents fell into arrears, creating further insecurity, a new danger of eviction, and another cycle of vulnerability and despair. These were the concerns that most troubled the farmer, and that provided the most fruitful possibilities for political exploitation to politicians seeking support from the Irish tenantry.

The nationalists of the 1830s and 1840s were cognizant of the farmers' problems, which were discussed publicly and at great length in Parliament and in the press during this period. But for various reasons, few of them were willing to take up the issues. O'Connell was greatly concerned that his Repeal movement remain a constitutional movement and not degenerate into the violent and insurrectionary upheavals that were characteristic of earlier agrarian movements such as the "Whiteboys" and "Steelboys" of the eighteenth century. Because of his hatred of violence and his fear that the introduction of the land question might arouse the peasants' passions to uncontrollable limits, he gave lip service to land reform but did little to promote it. As Lecky wrote of O'Connell: ". . . although he often used very violent and unjustifiable language towards individual landlords, he never encouraged those socialistic notions about land which since his death have been so prevalent: and he never forgave Arthur O'Connor for having, as he heard, a plan for the equal division of the land."[5] And O'Connell's successors, the vocally nationalistic Young Irelanders, were

guilty of the same neglect, but for different reasons. Most of these young
men were intellectuals concerned more with the ideological content of
nationalism than with its practical effects. By identifying Irish nationalism
with the Gaelic racial heritage, they imbued it with a cultural quality and
a vigor that O'Connell's moderate program had never been able to achieve.
But their absorption with ideological questions caused them to overlook
the more prosaic issues that were so important to the farmers, with the
result that when some of their members fled in 1848 to the countryside to
raise an insurrection, the Queen's troops in pursuit, they found themselves
unable to arouse much interest among the peasants, and their "rising"
never got off the ground.[6]

Among the Young Ireland intellectuals, only two, James Fintan Lalor
and Charles Gavan Duffy, addressed themselves to the farmers' problems.
Lalor, anticipating Davitt's "new departure" by three decades, formulated
a plan for merging the national and land reform issues into a single political
movement aimed at the liberation of both Ireland and the tenant-farmer.
The plan might have succeeded in enticing the farmers into politics had
Lalor had the opportunity to develop and enact it, but his untimely death
in 1849 removed his influence from the national scene and relegated his
proposal to the library shelf until, in 1878, Davitt presented it in a new
form. Duffy, as publisher of the *Nation*, often devoted a good deal of space
to discussions of land tenure, but his full conversion to land reform did
not occur until after the 1848 rising, and when he finally decided to espouse
the cause without reservations by founding the Tenant League in 1850,
he did so not as a nationalist but as a Tenant-Righter.[7]

Leadership did not, of course, end at the boundaries of Dublin. During
the thirties and forties, there were throughout the country many partisans
active in promoting Repeal and organizing public opinion behind it. In
the towns, as I mentioned, much of this activity seems to have been carried
on by the townsmen themselves. But in the countryside most of the local
leadership was provided by the priests and curates, whom O'Connell had
brought into politics during his Catholic emancipation movement in the
1820s. Exerting a powerful moral influence on the Catholic peasantry, the
priests were ideally placed to guide the peasants politically, and from the
late twenties until about the middle of the sixties they dominated popular
local politics. The high point in their influence appears to have come in
the fifties, when they were active in the Tenant-Right movement and in
electoral campaigns contested by Tenant-Right candidates.[8] As political

leaders the priests were more sensitive to the farmers' needs than were the leaders on the national level. The first Tenant-Right society was founded in 1849 by two Kilkenny curates who believed that the nationalist movements had not given sufficient attention to the land question.[9]

Clerical leadership, however, had certain disadvantages. The very fact that the priests were responsible for the moral education of the people often limited their political effectiveness. In their approach they tended to be conservative, and their unwillingness to condone forceful and revolutionary measures, which they considered morally corrosive, often placed them at odds with the more militant nationalists. Their conservatism was well suited to the constitutional nationalism of O'Connell, but as nationalism grew more radical, first under the auspices of the Young Irelanders and later, in the 1860s, under the tutelage of the Irish Republican, or Fenian, Brotherhood, the conservatism of the clerical leadership in politics began to be increasingly divisive. The more extreme Young Irelanders, for example, were never convinced of the sincerity of the clergy in politics, and the clergy were suspicious of both the advanced politics and the ecumenical educational views of the *Nation* group. An even more serious drawback to clerical leadership in politics, especially after the debacle of the Young Ireland rising in 1848, was the appointment of Paul Cullen as archbishop of Armagh and primate of all Ireland in late 1849, and apostolic delegate of the Holy See in early 1850. Cullen, who was very much the ultramontane conservative, saw the radical politics and the liberal educational views of the Young Ireland party as anathemas. Cullen was sure he saw the hand of Mazzini and Young Italy in Young Ireland, and he viewed the leadership of the Tenant-Right movement as tinged with those principles. When he was then translated to the more prestigious See of Dublin in 1852, therefore, he did as much as he could to dampen the political propensities of the Irish clergy, high and low, both at home and at Rome, as far as Tenant-Right politics and the Independent Irish party were concerned. During the 1860s, moreover, Cullen consistently condemned the Fenian Brotherhood by name, and no one did more than he to persuade the Irish bishops to secure a formal condemnation of the brotherhood by Rome early in 1870. Then, in refusing to countenance the Home Rule movement in the 1870s because he thought its leadership at once too Protestant and too Fenian, Cullen prevented the largest part of the clergy from taking up leadership positions in the movement. The withdrawal of the clergy from the kind of politics disapproved of by Cullen over a period of

nearly three decades, however, not only had the result of making even
constitutional politics more radical, but also resulted in laymen taking a
more active part in politics at both the national and local levels.[10]

Because of the backwardness of the peasantry and the inadequacies of
the existing leadership, there was a clear need during the middle decades
of the nineteenth century for a new class of leaders who would be committed without reservation to land reform, and who would not be diverted
by conflicts of interest from pursuing whatever policies were necessary to
achieve the desired political end. Beginning about the time of the Great
Famine, a series of developments occurring simultaneously set in motion
in Ireland a social revolution of major proportions, out of which there
emerged a new secular leadership. One group of developments, which
might be called a communication revolution, forged both a physical and
cultural link within and between Irish communities. In 1851, railway trunk
lines were completed, linking Dublin with the three other major cities—
Cork, Galway, and Belfast. Within twenty years, branch lines were extended from these points into all the surrounding hinterlands.[11] After 1851
a passenger trip from Dublin to Galway was reduced from twenty-six to
ten hours, and the fare was reduced by about half.[12] Postal service grew
so efficient that a letter posted in London before the close of a business
day would arrive in Cork before the close of business on the following
day.[13] During the sixties, the railways began to erect telegraph lines along
their trunk lines and many of their branches,[14] so that businessmen in the
provinces were able to learn of market conditions within hours after market
closings. A fringe benefit of the telegraph accrued to political leaders, who
were able to send instructions to lieutenants in the provinces in minutes,
thus facilitating the coordination of political operations. To recognize the
political significance of the telegraph, one need only consider that Parnell
issued instructions rarely by letter, but almost always by telegraph.

But perhaps the most important political aspect of the telegraph was its
use for the transmission of news.[15] For a population such as Ireland's, who
were so sorely in need of common experiences and access to information
about political developments, the press played a crucial role. Because of
news transmissions by telegraph, every newspaper in Ireland was able to
report important events and print the speeches of the important leaders
on practically the same day. The result, which was the converging of
experience rather than the diffusing of it, had inestimable consequences
for the development of a national consciousness. Although it would be
difficult to show a positive connection between the speeding-up of com-

munication and the growing politicization of the Irish people, one can hardly imagine a Land League or National League in O'Connell's day, when, as one reporter put it in 1867, "the citizens had a king's speech in perhaps three or four days, perhaps in the course of a week."[16] And while the telegraph brought the news more quickly to the people, the people at the same time became more capable of reading and understanding it. The National School system, founded in 1831, was far from perfect, but through it the Irish people grew literate. By 1871 about half the population were able to both read and write—which represented an improvement of about 30 percent over thirty years earlier—while the percentage who could neither read nor write decreased from about 50 percent to 33 percent.[17]

While the communication revolution altered the manners and customs of the people, another even more far-reaching development completely changed their economic condition. Prior to the Great Famine, Irish society was made up largely of small, subsistence farmers who planted crops and depended for their sustenance and livelihood on one principal crop—the potato. Population congestion was the normal condition, but it was particularly severe in the far south and west, reaching disastrous proportions in the province of Connaught and the western regions of Ulster where the land was least fertile. It was only slightly less severe in eastern Ulster and the northern half of Leinster, where farm sizes were small but the land was more fertile, and where alternative employment was available. Slightly less congested and less vulnerable were the south-central counties in the area ranging from Dublin southward along the east coast to Wexford and westward to the mouth of the Shannon River. In these counties agriculture was more diversified and farm sizes somewhat larger. The eastern coastal counties were important grain-producing counties, while those of the west in the fertile grasslands of northern Munster emphasized cattle, sheep, and dairy products. The largest farms of Ireland were in County Limerick and contiguous portions of Clare, Tipperary, and Cork, where a thriving cattle trade had been developing since the middle of the eighteenth century. Indeed, the effect of the industrial revolution and a rapidly increasing population in England at the end of the eighteenth century, had resulted in an increased demand for all Irish agricultural products. During the wars of the French Revolution and the Imperium, however, grain prices soared and the Irish agricultural sector responded smartly to the demand. When the wars with the French concluded in 1815, the bottom dropped out of the grain market, and the Irish farmers began the painful process of reconverting from tillage to pasture. Rapid population increase in Ireland, meanwhile, and the consequent subdivision of farms into smaller and smaller holdings, made it only more difficult to turn tillage into pasture. In a word, the Irish people were caught in the cruel vice of economic necessity and social need.

The awful turning point in this state of affairs was the Great Famine. The potato blight, which impaired the harvest of 1845 and destroyed that of 1846, was followed by winters among the fiercest in memory. The Irish peasantry, beseiged by hunger and disease and neglected by a government that came forward with too little too late, perished by the hundred thousands or made their way into the towns. Those fortunate enough to obtain passage moved to America or England, where they were eventually absorbed in the industrial cities. Within three years the population was reduced by two million, which was one-fourth of the pre-Famine figure. The heaviest decreases occurred among the laborers, cottiers, and those small farmers who occupied fewer than five acres. By the end of the decade the pressure on the land was relieved: the smallest, most inefficient farmers had been cleared off of the land; in the towns there was a new class of discontented, landless laborers who stood ready to support radical causes.[18]

The land clearance of the Famine marked the end of the first stage in a progression of events that began in 1815 and within twenty-five years completed the transformation of the Irish economy from one based on tillage farming to one centered around a thriving cattle trade. The second stage was an unprecedented rise in the price of livestock and dairy products between 1850 and 1876, caused by increased demands for these products in England. The high prices encouraged a shift to livestock production in Ireland, and the shift was facilitated by the availability of large tracts of land that had been cleared during the Famine.[19] At the same time, the railways, built during the early part of the period, opened up the hinterlands to the world market, encouraging a further shift from arable to pasture land in areas where livestock farming had formerly been unprofitable.[20] Everywhere in Ireland during the post-Famine years new grazing lands opened up and whole regions were converted to pasture as farmers expanded their holdings or carved out portions of existing holdings for pasture.

Among the first regions to feel the impact of the cattle boom was North Munster, the region where cattle grazing had been the main agricultural activity before the Famine. As early as 1851, the town fathers of Limerick began laying plans for the establishment of a cattle fair to end all fairs.[21] The Great Munster fair opened in April 1853, and was an immediate success. From surrounding Limerick, Clare, and Kerry farmers drove their herds to the fair, while the Waterford and Limerick Railway brought in additional herds from the counties to the south and east, depositing them on a special platform built by the railway company for that purpose. Buyers came to the fair from points as far distant as London and Liverpool, "whilst [according to the *Limerick Chronicle*] the jaded horses of the city cars told their own tale of work in the busy scene."[22] Some of those who attended were heard to say that the fair surpassed even the great, ancient fair at Ballinasloe. To the northeast and east of Limerick in the counties of the southern Leinster midlands, cattle grazing had also been a principal activity before the famine. In these counties—Kildare, Kings, Queens, and Kilkenny—tillage farming became virtually extinct during the post-Famine period. Just to the north, in the midland plains of Meath and Westmeath, the transition was most striking of all. Previously a region devoted predominantly to small farm tillage agriculture, this entire area was converted to grassland, and by 1870 it contained some of the largest and best stocked farms in Ireland.

Few localities were untouched by the cattle boom. In eastern Ulster farms remained small, largely because this was an important flax-producing center, and flax was in great demand during this period. Yet even there farmers fenced off portions of their land for the grazing of livestock, so that eastern Ulster became the second most important transition area in the country (next to Meath and Westmeath). The transition was somewhat less striking in the corn counties along the southeastern seaboard and in eastern Cork. The reason for this was that grain prices remained stable, so that farmers in these counties saw no reason to change over to pasture. In the entire country there was only one region where pre-Famine agricultural conditions persisted. This was the region along the western coast consisting of most of Connaught, the peninsular districts of the southwest, and County Donegal in the north. In these mountainous, wind-blown reaches, dense populations still crowded onto small, unproductive holdings continued to be the norm well into the twentieth century.[23] Yet by 1880 even in Mayo, one of the poorest of the western counties, two-thirds of its land under cultivation was in farms larger than thirty acres.[24] This suggests the existence there of a small but important class of graziers.

The economic prosperity of the third quarter of the nineteenth century, therefore, pervaded practically all of Ireland, and though all classes benefitted from it, none benefitted so much as the farmer engaged in livestock farming. It was from this newly prosperous class that the new rural leadership arose during the two decades following the Great Famine. They were able to emerge as leaders not only because of their wealth but because in a number of other ways they formed an elite group among the Irish farming class. Because of their importance to political organization in general and to organized agitation on the boards of guardians in particular, it is necessary to pay some attention to this particular group of farmers.

The Farmer Elite

C. M. Arensberg and S. T. Kimball, in their classic study of Irish rural society in the 1930s, offer a profile of rural Ireland drawn from data gathered largely in County Clare, an area that contained a balanced cross-section of the Irish rural population.[25] In that often-cited study, to which one must turn because of the lack of similar systematic studies of the nineteenth century, the authors found not one but two classes of Irish farmers, which they called the "large" farmers and "small" farmers.[26] The distinction was not based on farm sizes alone, though to be sure farm sizes made up a part of the overall definition. Rather, it was based on an entirely different set of social and economic norms under which the two classes operated. The small farmers, first of all, derived their principal income from raising crops, usually in great variety, which they sold largely for local and domestic consumption. They usually kept a few milch cows as well, selling the milk that their families did not consume and using the cows for breeding young stock. The calves that they did not need to replenish their own stock they also sold on the market, deriving from these sales a principal source of cash income which they used to pay rent and purchase consumer goods. Because their farms were small—usually not larger than fifteen to thirty acres—their chief capital asset was their labor, of which there was an abundant and inexpensive supply in their families. Farming for the small farmer was a family enterprise, and because the organization of the farm centered around the family, family ties and allegiances governed the attitudes and social relationships of the small farmer class.

Against this frame of reference, the large farmers stood in complete contrast. The large farmers usually were cattle graziers who occupied large tracts of grassland, meadow, and bog, usually in districts where the land was devoted solely to that purpose. Although the graziers set aside a small portion of their farms for raising crops, the crops were for family consumption or animal feed, not for income. They derived their income from the sale of animals, either two- or three-year-old store cattle or dairy stock, or the sale of milk and dairy products derived from the stock. Their principal markets were not local but national and international. Cattle grazing being an activity requiring a relatively small amount of labor, the graziers' chief capital assets were in their herds and pasturelands, and such labor as they required they were able to hire for wages. Thus they were much more directly involved in the money economy than the small farmers were, and their families were more free to pursue personal interests and goals. With hired labor to perform the chores, the grazier himself was as much a manager and businessman as he was a farmer, and having more leisure time as well as a greater need to be in contact with the market centers, his exposure to the world outside his community was much more frequent and regular than was the small farmer's. Thus the grazier differed from the small farmer in many ways—in the way that he organized his life and his farm, in his daily contacts and his handling of money, and in his orientation toward other people, which was outward toward society rather than inward toward the family.

The two classes were not, however, isolated from each other; on the contrary, each performed essential services for the other in ways that helped to integrate society and establish a continuous link between the small farmer and the external world. The binding agent was cattle or sheep. The small farmers needed an outlet for their young livestock but were ill-equipped in terms of financial and business resources to deal directly on the open market. Nor did they possess the acreage that was required for grazing and storing their herds beyond the yearling or two-year stage. The large farmers, therefore, purchased the young livestock for cash and used it to augment their own herds. Then, at the suitable time, they sent the stock on to other graziers near port cities for fattening and subsequent sale to dealers and packers. The money and goods thus obtained at the market place filtered back down to the small farmer, completing the cycle. In this way the livestock trade joined together in common interest not only the small farmer and large farmer but also farmers in different communities, not to mention the drovers, dealers, leather manufacturers, quay stewards, shippers, and others who derived their income directly or indirectly from cattle. Within this scheme, the cattle grazier was the central figure, standing with one foot planted in the town and the other in the country and embodying in his own occupational role the worlds of both the farmer and the businessman.

These were the conditions that Arensberg and Kimball found existing in the 1930s. They were no doubt much more clearly defined then than they were a half-century earlier, but the two classes were clearly in existence even before the Great Famine. Lord Clements, for example, when writing his pamphlet on the poor law bill in 1837, referred to the two classes in offering an argument for elected guardians to be granted salaries for their services. His reasoning was that if guardians were not paid, the boards of guardians would fall into the hands of the cattle graziers:

> There are very many districts, where the arable farms are so small, that the occupiers cannot be expected to give their gratuitous attendance; and if the Central Commission should disregard this peculiarity,—and should not stimulate a selection of these farmers, both by urgent advice and also by payment, in cases where this may be found necessary,—the whole management of the poor will be thrown into the hands of a class who are not employers of labour; that is, of the graziers. But the graziers on that very account will be indifferent in their attendance; and, from the peculiar nature of their business, being absent frequently at distant fairs in the spring and autumn, will be irregular: so that there will be an inefficient and irregular attendance at the Board of Guardians.[27]

Amazingly accurate in his predictions, Lord Clements did not, however, derive his perceptions from a crystal ball. He based his argument on two reports of the English Poor Law Commissioners, who reported a similar development on the boards of guardians in England. However, as his statement reveals, there was in Ireland before the Famine a class of cattle graziers who were perceived as a distinct class of farmers having somewhat different interests from the small farmers and a potential for using their advantageous position to assert themselves politically. If this were true before the Famine, it became doubly true after the cattle boom of the post-Famine years.

Even in 1870 the graziers did not constitute a very large segment of the farming population. A precise estimate of their proportion among the population is not attainable, not because of the lack of data but because of the vagueness of what constituted a cattle grazier. The large farmers and small farmers were not separated by a wide gap, but rather blended gradually into each other as the proportions of their income derived from grazing increased or decreased. A rough estimate, however, can be gained from examining farm sizes in relation to the kind of agriculture performed on them, which enables one to judge the proportion of farms engaged principally in cattle grazing. The data in Table 3 show the percentage of land in crops, grass, and waste by size of farm in the year 1871.

We see in the table that farm size was a fairly accurate guide to the kind of agriculture farmers engaged in. The percentage of crops relative to grassland decreased with each increase in farm size. At five to fifteen acres and fifteen to thirty acres the two were almost evenly balanced, but over thirty acres the ratio widened significantly at each level in favor of grassland. At over 500 acres the percentage of land in crops was negligible. Among the middle-sized groups (5–15, 15–30, and perhaps even 30–50 acres), the balance was close enough to make it difficult to say whether the farmers in these classifications were cattle graziers of the kind described by Arensberg and Kimball. Clearly at the fifty- to 100-acre level the proportion of grassland to crops was wide enough to permit the assumption that the farmers in this group derived most of their income from livestock. The assumption holds truer for the farms above 100 acres, because the higher proportion in grass reflected a vastly larger amount of land devoted to grazing. Using fifty acres as a safe cutoff point, therefore, one can say that the grazier class constituted only about 15 percent of the population— the top 15 percent in terms of land occupancy if not also in terms of economic wealth. One can hardly imagine a farmer who occupied a farm of, say 100 acres—and who consequently fell into the top 5 percent of farmers in land size—not being one of the more prosperous farmers in Ireland. For our purposes, at any rate, we shall assume the existence of a direct relationship between farm size and economic wealth.

Proportionally few in number, the graziers nevertheless were extremely active in local politics after the Famine. In fact, it would not be an exaggeration to say that they virtually monopolized the political positions both in and out of government that were open to the farmer class during this period. New opportunities opened up in the poor law administration,

TABLE 3

Percentage of Land in Crops, Grass, and Waste by Size of Farm, 1871

Size of Farm (Acres)	Proportion of Farms	Crops	Grass	Bog and Waste
Less than 1	8.2%	85.1%	5.5%	8.4%
1–5	12.6	63.5	27.5	7.9
5–15	28.9	47.4	42.9	9.0
15–30	23.4	40.6	48.1	10.7
30–50	12.3	35.3	51.1	12.8
50–100	9.3	28.9	54.8	15.1
100–200	3.6	21.3	57.2	19.4
200–500	1.4	12.7	52.5	31.4
Over 500	.3	3.2	33.2	60.3
All Ireland	100.0	27.7	49.6	21.0

Source: Barbara Lewis Solow, *The Land Question and the Irish Economy 1870–1903* (Cambridge, Mass.: Harvard University Press, 1971), p. 108.

Note: Percentages do not add up to 100 because of minor omissions, e.g., timber plantations.

supervised after 1847 by the new Irish Poor Law Commission set up in Dublin. In 1851 the commission assumed responsibility for medical care, taking over the supervision of the network of dispensaries and infirmaries from county government.[28] Local administration of the dispensaries was assigned to the boards of guardians, who appointed dispensary committees from among their own members. Most Irishmen probably did not think of the posts on boards of guardians as political offices, since the boards' functions were solely administrative. By any objective standards, however, the board offices, at least the elective ones, clearly contained a political dimension. Since the assent of the electorate was necessary to achieve an office, the achievement represented for the holder a certain amount of influence and status among the tenantry. Moreover, the functions of the office involved the exertion of influence on governmental policy. If, therefore, electoral influence and governmental influence make up any part of the definition of politics, then the elective offices were as much political in character as they were administrative.

That is not to say that the holders of the offices were necessarily partisan or even conscious of having political goals. Most guardians prior to the period of the Land League probably regarded their posts as status symbols: the recognition of their right, won at the ballot box, to preside in an exclusive atmosphere and participate with the upper crust of rural society in making important community decisions. The element of social exclusivity was so prevalent among the boards that members of the press often referred to them depreciatingly as "social clubs" and "debating societies." Few descriptions are available of the character of elected guardians as a group, and those that do exist are mostly descriptions written in the 1880s by nationalist newspapermen seeking to disparage the conservative guardians, who they felt did not sufficiently represent the "people." One such account, however, deserves to be quoted because the journalist, in this case the editor of the *Clare Advertiser*, seems to have gained a few worthwhile insights into the character and motivations of the earlier guardians. In an 1883 editorial entitled "What is a Guardian?" he wrote:

> The leading motive for seeking the office [in the case of industrious farmers or middle men] used to be that it gained them entree into a kind of club, where they could meet and converse with their equals, insinuate themselves into favor with those who were a step or two higher on the social ladder, and contemplate at a distance and with sufficient awe, the Mandarin or two, who at intervals might deign to shine on them. It was much too to be chosen to look after the poor rates of a district, to be a frequent theme of conversation to the neighbors, and to be the proprietor of an official book [probably the official guardians' handbook] written in rubrics, producing, strange to say,

such an effect upon the Dispensary Doctor as a red flag on a certain beast. Then, if there is such good luck as an election of a doctor! It is Danae wooed by Jupiter; a golden opportunity of disinterested patriotism. These, and such as these, were and may still be moving influences no doubt: but the leading motive for the office of PLG used to be—the ambition to rub against a squireen or a JP or an MP.[29]

As one can judge from the editor's description, the boards of guardians provided the perfect setting for the bourgeois with an interest in expanding his horizons: both social and political advancement and no doubt some economic benefits, derived from new business contacts, awaited the aggressive farmer or shopkeeper who sought entry into the public service as a P.L.G. It was inevitable that the available places on the boards should have been sought after and won by members of the cattle grazier class, not only because—as Lord Clements had observed in 1837—they had the time and economic resources necessary for holding an unsalaried office, but because the opportunities for social and political advancement accorded with their aspirations as members of a newly arrived social elite.

An examination of the occupations and landholdings of elected guardians in the 1870s reveals that the graziers were, indeed, well represented on the boards. One can take, for example, the tenant-occupiers who held board offices in 1877. It will be recalled from the analysis in the last chapter that the 489 board offices were distributed among 430 landowners and fifty-nine tenants. With the use of a number of commercial directories in combination with the valuation records, the occupations and landholdings of forty-one of the tenants were identified. The occupational distribution is shown in Table 4.

TABLE 4

Occupations of the Tenant-Occupiers Who Were Board Officers in 1877

Occupation	Number	Percent
Farmers	21	35.6
Shopkeepers	7	11.8
Merchants	5	8.5
Bank managers	2	3.4
Professionals	2	3.4
Civil servants	1	1.7
Business agents	1	1.7
Publicans	1	1.7
M.P.'s	1	1.7
Unidentified	18	30.5
Total	59	100.0

Source: See the Methodological Appendix.

As the table reveals, farmers headed the list with about three times as many officers as the group below them, the shopkeepers, and a slightly higher proportion than all the other identified classes combined. Commercial directories like the ones used here tend to be biased in favor of town occupations; therefore, it is easier to identify shopkeepers, professionals, and the like than farmers. So it is likely that the unidentified group were mostly farmers. If that were indeed the case, the proportion of farmers to the other groups would be considerably higher than the table shown. The town classes, especially shopkeepers and merchants, were surprisingly strong in the board offices, considering that they usually held no more than 20 percent of the elective seats on the rural boards. Town dwellers were, on the whole, considerably more active politically than farmers, and their occupations better prepared them for assuming managerial positions. Also, their businesses and professions brought them into more regular contact with landowners and land agents, who had the final voice over officer appointments. This may explain the high proportion of townsmen among the officers.

It is the twenty-one farmers we are interested in here. To determine whether they were small or large farmers we need to know the sizes of their farms. I selected a dozen names at random from among the twenty-one farm officers and ascertained both the acreage and valuations of the holdings on which they resided. The results, shown in Table 5, indicate

TABLE 5

Names, Addresses, Unions, Acreage, and Valuations of Twelve Sample Farmers Holding Board of Guardians Offices in 1877

Name	Address	Union	Acres	Valuation
William Bolster	Tullerboy	Kilmallock	303	£241
Michael Meagher	Monanore	Nenagh	212	73
James Kelly	Crakenstown	Dunshaughlin	189	198
William Mitchell	Castlefleming	Donaghmore	179	105
Patrick Murray	Ballynaskea	Delvin	177	134
William Jones	Knockeen	Clogheen	152	133
Daniel Maher	Thurles	Thurles	102	134
E. R. O'Farrell	Fary	New Ross	94	44
Patrick D. Clery	Fortboy	Kilmallock	50	59
Francis Geraghty	Finnalaghta	Mohill	50	21
Chas. McCarthy	Newcastle	Newcastle	49	83
Jonathan Dondican	High Park	Dromore	49	14
Average			133.8	£103.3

Sources: For names and addresses, *Thom's* (1878); for acres and valuations, *V.R.* (1877), under addresses cited.

that the farmers in the sample were large farmers, probably of the cattle grazier class. The farms of nine of the twelve had a £50 valuation; a tenth was valued at £44. The first seven names on the list were well above the 100-acre level, which placed them within the top 14 percent of farmers in terms of farm size. Therefore at least seven, probably ten of the sample farmers were men who would be considered graziers. The remaining two (Francis Geraghty and Jonathan Dondican) showed valuations that were relatively small and that may have placed them in the small-farmer class, though their farms were well above average size in the counties where they lived (Leitrim and Sligo).[30]

It is possible, one might argue, that the foregoing findings have been biased by the sample. All these farmers were officers, and it could be that although large farmers tended to hold board offices, they were actually a small group among the guardians as a whole. While it would be impossible to refute this argument without taking a broad sample of non-officer guardians—a chore that would be extremely difficult and time consuming because addresses were not given for non-officers—some verification of the findings can be supplied. In an attempt to ascertain the social composition of the boards of guardians in Connaught, I examined the entire valuation records for 1873 for the unions of Castlebar and Westport, seeking to locate the holdings of guardians whose names I found in the minute books of the two unions. In all, fifteen farmers' holdings were identified; their valuations (not acres) are shown in Table 6. Although the valuations of the fifteen varied widely, the list by and large paralleled closely that of the officers in Table 5. One farmer, Thomas Prendergast, had a valuation (£12) similar to that of the smallest landholding officer (Jonathan Dondican, £14); two others stood between £20–50; the remainder were all above £50, with about half (as in the case of the officers) ranging over £100.

In County Mayo, land values averaged about one pound for every four acres. If even half of this figure (one pound for every two acres) is applied to the valuations on the list in Table 6, then every farmer except Prendergast occupied farms of more than fifty acres. At least half the farms were in the hundreds of acres. There are additional facts that these statistics do not reveal, which can be known only by tracing the personal histories of the guardians, such as the fact that John Louden, who later became a Land League leader, was the son and heir of George P. Louden, who held 7,000 acres of land in the Westport union[31] and was therefore probably the largest tenant-occupier in Mayo, if not in all Ireland. These landholding statistics, in other words, do not take into account family

TABLE 6

Names, Unions, and Valuations of Holdings of Tenant-Farmers on the
Castlebar and Westport Boards of Guardians in 1873

Name	Union	Valuation[a]
William Nally	Castlebar	400
Edward Cannon	Castlebar	250
Patrick Daly	Castlebar	246
H. C. Larminie	Castlebar	234
Thomas Brennan	Castlebar	124
Thomas J. Gibbons	Westport	123
William Evans	Westport	118
John Louden	Westport	107
William Fahy	Westport	73
Malachi Tuohy	Castlebar	61
Patrick McGirr	Westport	59
James Hughes	Castlebar	57
Michael McHale	Westport	36
Patrick McHale	Westport	29
Thomas Prendergast	Westport	12
Average valuation		128.6

Sources: For names, Castlebar minute books, mss. 12400–12401 (1873); Westport minute books, mss. 12646–12650 (1873). For valuations, *V.R.* (1873), passim.

Note: The list does not contain all the tenant-farmers on the two boards but only those whose names were given in the board's minute books for 1873 as having attended meetings. It was not possible to get the names of those who did not attend, since the union clerks did not list them in the books. In all, three elected guardians in Castlebar and four in Westport remained unidentified.

[a] These valuations are minimums. The home addresses of the guardians were not given in the minute books, so all holdings to which reference was made for each guardian in the valuation records were taken into account. Since compiling valuations by this method is highly inexact because of the thousands of names one must go through to find the names of the guardians, it is more than possible that some holdings in the unions were overlooked.

connections and prospective holdings, both of which were important factors in determining social status. If, therefore, these two samples—the one a shallow sample of national scope, the other an in-depth sample of a small region—were at all representative of boards of guardians in general, one can conclude from them that the cattle graziers exercised a near monopoly over the rural elected seats not held by land agents and bailiffs.

The boards, however, were not the sum total of local politics in nineteenth-century Ireland, nor the only outlet for the large farmers' political energies. Some farmers—in many cases the same ones who sat on the boards of guardians—were very much concerned with political issues, especially issues involving questions of land tenure. Nationalist leaders before Isaac Butt were largely unresponsive to demands for raising these questions, so opportunities for reform-minded farmers within the nationalist context were few. The farmers, therefore, were compelled to make their own opportunities, which they did by launching the Tenant-Right movement. The movement began at the very end of the 1840s, at a time when public attention, because of the Famine, was focused on farmers' problems, and the failure of the Young Ireland rising had left a vacuum in popular politics. The first Tenant-Right society had been founded in Kilkenny in 1849. The goal of the organization was land reform, to be achieved by strictly constitutional means, that is, by pressures applied to Parliament through the Irish representation. The specific objectives were what later came to be known as the "three F's": fixity of tenure, which guaranteed the tenant security in his holding as long as he continued to pay his rent; fair rent, which was to be assessed by an independent tribunal; and free sale, which allowed the tenant to sell his "good will," in his right of occupancy to the incoming tenant.

The eagerness with which the farmers took up the new cause was evident in the rapid progress of the movement. By the end of 1850 there were at least two dozen Tenant-Right societies in Ireland,[32] and in subsequent years an undetermined number of others were added. In August 1850 the Young Irelander Gavan Duffy and another journalist, Frederick Lucas, founded the Tenant League, a national counterpart to the local societies, located in Dublin. The league immediately set out to procure commitments from Irish representatives and prospective representatives seeking popular support. It managed to gain commitments on the Tenant-Right program from about fifty M.P.'s, all break-away Liberals, who, in 1852, established themselves as a new party known as the Independent Irish party. Together, the party, its extraparliamentary wing, the league, and the local societies, formed the most coherent agrarian movement Ireland had had up to that time. But the movement lacked the dynamic and imaginative leadership that O'Connell and Parnell later were able to provide their own movements. Duffy and Lucas neglected to cultivate and consolidate the support of the local societies, while the parliamentary party was riddled by internal discord and political opportunism. The party itself was composed largely of landowners and professional men whose sincere dedication to land reform was questionable, at least in the eyes of farmers. Because of these and other weaknesses the league and party disintegrated in 1859, never achieving the hoped-for land reforms. However, in 1870 Gladstone, who had been influenced by the arguments of the Tenant-Righters and was then prime minister, secured passage of a moderately comprehensive land act, which included provisions for compensation for certain classes of evicted tenants, as well as a relatively liberal land purchase scheme that had been proposed by John Bright.

The Tenant-Right movement did not, however, terminate with the demise of the national organization. Local Tenant-Right societies going under the names of Tenants' Defense Associations, Farmers' Clubs, and Independent Clubs re-emerged in the 1870s, exerting a powerful influence on local and national politics until finally, during the early 1880s, they were subsumed by the Land League. In seeking an explanation for the durability of the Tenant-Right movement, the most obvious one that comes to mind is that it was the only movement prior to the Land League that addressed itself without reservation to farmers' problems. Irish farmers were always most attentive to bread-and-butter issues. But another reason, which is more important because it explains *why* it addressed itself to farmers' problems, was that the movement both resulted from and signified the growing politicization of the farmers. Unlike Catholic emancipation, Repeal, Young Ireland, Fenianism, and even Home Rule—all of which were political movements established by national political figures and then extended into the localities—Tenant-Right began at the grass-roots level and expanded upwards. The grass-roots character of the movement was the reason that, when the Tenant League collapsed and the Independent Irish Party dissolved, many of the local branches were able to survive or later revive. They drew their strength from the farmers, not the national leadership.

Not all classes of farmers, however, were represented in the local Tenant-Right societies, even though the societies' goals may have reflected the aspirations of all farmers. By all indications—and here again, the evidence is not satisfactory—their members were mostly large farmers. Conor Cruise O'Brien, in connection with his study of Parnell, gained the distinct impression that these bodies were generally "relics of the tenant right movement of the fifties, and on the whole they seem to have represented a more prosperous class of farmers than did the Land League".[33] In a more concrete context, Samuel D. Clark, a sociologist who has studied the social origins of the Land League and has had the opportunity to examine the farmers' clubs of the seventies in detail, also has the impression that almost all the members were prosperous farmers. This was certainly the case with the one club that he studied most extensively, the Limerick and Clare Farmers' Club, at one of whose meetings in the 1870s a member actually stated "we are all cattle graziers."[34]

The locations of major Tenant-Right activity also suggest heavy participation by cattle graziers and other prosperous farmers. Of some thirty Tenant-Right societies pinpointed by John H. Whyte as having been established in 1849 and 1850, seventeen were located in a narrow band of territory reaching from Wexford to Limerick, and the majority of these were clustered in counties Kilkenny and Tipperary—among the most important livestock regions in Ireland.[35] To discover whether any major shift occurred over time, I went through every issue of the *Nation* for 1877 and marked down the location of every local political club mentioned as holding meetings during that year. The *Nation*, it might be pointed out, was meticulous about reporting meetings of popular political organizations. The clubs mentioned were the following: the Kilkenny Tenants' Defense Association (T.D.A.), the Limerick (formerly Limerick and Clare) Farmers' Club, the North Kerry T.D.A., the Ballinasloe T.D.A., and the Mallow Farmers' Club. There were, in addition, Independent clubs in Wexford and Queens counties that listed Tenant-Right among their goals, and also a Home Rule club in Edenderry (Kings County) that, though formally connected with the Home Rule movement, counted many Tenant-Righters among its membership. These were the only clubs operative in 1877 outside of one or two others which held only one meeting during the entire year. Tenant-Right activity, then, had quieted down considerably since the early days of the movement, yet the region in which the 1877 clubs were concentrated was roughly the same one that contained most of the early societies. On a map of Ireland it can be defined by a line drawn from Dublin westward to Ballinasloe (Galway), southward to Tralee (Kerry), eastward to Wexford, and north again to Dublin but excluding Carlow and Wicklow. Not only does this line define roughly the outer limits of organized local political activity in 1877; it also defines almost precisely the region containing the highest and oldest concentration of livestock farms in the south of Ireland. While this correlation does not prove that the members of the political clubs were cattle graziers, it does suggest the existence of a high level of political consciousness and receptivity to organized action among the farmers in the grazing region. Taken together with other evidence, it indicates some connection between tenant wealth and tenant political organization in the 1870s.

There were no doubt factors other than wealth involved. The counties within the politically active region were among the most Catholic counties in Ireland. The Catholic portions of their populations ranged from 85 percent in Kildare to 95 percent in Limerick and Kerry.[36] Significantly, the region along the southeastern coast that made up the old English Pale—north Wexford, Carlow, Wicklow, and Dublin (county)—was devoid of Tenant-Right societies, although the farms in this area were generally as large as those in the politically active counties to the west. One reason might be that these counties had the largest Protestant populations in the south of Ireland (Carlow, 11 percent; Wicklow, 36 percent; and Dublin, 24 percent in 1881),[37] and the best farm lands were in the hands of the Protestant farmers. Although Tenant-Right was not particularly a Catholic movement, it was a movement directed against landlords whose racial and religious origins were the same as those of the Protestant farmers. It may well be that the farmers of the Pale counties had, over the generations, made their peace with the landlords and considered themselves part of the social and political establishment. Whatever the reason, political agitation involving Irish tenant-farmers in the three southern provinces seems to have been weakest in the Pale counties, and this continued to hold true in subsequent years, as I will demonstrate later.

During the quarter-century following the Great Famine, then, there developed in Ireland an agrarian elite which dominated the social, economic, and political life of the farming classes. Socially mobile and economically independent to a degree unprecedented in Irish agrarian history, the large farmers—who constituted a new rural upper middle class—turned to politics as a means of fulfilling their social and economic aspirations. This combination of independence and rising aspirations represented a potential threat to the privileged position of the landed interest in local government, for the farmers' quest for a higher status in the community might eventually lead them into claiming as their own right the privilege of exercising authority over the proceedings of the boards of guardians, and holding the honored positions monopolized by the ex-officios. Until about 1870, however, the threat remained only potential, largely because the boards in the beginning were not considered to be political bodies. The tenants who joined them, whatever their motives, and the ex-officios both considered themselves administrators and confined their activities to the purposes for which the boards had been established. Any radical ideas the elected guardians might have had, they either kept to themselves or reserved for the discussions in the Tenant-Right societies. This compartmentalization of roles operated against the politicization of the boards, and was part of a wider pattern of political particularism that operated against the politicization of the Irish tenantry as a whole.

The Farmer Elite and Home Rule

When Isaac Butt rose to prominence as a national figure toward the end of the 1860s, Irish popular politics was atomized into a number of disparate, ostensibly unbridgeable factions. The old division between nationalist and land reformer, which had appeared in the Repeal and Tenant-Right movements, still existed and had been aggravated by the emergence of the Fenian Amnesty movement in the aftermath of the collapse of the Fenian conspiracy in their insurrection in March of 1867. Before its demise, the Fenian Brotherhood had, in fact, made very few recruits among the tenant-farming class. In emphasizing its goals of overthrowing English rule by force of arms and setting up an Irish republic, the Brotherhood appealed mainly to those who had little to lose—the younger and poorer classes of the towns, laborers, artisans, shopboys, domestic servants, and some farmers' sons. Part of the reason that the Brotherhood failed to attract the support of tenant farmers was its lack of any policy on land reform. Michael Davitt, who served his political apprenticeship as a Fenian, in later years attributed the failure of the movement to the fact that the Brotherhood was not an agrarian association.[38] The farmers might wish the Fenians well in the abstract, but they apparently were not prepared to make a serious sacrifice for what was little better than buying the proverbial pig in a poke.

The Fenian leaders, moreover, had also aggravated the division over national and agrarian goals by espousing methods of agitation that made the agrarian leaders uncomfortable. Their advocacy of physical force as a means of achieving their objectives represented a return to the republicanism of 1798—a brand of nationalism that O'Connell had done all in his power, with some success, to eradicate. Land agitation, at the same time, took an opposite turn, away from the secret, oath-bound, and violent methods employed by the "Whiteboys" and "Steelboys" of the previous century to the open, peaceable, and constitutional methods of Tenant-Right. The temperate attitudes of the Tenant-Right farmers are not difficult to explain if one keeps in mind their social character. A contributor to the *Dublin Magazine* in 1861 recognized this attitude among large farmers and attributed it to their growing wealth and social position, resulting from what he believed to be a "social revolution" in progress. The pauper class of pre-Famine times, he observed, was gone, and in its place was "a class of farmers more prosperous than they could ever have imagined." The new farmer, who could be found "everywhere, as for example in the counties of Tipperary, Cork, or Limerick," held "twice or thrice as much land as he held in 1849 or 1850," and his land was "better stocked or tilled, as the results of larger dealings have enabled the cultivator to extend his enterprise." The farmer who had been a beggar only twelve years earlier was now "disinclined to agitation, and more anxious . . . that his newspaper shall report correctly the prices of stock at the great fairs of Munster, Banagher, and Ballinasloe, than the speeches of the O'Donoghue himself." Politically, he was "dependable," having "no subversive ideas," and though Catholic, "not willing to be ultramontane."[39] Such was the effect of the cattle boom.

Violence is the instrument of the poor, and it is not surprising that the Fenians' strongest following should have come from the urban working classes. But the prosperous farmers had little to gain by advocating physical force methods that, once set loose, might easily be used against their own persons or property. Rick-burnings, cattle-maimings, and other outrages committed in great numbers by the Fenians offered evidence enough of their lack of respect for property. An 1870 advertisement in the *Newspaper Press Directory* placed by the Cork *Southern Reporter* perhaps best expressed the large farmers' attitude toward violence in general and Fenianism in particular. In the advertisement the *Reporter* declared itself to be a newspaper that

> advocates the ideas of the Liberal Party, and strongly discourages "Irish Republics" and similar chimeras. It strenuously urges the redress of many grievances by strictly constitutional methods. It does not sympathize with the "nationalist" party, and is devoted to both liberty and order. It is the sole organ in the south of Ireland of the moderate Liberal Party, the upper middle classes, viz., those who have something to lose.[40]

The Cork *Southern Reporter* undoubtedly represented the upper limit in the attempt at this time to revitalize the Liberal party in Ireland. Indeed, at the time of the advertisement Gladstone was doing his best to come to terms with those most partial to Tenant-Right by enacting the Land Act of 1870. No class could have been more useful, in fact, to the concept of the Gladstonian Irish-Liberal alliance than those large tenant farmers who constituted the rural "upper middle classes" in the south of Ireland.

Fenianism, therefore, offered the large farmers little that they could use; because Fenianism was the outward expression of Irish nationalism, most of these farmers avoided being too closely associated with that brand of nationalism during the sixties. But events soon altered that picture. Toward the end of the sixties Isaac Butt, a Protestant barrister who had been receiving national attention for his efforts in defending Fenian suspects, began to reconstruct Irish nationalism on the ashes of the Fenian debacle, basing his program on the novel plan known as Home Rule. The plan represented a compromise between the demand for total severance of the

British connection and the contrary demand for continuance of the Act of Union. A separate parliament was to be established in Ireland to deal with Irish internal affairs, while Ireland would continue to send representatives to Westminster, which would legislate in matters concerning the whole United Kingdom. This simple goal was to be sought through constitutional channels by an Irish parliamentary party supported by an extraparliamentary organization. Such a movement, Butt reckoned correctly, would have the advantage of appealing to a broad cross-section of the Irish population, including the more influential elements—businessmen, landowners, and respectable farmers. In May 1870, he proposed the plan to a group of businessmen and landowners meeting in Dublin, and before the group disbanded they founded the Home Government Association, the parent organization of the Home Rule movement.

The story of the Home Rule movement under Butt's leadership was one of rags to riches—and then to bankruptcy. Up to 1874 it made great strides forward, winning support from nationalists, land reformers, Liberals, and Conservatives; it sparked the establishment of about twenty affiliated associations in the localities and surprised even its own followers by seeing fifty-nine of the Irish parliamentary seats in the 1874 general election go to men pledged to Home Rule. This string of successes was followed, however, by five years of internal dissention, defection, schism, and finally, by the time of Butt's death in 1879, stagnation. Much of the later difficulty was a product of Butt's own misdirected leadership and his unwillingness to place political necessity above his personal preferences. Butt's vision was to found a political movement that would not only achieve self-government for Ireland, but would also reconcile all elements of the Irish population—Protestants and Catholics, landlords and tenants, and unionists and separatists.[41] The issue on which he chose to construct his vision, Home Rule, was not ostensibly unrealistic as a reconciling issue. There were a great many people in the country who could in good conscience agree to a greater measure of self-government for Ireland, including members of the Protestant Ascendancy. Many Conservative landlords were dissatisfied with the Liberal government's handling of Irish affairs under Gladstone. In 1869 that government had deprived the Church of Ireland of the privileged legal and economic position it had always held, and the following year it made incursions into the autonomy of Irish landlords by compelling them, under the Land Act of 1870, to pay evicted tenants compensation for improvements and disturbance. The compensation was not great, but the landlords viewed the act as an ominous precedent which could lead to legislation in the future that might cut more deeply into their property rights. For some of these landlords, Home Rule appeared to offer a viable alternative to Gladstonian liberalism. They might stand a better chance of stemming further reform in an Irish parliament, where their prestige and power would probably make them the dominant element, than in a hostile English Parliament where they were in the minority.[42] The Home Government Association in its early years was dominated by men with motives such as these.

The tenants, of course, would be receptive to any program leading to Irish self-government, and the large number of Protestant landlords who joined the movement in the beginning gave some tenants cause to believe that the landlords were beginning to come around to their point of view on the national question. The enrollment of a few prominent Fenians during the first few months of the Home Government Association's operation further reinforced their belief.[43] Another attractive feature of the movement, particularly for the more prosperous inhabitants of the towns and countryside, was its constitutional character. Not since the Repeal movement, if the abortive National Association of the 1860s is discounted, had the large farmers and shopkeepers, most of whom were advocates of law and order, had an opportunity to participate in a nationalist cause that was not violent and revolutionary. The constitutional nationalism of Home Rule consequently attracted those classes of tenants who had remained aloof from Fenianism. The Home Rule associations in the provinces enlisted few laborers and artisans but consisted mainly of shopkeepers, publicans, journalists, and farmers. The largest of them, the Edenderry Home Rule Association, appears to have been composed almost entirely of farmers, and the Tenant-Right societies universally adopted the Home Rule program as part of their goals.

As this heterogeneous membership demonstrates, Butt was not unrealistic in his belief that Home Rule could be a healing device. However, the continued success of the alliance would only be possible as long as all minds were focused on the single question of Home Rule, because that was the only issue on which the supporters were in universal agreement. But for many of the tenant supporters other issues were paramount. Land reform continued to hold the central position for the farmers, who believed that the Land Act of 1870 had not gone far enough. Its compensation benefits, first of all, did not extend to large farmers, and no provision was made for preventing evictions and reducing rent. Thus the "three F's"—fixity of tenure, free sale, and fair rent—remained yet to be achieved. A second important question involved Catholic education. Ever since the launching of the Catholic University of Ireland in 1854, the Catholic bishops had been attempting to secure both a charter and an endowment for their institution. Though tentative negotiations had been inaugurated by both the government and the bishops in the 1860s, they had broken down over the issue of allowing Catholic laymen a voice in the governing of the university. The bishops were determined to maintain their authority over all levels of education; to them and their clergy the achievement of a denominational system of education under their control was as important as achieving the "three F's" was to the tenant-farmers of Ireland.

There was no inherent relationship between these reform issues and Home Rule, yet clearly the reforms were part of the benefits the tenants hoped to receive from an Irish parliament. When, therefore, Home Rule candidates seeking election to Parliament turned to the tenants for their votes, the voters inevitably demanded and in many cases received promises to incorporate their favored programs in the goals of the party. In a by-election in February 1871, Mitchell Henry won a seat for Galway on a denominational education platform, and the following September Butt himself secured one of the Limerick constituencies mainly on the issue of Tenant-Right. In other by-elections held during this period, Conservative Home Rulers who limited themselves to Home Rule alone all lost or were forced by lack of support to withdraw.[44] It thus became obvious early on that Home Rule by itself did not have sufficient appeal to attract supporters from the popular side.

For the first three years, as a result of voter pressures, the movement took on an increasingly popular character, causing many of the early Conservative supporters to disappear. The turning point came in the spring of 1873, when the Gladstone administration introduced a university bill that continued the subsidies for the Protestant universities but offered no concessions as far as endowment was concerned to the Catholics. The Roman Catholic bishops declared against it, and the bulk of Gladstone's Irish supporters, under episcopal pressure, voted against it, bringing about the bill's defeat. Having nothing further to gain from the government, some of the bishops began to look more favorably upon Home Rule, while Liberal M.P.'s, with an eye toward the forthcoming general election, began to consider the disadvantages of being linked to the now unpopular Gladstonian government, and decided that their future prospects might be better served by Home Rule. In November 1873, a meeting was held at the Rotunda; the Home Government Association was dissolved, and a new organization, the Home Rule League, was set up in its place. Though the avowed goal of the organization was Home Rule, and only Home Rule, its membership was dominated by men who took the popular side on all issues. In January 1874, Parliament was suddenly dissolved, and in the general election that followed, fifty-nine candidates pledged to Home Rule won parliamentary seats.

The movement might have achieved even more had Butt been willing to concede the failure of his plan for a great synthesis of all classes and parties and allowed himself to be carried along by the popular tide. However, even after the general election he continued to woo both Conservative landowners and tenants by declaring, in his official capacity as party leader, that Home Rule was still the only goal of the movement, while unofficially promising his support for land and educational reforms. But he was unable to sustain this unpopular position indefinitely, and in 1874 and 1875 he introduced two land bills, both unsuccessful, whose terms he deliberately held within moderate limits so as to give the least possible offense to the Conservative supporters. The bills pleased no one and irritated many on both sides; the Tenant-Right newspaper, the *Kilkenny Journal*, argued the farmers' viewpoint that the measures were not strong enough, while the Conservative Home Rule M.P.'s attacked them as diversions from the original goals of the League. In 1876 Butt recovered some of his credit with the Tenant-Righters by introducing another, stronger land bill. The reaction from the right, however, was even stronger than before. One landowner, The O'Conor Don, speaking for the others, depicted it in the most vehement terms as a bill detrimental to the rights of property. Such a statement coming from a member of the Home Rule Party aroused the farmers' suspicions even further and destroyed whatever credibility remained to the league and the party. Tenants who had supported the movement in earlier years deserted in large numbers, and when, after 1876, Butt finally moved on the education question and introduced a university bill, the Protestant landowners who had remained with the movement deserted as well.[45]

In the meantime, another issue arose with respect to which Butt again found himself on the unpopular side. The issue involved the methods of promoting Home Rule in Parliament. Although under the Home Rule program physical force as a method of agitation was ruled out, there was still room within the constitutional framework for the application of forceful tactics. Irish Catholic tenants always admired most those leaders who confronted the British establishment aggressively, and to see the British government suffer an indignity at the hands of an Irishman was perhaps their greatest source of enjoyment. Beginning in 1875 the Irish were offered many such opportunities for rejoicing in the activities of a small group of Home Rule M.P.'s known as the "obstructionists." The group, which had a core of about six members at its high point, was led by Joseph Biggar, a Protestant from Belfast who won a seat for Cavan in 1874, and by Charles Stewart Parnell, who joined the party as representative for Meath in 1875. These obstructionists operated on the principle that the denial of Ireland's right to self-government could best be countered by Ireland's similar denial of the British government's right to conduct its public business. Whenever a bill was introduced that they considered to be against Ireland's best interests, they expressed their opposition by capturing the floor and making long-winded speeches for hours on end. The tactic threw Parliament into confusion, outraged its members, and obstructed its proceedings; although it did not succeed in impeding legislation, it did succeed in popularizing and winning friends for Home Rule in Ireland.

To tamper in this way with the legitimate rules of Parliament was an action that Isaac Butt could not condone or endure. He was deeply fond of the British people as a people, and he considered the British constitution the most perfect constitution ever devised. To apply the rules of Parliament against Parliament itself was to subvert the constitution, and this was not Butt's definition of constitutional action. What Butt did not realize, however, was that the obstructionists had, to a very large degree, captured the political imagination of that portion of Irish nationalist opinion that was considered "advanced," and to that opinion Home Rule meant, above all, that Ireland should be governed according to Irish ideas and needs rather than the English version of those ideas and needs. Because he was not really able to make that distinction, Butt voiced his opposition to obstruction, first privately, then openly, and in time the more conservative members of the party rallied around him, while those of more radical inclination joined the obstructionists under the emerging leadership of Parnell. By the end of 1877, the year of greatest obstructionist activity, the Party was irreconcilably divided between obstructionists and anti-obstructionists, with an array of members standing at points between.[46] Thus as the 1870s drew to a close, the Home Rule movement was at its lowest point since its establishment, its party rent by factionalism over both methods and goals and its extraparliamentary wing discredited and divested of its most important support. Perhaps the best indication of the downward course of the movement was in the fact that the number of local Home Rule clubs, which during the early seventies had reached about twenty, was reduced by 1877 to only one club—the Edenderry Home Rule Club in Kings County. Such was the opportunity offered to, and lost, by Isaac Butt.

Frustrated and in poor health, Butt died in May 1879, without realizing his vision of an Ireland governed by Irish men of reason and good will representing all classes. Indeed, the vision had been doomed from the beginning because it did not take into account the political realities of Ireland in the nineteenth century. Nevertheless, Butt had made some substantial contributions to Irish politics, the effects of which did not become apparent until the next decade. His Home Rule program, first of all, had remained unchanged, and in the more capable hands of Parnell it subsequently proved to be an issue attractive enough to form the basis for an effective political movement. Second, although the Home Rule League did not survive, the party did, and in 1880 it became the focal point for a renewed and expanded extraparliamentary organization—the Land League—which did not, like its predecessor, neglect the demands of the farmers. Third, Butt's land bills, though moderate by later standards, served to focus public attention on the waning cause of Tenant-Right, thus keeping alive the farmers' hopes for reform. As Michael Davitt said of Butt, "He may be said to have been the reforming link between Gavan Duffy's Tenant League and the Land League, and to have handed on the endless struggle of the Celtic peasantry for the soil from the movement destroyed by Cardinal Cullen . . . in the fifties, to the leadership of Mr. Parnell in the agrarian uprising of 1879."[47]

In summing up Butt's achievements, furthermore, one must not overlook his considerable contribution to organized political agitation in the Irish localities. The Home Rule Clubs founded early in the decade did not survive, but the Home Rule program was taken up and incorporated into the programs of the Tenant-Right and Independent clubs, which did survive. As stated earlier, these organizations, composed mostly of large farmers, had in the past shunned Irish nationalism because of its revolutionary and violent connotations. By the end of the decade, largely as a result of the revival of Repealist constitutionalism, the members of these clubs were firmly nationalistic. Like the Home Rule League and party, they were also seriously divided on the obstruction issue. On the whole, Parnell's aggressive policies seem to have been most warmly received by the Tenant-Right clubs, and most consistently opposed by majorities in the Queens County Independent Club and Edenderry Home Rule Club.[48] But these tactical differences aside, the fundamental issues of the day—land reform, Home Rule, and Catholic education—were issues on which most of the members of the local organizations were in common agreement. In a policy statement issued by the Queens County Independent Club in 1877, for example, the members declared the organization "dedicated to materially promoting the interests and welfare of the country by constitutional means," by which they meant, more specifically, "Home Rule, Tenant-Right, and a proper system of education" (the word "proper" in this case being a euphemism for "denominational").⁴⁹ Similarly, the *Kilkenny Journal* expressed the Tenant-Righters' viewpoint by suggesting that the Home Rule League be replaced by a "truly national organization devoted to Home Rule, Tenant-Right, and denominational education."⁵⁰ It is significant of Butt's impact that in both cases Home Rule headed the list of priorities.

In advocating a program devoted to both land reform and self-government, the political clubs anticipated the Land League by about three or four years. It is not surprising, therefore, that when Davitt stepped forward in 1879 with his proposal for a movement based precisely on that double goal, he was able to enlist the aid of the clubs' members in getting the movement started and providing its leadership in the localities. Inasmuch as these influential local politicians owed their conversion to nationalism to Isaac Butt and his constitutional Home Rule program, Butt's contribution to later organized agitation was substantial. The effect of his accomplishment was felt in the localities even before the founding of the Land League. While on the national level Butt, Parnell, Biggar, and the rest of the Home Rule party wrangled over which issues and methods should be employed in presenting Ireland's case to Parliament, the local nationalists were themselves busy wondering what they could do to promote the national cause. The world in which the M.P.'s moved was a universe apart from theirs: only powerful landowners and the few dozen tenant-occupiers who represented Irish constituencies were permitted the privilege of entering the halls and offices of those at Westminster who directed the course of the British empire. Much less glamorous was the political world of the Irish countryman, whose influence was limited to whatever impact he might make on his fellow countrymen in the pub, in the hotel meeting room, or on the speakers' stand.

Still, there was one public office open to local nationalists that offered unlimited opportunities for political action within constitutional limits. The office of P.L.G. was the local Irish version of the office of M.P. Membership in it required election, and elections could be used to test one's personal popularity, the popularity of the program, and the electoral effectiveness of the local organization if there happened to be one. The board itself resembled Parliament in the division of its members into a dominant pro-British element and a subject Irish element, and it had control over about half the local government purse. Its proceedings, moreover, were governed by the rules of parliamentary procedure, and resolutions passed by a majority of the board could be forwarded to higher authorities as representative of the corporate opinion of the board. Finally, at the top, there stood the board offices, occupied by prominent landowners, most of them English by descent; many were Peers of the Realm holding seats in the House of Lords. Could not a transfer of power from the hands of these notables to those of the popular representatives be interpreted as a change of government from the British to the Irish party—a kind of victory for Home Rule within the local community? Opportunities for confrontation and publicization offered themselves at every step of the way, and inevitably, although at first slowly, local nationalists began to recognize these opportunities and turn their eyes toward the workhouse boardrooms.

The Origins of Board "Nationalization"

From the middle of the 1850s to the early 1870s the effects of the general prosperity, organizational experience, and continual exposure to anti-British and anti-landlord propaganda, not to mention the addition of new, younger guardians whose attitudes had been formed and nurtured by the teachings of O'Connell, Lalor, Duffy, and James Stephens, all combined to create a new and growing attitude of independence among elected guardians. The new independence and heightened political consciousness were transformed on the boards into a greater eagerness of elected guardians to initiate or respond to political appeals. By 1868, almost every important issue brought forth flurries of resolutions and petitions from boards in the south and west. One such issue which arose in the late sixties was a proposal, promoted by Isaac Butt, that the government grant amnesty to the imprisoned Fenians. In 1871, three boards in Mayo signed their corporate names to an amnesty petition that had been initiated by two members of the Castlebar board.[51] Home Rule proved, however, to be the issue with the widest appeal. In 1872 the Dublin Corporation drew up a resolution calling for Home Rule and circulated it among the boards of guardians. An incomplete count of the responses showed that at least twenty-six boards had responded by approving the resolution.[52] By the beginning of the 1870s, then, the boards had already begun to perform an important function in popular politics by acting as a network for the dissemination of political propaganda.

It was partly in connection with this function that the idea first arose that the boards and their offices belonged by right and justice to the common people. The incident of Alexander O'Connor Eccles and the 1872 Roscommon Home Rule Association was described in the Prologue. On that occasion, the action taken by the elected guardians resulting in the resignation of the ex-officio officers had been stimulated by the founding six weeks earlier of the Roscommon Home Rule Association. Although the elected guardians' victory was unanticipated and brief, the guardians who carried it off readily recognized its nationalist implications. This was evident not only in the board's proceedings, but also in the debate in the press between Alexander Eccles and William Tully in which Eccles argued that his action against the ex-officios had been a blow delivered for Ireland. The incident at Roscommon forged a link between the national and social questions by applying the national principle to a concrete local situation. The nationalists' attempt to assert Ireland's right to self-government, in other words, had been transmuted into a struggle between landlords and tenants for local political authority.

At about the same time the guardians of another union, Kilmallock, at the very center of the prosperous North Munster dairyland district, arrived at the same synthesis by an opposite route. In 1870, the chair of the Kilmallock board became vacant with the death of its chairman, an ex-officio named Robert Dawson. Four years earlier, a group of farmers and Limerick townsmen had founded the Limerick, Clare, and Tipperary Farmers' Club; at least five members of the club, including its president, a wealthy cattle grazier named William Bolster, were P.L.G.'s on the Kilmallock board. The death of the board chairman provided the members of the new organization with an opportunity to test the strength of the club; accordingly, the members who were on the Kilmallock board decided to contest the chairmanship, putting forward the name of their own leader, Bolster. In a heated contest between the elected and ex-officio guardians in which, according to a later report, several of the ex-officios sided with the elected guardians, Bolster defeated the ex-officios' candidate. He served out the remaining two months of the term, then won reelection in the scheduled election in April, carrying the other offices as well.[53]

In the two years following Bolster's reelection, the board of guardians became the focal point of an immense struggle for power between the landlords and tenants of the Kilmallock union—a struggle carried on in the boardroom as well as the electoral divisions. In 1871, the defeat of several radical elected guardians in the general poor law election enabled the ex-officios to recoup the three offices. They accomplished the unseating of the radicals, if the elected guardians' spokesmen are to be believed, through liberal use of intimidating tactics upon the electorate. In the election the next year, intimidation was rife again; one landlord was said to have brought his pack of hunting hounds to the houses of his tenants in an attempt to frighten them into voting for his candidate in the division. However, as one of the popular guardians later remarked, "That gentleman might well have stopped at home and not brought his beagles—his hungry beagles, snarling to the doors of his tenants," because the voters held fast behind the popular element and returned a sufficient number of supporters to secure the reelection of Bolster and two other tenants to the chairmanships.[54] The ex-officios who lost their offices that year were the last ever to be elected to the chairmanships of the Kilmallock board of guardians. Bolster was reelected chairman each subsequent year until 1879, and he was succeeded by other elected guardians representing the popular viewpoint. The same was also true of the other offices. The 1872 election in Kilmallock, therefore, was the first election in which elected guardians were able to win and maintain control of an Irish board of guardians; because it was the first of many to come, it may be considered the starting point of a developing revolution in Irish local government.

Until 1872, however, the conflict in Kilmallock was an isolated event confined to one union and having no basis in a broader plan for reform of the boards of guardians. It had no connection with Irish nationalism but emerged from the continuing conflict between landlord and tenant which the members of the Limerick farmers' club had extended into the political sphere. That is not to say that there were no nationalists among the members of the farmers' club. One of its members, William H. O'Sullivan, like Bolster a wealthy farmer, had been a nationally prominent leader of the Fenian movement. With the collapse of the Fenian rising he had turned his attention to the Tenant-Right movement and became a founder of the Limerick, Clare, and Tipperary Farmers' Club. After Isaac Butt introduced his program for Home Rule, O'Sullivan quickly espoused the new cause as the foremost spokesman for Home Rule at the Farmers' Club. He joined the Home Rule League when it was founded in 1873, and in the general election of 1874 contested and won a parliamentary seat for Limerick. O'Sullivan, a professional agitator and politician, was also a P.L.G.

on the Kilmallock board, and his orientation toward nationalism as well as his experience in national politics permitted him insight into the wider implications of the events in Kilmallock. Speaking to the board on the occasion of Bolster's election in 1872 he told the members: "I am proud that Kilmallock was the first to set an example to other boards in Ireland, and I sincerely trust that the example will be taken up by the whole country until we are able to rise as one man to demand our right to an independent legislature."[55]

The Kilmallock officers' election took place on April 5, 1872. This was two days after the founding of the Roscommon Home Rule Association and six weeks before the Roscommon board of guardians' meeting at which the elected guardians forced Lord Crofton's resignation. The coincidence of these two apparently unrelated events—the one arising out of the application of nationalism to a local situation, the other out of a local power struggle which was later interpreted as a nationalist action—were indicative of the rapid convergence of the social and national issues after the introduction of Home Rule. The examples set by Kilmallock and Roscommon were not taken up immediately by other boards. Most voters and most nationalist guardians were still not convinced in 1872 that bringing politics into the boardroom was necessarily the ethically or even tactically correct thing to do. Even in Roscommon, the nationalists' victory could not be sustained. After the return of the ex-officios to office in 1872, eight more years passed before the nationalist P.L.G.'s were able to win enough electoral support to offer another successful challenge to the ex-officios. Thomas Mapother was finally installed as permanent chairman in 1880.

For militants like Eccles and O'Sullivan, who wanted to see an immediate attack launched against the ex-officios, the most immediate need in 1872 was to convince their fellow nationalists of the wisdom of such action. The moderate nationalists had to be shown that the boards of guardians had a positive role to fulfill in national politics. This need for a justification prompted some contemporary nationalist ideologues to begin thinking about the boards of guardians and how they might fit into the struggle for national independence. In 1873, the Roscommon Home Rulers decided to make another attempt at winning the chair, and with that end in mind put up three candidates in the general poor law election. During the campaign, Eccles published in the *Roscommon Messenger* an editorial on the Home Rulers' preparations that ended with the plea: "Surely we can never expect a British Senate to pay attention to our demands for Home Rule if we have not the moral courage to elect a poor law Guardian on that principle.

Before we can exert influence across the Channel we must be able to regulate affairs at home, and the Land Act has left the people sufficiently independent to do it, if they have but the moral courage."[56] This line of reasoning—that through local self-government the Irish people could prove their capability of national self-government—appealed particularly to moderate and conservative nationalists, who employed the argument on many boards of guardians in subsequent years. At Roscommon in 1873 it had little effect, for none of the three Home Rule candidates was elected.

But the efforts of the Roscommon Home Rulers were not wasted, for their activities came to the attention of the editorial staff of the *Nation*, who always took a keen interest in local nationalist actions. Just before the 1873 poor law election the *Nation* reprinted the *Messenger* editorial, noting that the Roscommon home rulers were "preparing for the coming great Home Rule battle."[57] It was probably the first time that a local poor law contest received exposure in a newspaper with national circulation. The article undoubtedly lent respectability to the militants' cause. The next step came later in 1873 when, just prior to the convening of the Rotunda meeting at which the Home Rule League was founded, the secretaries of the Home Government Association issued invitations to the boards of guardians "to join in the demand for an Irish parliament." This appeal, representing in effect the national organization's sanction of political activity on the boards, had an immediate effect on moderates and others who had previously disapproved of it on the ground that it might be damaging to the cause. William Tully in Roscommon reported the invitation in the *Journal*, and announced that henceforth he would abandon his previous opposition to the introduction of "polemical" questions into poor law boardrooms. His opposition, he said, had been founded on the consideration that the boards of guardians were not truly representative bodies inasmuch as half their membership were J.P.'s, but the new editorial position was based on the consideration that "the promoters of the cause of self-rule should avail themselves of every opportunity to forward the cause."[58] The new editorial position represented a fundamental reorientation in Tully's attitude not just toward the boards of guardians, but toward politics in general: it was no longer necessary to justify political acts by reference to legal or established values; the tactical value of the act was itself sufficient justification.

The following summer, just after the adjournment of Parliament in August, the *Nation* joined in the discussion again with an editorial that raised the local government issue to a higher ideological plane. The session that had just ended was the first in which the new, expanded Home Rule party had participated. Throughout the session, public excitement over the Home Rule League's victories in the January election remained high, but with the adjourning of Parliament for six months the possibility arose that public interest might wane and the momentum built up by the election be lost. Attempting to counter this threat, the *Nation* published its editorial, pointing out that a good deal of work had to be done during the six months before the opening of the next session. The people, first of all, had to demand Home Rule and maintain that demand until it was fully conceded. With that end in mind, the partisans of Home Rule had to spur themselves to greater exertions to educate the whole people to the nature of the principles in conflict. Secondly, a constant endeavor had to be kept up to "nationalise" more and still more the whole life of the country. "Every position which is open to popular election must be captured and held for Ireland—all poor law boards, town councils, parliamentary representation—all should be made strongholds of Irish feeling." To this end, the registries of the electors should be continually watched and kept right.

Why was this activity so important? Because —(the *Nation* continued):

Here is work which the people in every locality can do for themselves, and the effects of which would be simply incalculable. Here is a way open in which intelligent and patriotic young men in every part of Ireland can help in their own country's cause. How often do we not hear of boards that could be nationalised, and boroughs and counties that could be won, if only a few energetic men would take the matter in hand and rouse to the good work their well-meaning and willing, but woefully apathetic neighbors? Why is not the good work done? Some men who have talent enough to set it going, and do not lack the will, hold back through a sort of diffidence, waiting for more important persons to undertake it. This is a mistaken feeling on their part. If the important persons do not come to the front to perform a patriotic duty toward their country, then the unimportant persons should take their place, and not let the Irish cause suffer for want of honest men's help.[59]

Although intended as a spur to nationalist activity, the editorial was the most elaborate and concrete statement of aims for local nationalists to appear in print in the 1870s. As the editor saw it, a movement to "nationalise" the local boards could serve at least three useful purposes for the national cause. First, because the local bodies were closer to the people than the national organization, nationalization would enable the people of every locality to participate personally and directly in the national movement. In the hands of "a few energetic men" this could have the effect of politicizing ("arousing") the woefully apathetic mass. Second, the scope of the movement would be wide enough to enable "unimportant persons" who might otherwise be left out of politics to rise to positions of leadership. Third—and this was implicit in the timing of the editorial—a movement to nationalize the local bodies would lend continuity to the national movement by engaging the people in political activity during slack periods in the national agitation.

The challenge posed by the *Nation* was not broadly taken up during the seventies. By the beginning of 1880 only two boards of guardians—those of Kilmallock and Castletown (Cork)—had elected P.L.G.'s as chairmen. Electoral contests for board seats remained at a low level: only 235 contests were held in the 3,044 electoral divisions in 1878, most of these taking place in urban divisions.[60] On the other hand, there were signs, as the decade neared its end, of a new militance with regard to tenants' rights in local government, of rising impatience among elected guardians with their exclusion from the board offices, and of keener understanding among nationalists of the connection between tenant autonomy on the boards of guardians and the national movement for self-government.

These signs were most evident in those districts where tenant organizations existed and P.L.G.'s were affiliated with them. In the union of Naas, for example, the chairmanship of John Latouche, a J.P. with an estate valued at about £8,000, was constantly troubled by the obstructive tactics of Edward Fenelon, an elected guardian and 100-acre farmer,[61] who seized every opportunity to introduce Tenant-Right and Home Rule discussions into the board's proceedings. In 1877, at the meeting for the election of officers for the coming year, the names of Latouche and two incumbent ex-officios were put forward for reelection. Fenelon responded that he had no personal objection to any of the men named, two of whom were his neighbors, and that therefore he would not oppose their reelection. But he hoped that "one of those gentlemen will consider the feelings of the majority of the elected guardians" and would resign before the next year.[62] Latouche, a reasonable and amiable man, was touched by Fenelon's appeal and on the following week offered to resign his own chairmanship. The board protested strongly and refused to accept his resignation, but the following year the members decided by universal agreement that the elected guardians should have one of the seats, and Fenelon was unanimously elected deputy vice-chairman.[63] Fenelon was a member and regular attender of the Queens County Independent Club.

The neighboring Edenderry Home Rule Club was staffed almost entirely by P.L.G.'s from the Edenderry board of guardians. Three of the
club's five officers in 1877 were elected members of the board: Edward
Wyer, the president; Michael Costello, honorary secretary; and C. Jellicoe,
the treasurer.[64] At one of the club's meetings in 1877, Costello suggested
that the club make an attempt to nationalize the whole elected membership
of the board, and with that in mind he proposed enticing other guardians
to join the club by making all poor law guardians ex-officio members of
the club's executive council.[65] His proposal was never voted on, but his
use of the term "ex-officio" instead of, say, "honorary" was interesting and
suggestive. Costello may have had visions of converting the club into a
kind of tenants' counter-government, with P.L.G.'s holding the same position in it that the landlords held at the board of guardians.

At the same time, the national leadership came increasingly to recognize
the potential value of the boards to promotion of Home Rule. In October
1877 the executive council of the Home Rule League called a conference
to be held in Dublin in January, at which important policy questions were
to be discussed. In a circular notice distributed to the press the council
announced that the classes admissible to the conference were the Home
Rule Members of Parliament, two nominators of any Home Rule member
or candidate, the members of the Home Rule League, clergymen of every
religious persuasion, magistrates, members of the municipal corporations,
town or municipal commissioners, poor law guardians, and persons who
had been at any time members of the Home Rule Associations or Home
Rule League.[66] This interaction between the Home Rule League, the local
political clubs, and members of boards of guardians contributed to the
growth and maintenance of nationalist militance on the boards. Although
the impact of this militance on the composition of the board chairmanships
was negligible in the 1870s, it did have some effect on the composition of
the two lower offices, particularly in regions where the tenants were best
organized.

From a vantage-point in the late seventies, one would have to conclude
from the experience of the preceding ten years that the escalation of the
"nationalization" movement into a full-fledged war against landlord privilege would depend largely on the ability of the tenantry to organize.
Political activism on the boards was generally weak where there were no
outside political organizations, stronger where one or two of the elected
guardians were also members of a political club, and strongest of all (as in

Roscommon and Kilmallock) where the outside organization was active and had several members on the board. Just as the parliamentary Home Rule party had its Home Rule League to perform the organizational chores, conduct electoral campaigns, and publicize the goals of the party, so too did the nationalist element on the boards of guardians need the moral and organizational support of an extra-official wing to become effective enough and numerically strong enough to conduct a sustained campaign for the board offices. Most important of all, there was still that large, uncommitted element, made up mostly of the small farmers, who were as yet not fully politicized. Without their votes the nationalist element must continue to remain small, and the boards continue to be dominated by the ex-officios in combination with their agents, bailiffs, and friends. The solution to this problem could be found, once again, in organization.

Yet as the 1870s drew to a close, conditions arose in another sphere, the economic sector, that had significant implications for political organization. The year 1876 was the most prosperous year for agriculture in Ireland's history to that time. Crop yields were at an all-time high and prices were at a peak. It was the third such boom year in a row. Under these conditions it was difficult to interest farmers in political or land reforms of any kind. But after 1876 the economic picture began to change; prices moved downward, slowly at first, then more rapidly, and by 1878 it was clear that the boom was over. To compound the difficulties, the newspapers announced late in 1878 that large shipments of cattle were being transported from America to supply the growing needs of England. This aggravated an already deteriorating situation in Ireland, whose economy depended so strongly on the livestock trade with England. Then, in the winter of 1879 came the crowning blow: crop failure, the worst since the Great Famine.[67] Such were the conditions when Michael Davitt, newly emerged from prison, arrived on the scene with his proposal for a new political movement.

3

{flourish} A New Departure in Local
Politics, 1879–1881

The Agitation in the West

COMING AS it had after two years of declining prosperity and two successive
bad harvests, the cold and wet winter of 1878–79 worked a dire hardship
on all classes of Irish society. The first and hardest hit was the farmer, but
by 1879 the town and country classes were so integrated economically that
any harsh and unrelieved pressure on the farmer also took its toll on the
shopkeeper, draper, publican, and any other townsman who depended
upon the farmer to purchase his goods or services. The interdependence
of the town and country classes had been largely a product of the long
prosperity itself. Under the affluent conditions Irish farmers had become
consumers of manufactured goods and of foodstuffs that were not locally
produced. To a far greater extent than in pre-Famine times, they depended
on the shopkeeper for their supply of consumer goods, and since the farmers received most of their income only once a year (at the time of the annual
harvest), the shopkeepers readily accommodated their expanding tastes by
extending them credit between harvests in the form of victuals, manufactured goods, seed, and farm supplies. During the early seventies the shopkeepers took advantage of these favorable conditions by borrowing large
sums of money from banks and extending their lending operations. Those
shopkeepers who operated in this manner as middlemen on a large scale
often gained the pejorative title of "gombeen men," but often the title was
undeserved, since their intent was usually little more than to supply the

farmers with goods they wanted and which they would not otherwise have been able to purchase.[1]

After the harvest the farmers repaid part of their debts, but during the 1870s their purchases far exceeded their incomes, so that each year a portion of their debt was carried over to the following year. Over time the accumulated debt was in many cases considerable. A witness before the Bessborough Commission of 1880–81 estimated that in many places farmers owed an average of three to five years' rent to the shopkeepers alone, and in some cases the amount owed was the equivalent of ten years' rent.[2] The fundamental weaknesses of this credit system were not apparent at the height of prosperity, but with the dampening of the economy after 1876 they became all too obvious. With the coming of the bad harvests of 1877–79 the farmers became unable to pay the shopkeepers, and the shopkeepers in their turn defaulted on their payments to the bank, with the result that the entire credit structure collapsed. When in the summer and autumn of 1879 the harvest showed the worst yields since the Great Famine, bankruptcies began to increase at an accelerating rate. Before 1880 the total number of bankruptcies registered under the Irish Bankruptcy and Insolvency Act of 1857 had been 289; in 1880 alone it was 130 and in the two succeeding years it rose to 237 and 330.[3] These figures reveal quite clearly how closely tied the interests of town and country were in Ireland.

The distress of 1879 carried over into 1880, but severe as it was, it did not approach the intensity of the Great Famine. Nevertheless, to those who were affected by it, it seemed to have all the earmarks of a return to the desolate conditions of the earlier period, and was all the more frustrating and intimidating because of its arrival at a time of unparalleled prosperity when the aspirations of the Irish shopkeeper and farmer alike were at an all-time high; thus, they began to seek ways and means of meeting the crisis that would not force them back into the impoverished conditions of thirty years earlier.

The first man to recognize and seize the opportunities afforded by this new wave of discontent was Michael Davitt. Davitt had been born in County Mayo, but when he was four years old his family had been evicted from their small peasant holding and removed to Lancashire, where he was raised. This early experience had left him with a hatred of the landlord system and a desire for social justice, as well as a doctrinaire nationalism, which led him as a young man to join the Fenians. As a result of his complicity in the Fenian uprising he was sent to prison, where he remained from 1870 until 1877. While in prison he had many opportunities to read widely and develop his ideas, and by the time of his release in December 1877, he had developed a plan for founding a revolutionary movement in Ireland by rallying the town and country classes behind a struggle against landlordism. The plan, essentially the same as that proposed thirty years earlier by James Fintan Lalor but apparently arrived at independently by Davitt, was based on the weapon of the rent strike. Davitt knew, as Lalor had before him, that the Irish town classes were not much interested in the land question and that the farmers were not greatly attracted to nationalism, but that the interests of the two classes came together on the issue of rent. All Irish tenants paid rents and all resented the exactions extracted from them by the landlords. With the onset of the distress of the late seventies and the need for the tenants to find a way of augmenting their income, the resentment against paying rent was further heightened, and Davitt, emerging from prison, saw that the time was favorable for putting his plan into action.

He went first to Parnell, who had been instrumental in securing his release, and stated his proposal, but Parnell, readily seeing the revolutionary implications of the scheme, declined to act as a promoter. Next Davitt went to America in the summer of 1878 to try to interest the exiled Fenians who were organized there under an association called the *Clan na Gael.* While in America he met John Devoy, a *Clan na Gael* leader, who took an interest in his idea and helped him work out the details of the scheme. For the rest of 1878 Davitt toured America, speaking to Irish-Americans about his program, which came to be known as the "new departure."[4] In its broadest outlines, the program consisted of a two-pronged attack upon both British rule and landlordism, aimed ultimately at securing self-government for Ireland and establishing an Irish peasant proprietary. Four general aims mentioned by Davitt in his various speeches were: (1) self-government as the chief goal for Ireland; (2) an independent and aggressive Irish party in the House of Commons; (3) the settlement of the land question including the prevention of evictions for nonpayment of rent, and the development of a class of owner-occupiers or peasant proprietary; and (4) the development of Irish industries, the improvement of peasants' dwellings, an education system that was not antinational, and the right of Irishmen to bear arms. To this list Devoy, speaking to a large meeting in Brooklyn on October 13, appended one additional objective that is of interest here because of its relevance to the boards of guardians. Devoy's suggestion, little noticed at the time and by historians since then, was that the nationalists should aim at controlling "not only the parliamentary representation of Ireland but also every public body in the country, from the little boards of poor law guardians and the town commissioners to the city corporations."[5] By the time Davitt left America the suggestion had been incorporated into the new departure program. Davitt, in his final speech in America on December 8, told his audience in Boston that the nationalist party in Ireland had a right to participate in everything concerning the political and social well-being of the Irish people, and to "stamp in this manner its nationalist convictions on everything from a local board of guardians to a representation in an alien parliament."[6] The local government struggle, therefore, was to be a part of the general war against landlordism and British rule.

Davitt's speeches failed to find their mark with the American audiences. The American Fenians were out of touch with the mood of their kinsmen in Ireland and were not fully aware of the impact that Butt's and Parnell's constitutional policies had made on the Irish nationalists. Still holding out a hope for the violent overthrow of British rule in Ireland, the American Fenians did not warm to the constitutional aspects of Davitt's scheme. Parnell also continued to withhold his support, but for the opposite reason. Davitt wrote to him from America asking whether he would undertake to lead the new movement, but Parnell, still reluctant to become involved with a scheme having revolutionary implications, again refused. At that point, in December 1878, Davitt returned to Ireland, still undaunted and determined to take his case directly to the Irish people. More than any other figure of his time Davitt possessed an instinctual capacity for sensing the moods and needs of the Irish common people. Upon returning to Ireland he did not go to the rich cattle regions of the Midlands where poverty was least felt and the populations, though highly politicized, were dominated by conservative nationalists; rather, he went directly to the west coast, where the distress was most extensive and radical sympathies always ran high, but political causes suffered from the lack of organization. He travelled first to Mayo, his native county, where, as he said, "Whiteboyism, Steelboys, Thrashers, and Ribbonmen had each their active adherents among the Mayo peasantry in times of agrarian troubles." There he found "a number of farmers, businessmen and others . . . intelligently anxious about the outlook, and all eager to take part in any movement that might promise some hope of relief from excessive rents."[7]

Davitt's birthplace was a village called Straide, which was in the Castlebar poor law union not far from the town of Castlebar and another village, Balla. It was in the region of these three towns that Davitt found his earliest and sturdiest support. Castlebar had been a Fenian stronghold, and three of the persons mentioned later by Davitt as being instrumental in originating the agitation were Fenians from the village of Balla.[8] The Fenians, of course, were experienced in matters of organization, and throughout the agitation of the following months Fenians throughout the West played an important role in organizing and publicizing meetings. But the Fenians were not the only persons in the West who were receptive to Davitt's teachings. There was another group whose members were unconnected with Fenianism, who were largely farmers or of farming stock and somewhat more prosperous than most of the Fenians, and who, though smaller in number than the Fenians, played at least an equal, perhaps a dominant, role in initiating the agitation. Constitutionalists by preference, most of these men were graziers, many of them members of boards of guardians or town councils, and all of them supporters of both Tenant-Right and Home Rule. They were the West Country counterpart of the farmer-politicians of the Midlands, the principal difference being that they were fewer in number and therefore less able to organize themselves politically. And the spokesman for this group in Castlebar was James Daly, owner, publisher, and editor of the *Connaught Telegraph*, who was cited earlier in this study for his testimony before the Select Committee on Poor Law Elections in 1878.

Although politically among the avant-garde, Daly was, in his social background and general attitudes, typical of the more prosperous class of rural countrymen who supported the political movements of the 1870s and 1880s. The eldest of eight brothers and sisters, Daly was born in 1838 and spent his early childhood amidst the death and despair of famine-stricken Mayo. Little is known about his father, except that his name was Charles and he was a farmer. The facts of James's early life are also obscure, but it is known that he was educated at the Errew monastery, a Franciscan brothers' monastery about five miles from Castlebar.[9] The school is reputed to have had a history of radical teaching. However, James apparently exhibited few radical tendencies during his teens and twenties. During the 1860s he occupied a farm of £45 valuation in Ballyshane townland, Breaghwy, which he rented from a local landlady, Harriet Gardiner,[10] and was also Miss Gardiner's bailiff.[11] Oral tradition has it, however, that on one occasion, probably sometime before 1869, he spoke out in defense of a tenant whom his employer had evicted, and either quit or was dismissed from his post. This incident appears to have marked his conversion to radicalism.

In 1869 Daly won a seat on the Castlebar board of guardians. That same year, he and another guardian, Charles O'Malley, a solicitor who had been active in the repeal movement during O'Connell's time, introduced a resolution at the board calling for amnesty for the Fenian prisoners. The resolution was passed by the board, suggesting—if such a resolution might be considered a measure of popular sympathy—that even by that year there were a number of supporters of popular causes on the board. At the time, Daly had not yet embarked on his career in journalism; his activities appear to have been confined to farming—probably cattle grazing, since his farm was 120 acres. His colleague, O'Malley, though a solicitor by profession, also occupied a farm of 160 acres, which he rented from Lord Lucan.[12]

During subsequent years, Daly moved toward an increasingly radical and activist political position. The *Nation* records him as speaking to a cheering crowd at Louisburgh, near Westport, in December 1875, calling for the establishment of a tenants' defense association in south Mayo "to maintain our rights against the landlord."[13] No such association appears to have been founded as a result of the meeting. The next year he made a further contribution to the radical cause by purchasing the old *Castlebar Telegraph and Connaught Ranger* (which had ceased publication in 1870) and renaming it the *Connaught Telegraph*, a newspaper that Davitt, in 1879, described as "one of the few papers in Ireland that honestly advocates the cause of the people."[14] Daly's declared purpose was "not to make a fortune, but to advocate the cause of the poor struggling tenantry."[15] His strong support for Isaac Butt in the early editions of the paper indicated his growing interest in nationalism during the mid-seventies, but by 1877 he began to reject Butt as a politician "who would not strip to fight," and became a supporter of Parnell and the obstructionists.[16] In this fashion he made his way toward the historic meeting at Irishtown in 1879.

The outdoor meeting at Irishtown, held on Sunday, April 20, 1879, was the meeting that initiated the agitation in the West. Davitt and Daly each tell different stories about how the famous meeting was launched. According to Davitt, a number of tenants in the village of Irishtown near Claremorris complained to him about a certain local landlord, Geoffrey Canon Burke, who, acting as executor for his recently deceased brother's estate, threatened to dispossess a number of tenants unless they paid the arrears that had accumulated in their rents. After listening to these complaints, Davitt, in consultation with a few local Fenian friends, suggested that a meeting be held to protest Canon Burke's action, to call for a reduction of rents, and to denounce the whole landlord system. A meeting was called for April 20,[17] and while Davitt's Fenian friends worked to collect an audience, Davitt used his influence to engage a list of prominent speakers. The meeting was then publicized in the *Connaught Telegraph*. Seven thousand people (Davitt's estimate) attended the meeting, which was presided over by James Daly. Davitt himself was not present because he missed the train from Dublin;[18] he did, however, forward a speech, which was read by Daly.

By Daly's account it was he, not Davitt, who originated the meeting. In a letter to his own newspaper the following winter he claimed that he had proposed the meeting to a group consisting of another James Daly, of Irishtown; Daniel O'Connor, also of Irishtown; Thomas Sweeney, a Claremorris shopkeeper; and John O'Kane, one of the persons mentioned by Davitt as helping *him* to organize the meeting.[19] Unless new evidence is uncovered, it is unlikely that the discrepancies in Davitt's and Daly's accounts will ever be reconciled. Daly's account, however, ought not to be rejected out of hand. Daly had a previous history of organizing mass demonstrations to protest rent increases, and the fact that he chaired the Irishtown meeting suggests that he played more than a nominal role in organizing that particular meeting. Furthermore, Daly wrote his account in the *Connaught Telegraph* less than one year after the event, when there were still many participants present who could have denied his claim, including the four persons he mentioned. Davitt, on the other hand, wrote his account in his *Fall of Feudalism in Ireland* twenty-four years later, when the question was hardly any longer debatable and Davitt's memory of the details might have grown vague. There is, of course, a third possibility, namely that both Davitt and Daly were searching at the time for an issue over which to hold a protest meeting, and when the Irishtown issue conveniently presented itself, both men seized upon it independently and were then brought together by a third party—perhaps the John O'Kane who is mentioned in both accounts.

Whatever might have been the truth, the meeting itself had far-reaching effects. The demonstration succeeded in convincing Canon Burke not only to withdraw his threats of dispossession, but to grant an abatement of 25 percent on rents on the estate. Word spread quickly of the success of the demonstration, largely because of the publicizing efforts of James Daly in the *Connaught Telegraph*, and requests for similar demonstrations began pouring in from all parts of the district. Within weeks and throughout the summer and fall of 1879 the west of Ireland was aflame with demonstrations attended by thousands and involving all of the local political talent the nationalists could muster. The most important side effect of the Irishtown meeting was that it brought Parnell into the movement. Though Parnell had refused on a number of occasions to become involved in the new agitation, after Irishtown he was confronted with the clear choice of either accepting the leadership of the agitation or dealing with it as an outsider; he joined the movement. On June 1, Parnell, Davitt, and Devoy met in Dublin, where presumably they cemented an agreement along the lines of Davitt's and Devoy's program. Just how firm the "cement" was is not known, for although Devoy later claimed that the decisions taken at the meeting consisted of a formal treaty between the three, both Davitt and Parnell denied that they had engaged in any such treaty.[20] Be that as it may, it appears that the local government question was brought up at the meeting, because in Devoy's *Recollections* he mentions that a "working agreement" was reached between the three leaders "on the basis of approval of that part of the proposition aimed at securing control of the local public bodies."[21]

The second of the "western meetings" was held on June 6 at Westport. Parnell spoke at this meeting and urged the people to organize against landlordism. Davitt also spoke, emphasizing essentially the same theme, and Daly was again the chairman.[22] The Westport meeting introduced the second of the two major local politicians who were most influential in founding the Land League, John Louden of Kiltannon in the Westport union. Louden, it was mentioned earlier, was the son of George P. Louden, probably the largest tenant-occupier in Mayo.[23] The Louden holdings consisted of 7,000 acres of grazing land ranging over and around Croaghpatrick mountain near the town of Westport. When George died in 1877, he left the entire estate to his son John.[24] Though Louden, like Daly, was to become an important figure in organizing the Land League, he was far from representative of the typical farmer whose cause he espoused. Groomed from an early age for a professional career, John entered King's Inn in Dublin in 1856, the records showing that he had not taken any prior degrees.[25] Assuming that he began his higher education at about twenty years of age—the normal age for a young man of his social position—he would have been born about the same time as James Daly and been in his early forties at the time of Irishtown. His activities between 1856 and 1865 are difficult to trace, but it is known that he spent most of this period in London,[26] probably grooming himself for his legal career. In 1870 he was called to the bar and returned to Westport to take up his practice. In 1872 he won a seat on the Westport board of guardians, no doubt under the patronage of his father, who was also an elected guardian and a principal tenant of both Lord Lucan and the Marquess of Sligo. Both father and son appear to have been fairly conservative in their activities on the board. In 1876 the elder Louden voted not to move a petition in support of Butt's land bill that year,[27] and the younger Louden, though not present on that occasion, never attempted to introduce political discussions into board meetings. Outside the board, however, John was politically active, having been a member of the Home Rule League from the time of its foundation, and one who began his career, as he later said, "by denouncing Mr. Butt for taking [the league] into the hands of the Conservative Party."[28] He told the Parnell Commission in 1888 that he had also been active in radical politics on the board of guardians from an early date, but this claim does not appear to have been borne out by the facts.

Louden had been present on the platform at Irishtown but had had no role in organizing the meeting. Westport, however, was his own territory, and in the organization of the Westport meeting he played a central role, including, so he claimed, financing the meeting out of his own pocket.[29] At the meeting itself Louden nominated Daly for the chairmanship and also spoke from the platform. While Davitt and Parnell spoke in generalities, emphasizing the depressed condition of the Irish peasantry, Louden's speech was more specific. He launched out against Lord John Browne, the man who was landlord of most of the people present, depicting him as a "harsh landlord who insists by a law process on tenants to pay poor rates who are exempted by an act of Parliament," and when he finished speaking, cries of "Three cheers for Louden!" and "He keeps Lord John Browne in his place!" were heard from the crowd. When Davitt spoke he again brought up the local government question, telling the audience that there were few honest representatives of the people on the boards of guardians and urging them to "secure local representation by electing such men as Mr. Louden and Mr. Daly as members of town boards and boards of guardians."[30]

From Irishtown onward Louden and Daly were found together on the platforms of most of the western meetings, making speeches and acting as chairmen when more prominent ones could not be found.[31] On August 16 Davitt and a number of nationalists from Mayo and Dublin gathered in Castlebar and founded the County Mayo Land League. Louden and Daly were present, the only ones who were not Fenians.[32] At the motion of Daly, Louden was elected president of the organization.[33] In subsequent months the two men continued participating in the agitation in important ways. Both were present when, on October 21, the Irish National Land League was founded in Dublin. Both were elected to the executive council and Louden became a member of the council's executive committee, which became the league's governing body. Parnell was elected president.[34] After the founding of the national organization Louden devoted most of his time to politics and became a well-known national figure. Daly appears to have had no political aspirations beyond local politics. He occasionally attended the league's meetings in Dublin, but for the most part he seemed content with leading the agitation in Mayo. That he was its leader, there seems to have been little question. William O'Brien, who toured the West during the summer of 1879, met Daly and recorded the meeting in his personal journal. So moved was he by Daly's charisma, his moral conviction, and his use of language, that twenty-five years later, when he wrote his own memoirs, he thought enough of the meeting to quote the entry he had made in his journal for that day, August 21, 1879, which reads in part:

3 o'clock. Missed James Daly, who is the storm-center of the agitation. Made out a parish priest, Canon McGee, who at first shivered at Daly's name and looked reserved. . . . Daly made me out later at the hotel and hailed the press as a deliverer. "It is the first time they ever discovered the unfortunate County Mayo on the map of Ireland. They were never done talking about the famine pits of Skibbereen, because there was a smart local doctor who wrote them up. Two hundred thousand people died of hunger in Mayo, after living on nettles and asses' flesh, and the world never said as much as 'God be merciful to them!' " A rough-spoken giant, with an inexhaustible fund of knowledge of the people and the quaintest mother-wit. Talked far into the night and told me stories of Mayo landlordism that followed me to bed like nightmares.[35]

Daly's journalistic style accorded well with O'Brien's personal description of him. Bellicose, abrasive, and liberal in its use of classical and literary references, his writing ranged in mood from formal, to righteous, to melancholy, to flippantly satirical, often from one issue to the next. Expert in the use of the epithet, Daly once referred to his landlord and former employer, Harriet Gardiner, as "a savage amazon," and to another landlord, J. Vesey Stoney, as "the heartless savage of Rossturk, the bigoted, brandy-marked despot." His use of language was similar to that of O'Brien himself, who entered journalism in 1881 as publisher of Parnell's party newspaper, *United Ireland*, and it might well be that O'Brien developed his style in part from his reading of the *Connaught Telegraph*.

Down to the end of 1879 the agitation remained largely confined to Connaught. Davitt's explanation of this was that the agitation was on the whole opposed by the clergy, and also that the leading nationalists outside the West, whose viewpoint was represented by the *Freeman's Journal*, remained hostile to Parnell and loyal to the conservative wing of the party.[36] However, in November 1879, an event occurred in Gurteen, Sligo, which quickly altered the picture. On November 2, Daly, Davitt, John Kileen (a Belfast barrister), and John Ferguson (a nationalist from Scotland) held a mass meeting at Gurteen at which Davitt made a violent attack upon rent and hinted at a coming combination of farmers and others who would sweep rent and landlords out of the country. The government, by this time frantically searching for a way to stem the agitation, arrested Daly, Davitt, and Kileen and tried them on the charge of sedition. The three made a farce of the trial, turning it into an indictment of British rule and landlordism and providing the nationalist press with an inexhaustible fund of humorous quotes with which to amuse their readers. Eventually the government, unable to find a jury to convict the three, dropped the charges. The victory of the nationalists and the humiliation of the British authorities was enough to turn the tide. The league's influence in the country rose sharply after the Sligo prosecutions, as branches began to spring up throughout the country.[37]

Board Nationalization under the New Departure

As the agitation in the West assumed a more and more national character, the "local bodies" portion of the new departure agreement receded into the background. Davitt does not appear to have mentioned the boards of guardians in any of the western meetings after Westport, and when the Mayo Land League was founded in August, though the question was mentioned in the charter, it was much watered down. The Mayo league, the charter said, was "to act as a vigilante committee in Mayo, noting the conduct of its grand jury, poor law guardians, town commissioners, and members of Parliament, and pronouncing on the manner in which their respective duties are performed, whenever the interests, social or political, of the people represented by this club render it expedient to do so."[38] Gone were the earlier references to "nationalizing" the boards and turning them into bastions of public opinion. The charter of the Irish National Land League did not bring up the matter at all. As for Parnell, he never mentioned the question in any of his speeches, and appeared to be completely indifferent toward the local government portion of the new departure. The first real opportunity for him to promote the local movement came at the time of the poor law elections in March 1880, when the league was at the point of its greatest expansion and nationalist enthusiasm in the country was high. A word or two of encouragement from Parnell might have done a great deal to stimulate voter interest in the elections, but Parnell did not speak out.

Parnell's silence may not have been so much a sign of his indifference toward the question as of his concern about other matters that were pressing heavily upon him at the time. During the first few months of 1880 his time and energies were completely absorbed by two other extremely important matters—a tour in America to raise funds for the Land League, and a general parliamentary election that arose suddenly during the very weeks when the poor law elections took place. Between January and March, Parnell and his young associate, John Dillon, were in America making speeches and soliciting contributions for the Land League and for the easing of distress in Ireland. Their tour was very successful, so much so that Parnell had to send for another associate, Timothy M. Healy, to help him attend to the multiplying requests for meetings. Early in March, the Queen dissolved Parliament, thus bringing to an end the Conservative Disraeli government, which had been in office since 1874. Parnell returned immediately to deal with the election campaign. It was an important election for Parnell—his first general opportunity since 1875 to test his popularity in the country and increase his support among his own party. Butt had died early in 1879, and William Shaw, a colorless politician who was more a Liberal than a Home Ruler, had been elected chairman of the party. Shaw had the support of a large majority of the party, many of whom were Irish Whigs, that is to say, supporters of the crown. These men were much more conservative than Parnell and not at all in accord with his Land League activities outside of Parliament or his obstructive policy within it.[39] Throughout March Parnell campaigned for men committed to his own position while contesting, himself, three constituencies, Cork city, County Mayo, and his own constituency in Meath.

In the general election Parnellites won some important victories. Parnell himself won his three contests, proving beyond a doubt his popularity in the country. Altogether fifty-three Home Rulers were returned, a decrease of seven in the number returned in 1874. Ten Whig landlords who had served under Butt and Shaw were unseated and replaced by ten middle-class Home Rulers. The difference was sufficient to turn the tide in

Parnell's favor. At a party caucus held after the election Parnell was chosen over Shaw as the new party chairman by a vote of twenty-three to eighteen. The majority of those who had voted against Parnell later refused to serve under him, and they were joined by some of the members who had not attended the meeting. But the dissidents did not form a new party of their own; some remained as independent Home Rulers, while others joined the Liberals. From May 1880 onward the only effective "Home Rule party" was that led by Parnell.[40] A second significant result of the election was the return to power of William Gladstone and the Liberal party. Gladstone had been the author of two great Irish reform measures—the disestablishment of the Church of Ireland and the Land Act of 1870—for which he had gained the respect of many in Ireland. In May 1880 the new Irish party could only view his election as a hopeful sign and wait to see what developed.

While the general election of 1880 was absorbing the attention of the Irish people, the poor law elections took place. As usual, they were held during the last week of March, which was two to three weeks before the parliamentary election. But the campaigning for the parliamentary election covered the entire month of March, completely overshadowing the local government elections. Poor law elections were never given more than superficial coverage in the press, but in 1880, with the competition from the national election, press coverage of them shrank to a fraction of what it was normally. In 1877, for example, the number of unions whose elections were reported in various national and provincial newspapers was thirty-eight, while in 1880 the same newspapers reported only nine.[41] But in spite of the distraction created by the national election, the local government question continued to be important to the people most directly affected by it. All indications are that local interest in the poor law elections increased in 1880 over earlier levels. In Castlebar, James Daly published in the *Connaught Telegraph* the first of many editorials on poor law elections, urging his readers to hold fast against landlord intimidation and reject the landlords' nominees, those "bailiffs, stewards, and flunkeys"—"creatures" whom the landlord "may command or sycophants whom he may cajole." Pointing out that the boards of guardians had become important institutions having jurisdiction over many areas in addition to poor relief, he argued that the existing power structure operated contrary to the interests of the Irish people. Guardians sent to the boards were entirely unrepresentative of the people, and the workhouses they controlled were "garrisons for the defence of landlordism." These same guardians opposed every national demand and supported every project that was anti-Irish: "They reject petitions in favor of Home Rule and adopt those favourable to imperial projects such as the presentation of a testimonial to a Royal Duke." Daly concluded, "Well, we have declared war—war within the constitution, within the law—against landlordism; shall we allow the workhouses to pass?"[42]

The most accurate method of determining whether the public shared Daly's interest in the elections would be to compare voter turnouts in 1880 with those of previous years. Unfortunately such an analysis is impossible to achieve, because poor law poll books have not survived, and the press before 1881 rarely reported the numbers of votes for candidates. How thoroughly a newspaper reported a given poor law election depended largely on the individual editor's interests. Some editors, like Daly or the editor of the *Leinster Express* were actively interested in local government and often provided full reports of local and regional poor law elections. Others, like the editor of the *Galway Vindicator*, were hardly interested at all and only provided the most essential information about the election in the union in which the paper was published. Another way to estimate public interest would be to compare the numbers of electoral contests in the different years. Press reportage of divisional contests was also haphazard, but newspapers often reported the numbers of contests in a union when they omitted all other information. It is possible, by comparing the contests in unions for which this information was given consistently from year to year, to arrive at some estimate of change in public interest within those selected unions, and—operating on the assumption that those unions were roughly representative of other unions in the country—to generalize from them about the level of public interest as a whole.

In 1880, for example, the number of contests in nine unions was reported, all nine of which had also been reported in 1877, the year which was selected earlier to describe pre-Land League conditions. The unions were fairly widely distributed over the various counties in the three southern provinces: Athy (Kildare), Naas (Kildare), Mallow (Cork), Tipperary, Limerick, Castlebar, Westport, Galway, and North Dublin. Table 7 lists, for each board, the province, the number of elected seats, the number and percentage of seats contested in 1877 and 1880, and the percentage increase or decrease in the latter year over the former.

As the table indicates, the number of contests in the nine unions more than doubled, from twenty-three in 1877 to forty-nine in 1880, in spite of a decrease of four contests in the unions of Tipperary and Mallow. The

TABLE 7

Poor Law Contests Held in Nine Poor Law Unions in 1877 and 1880 and
the Percentage Increase or Decrease in Contests

Union (Province)	No. Elected Seats	Seats Contested				Percentage Change
		1877	%	1880	%	
1. Westport (C)	21	0	0.0	10	47.6	+ 47.6
2. Castlebar (C)	18	0	0.0	6	33.3	+ 33.3
3. North Dublin (L)	33	4	12.1	11	33.3	+ 21.2
4. Galway (C)	37	1	2.7	7	18.9	+ 16.2
5. Naas (L)	33	0	0.0	1	3.0	+ 3.0
6. Limerick (M)	46	3	6.5	3	6.5	0.0
7. Athy (L)	29	2	6.9	2	6.9	0.0
8. Mallow (M)	23	7	30.4	6	26.1	− 4.3
9. Tipperary (M)	33	6	18.2	3	9.1	− 9.1
Total	273	23	8.4	49	17.9	+ 9.5

regional variations suggest a distinct relationship between agitation and
electoral activity. The sharpest increases were in the Connaught unions of
Westport and Castlebar, where the agitation first began. Galway, also
within the region covered by the western meetings, showed a substantial
increase, as did North Dublin, the Catholic part of the city which housed
the offices of the Irish National Land League. The high figure for North
Dublin, however, might not have been too significant, since the union had
long been a center of active poor law campaigning, and in 1880 the contests
there were not between nationalists and unionists but between the traditional Liberal and Conservative party organizations. According to the *Freeman's Journal* the Liberals picked up two seats in the North Dublin union
in the 1880 election, which was perhaps more a tribute to Gladstone than
to Parnell.[43] Interestingly, the least active unions were those in the midland
counties where the political clubs of the seventies had been strongest. The
Tenant-Right unions of Limerick, Tipperary, and Mallow were among
the four lowest on the list, suggesting that the Land League's influence
within this region was still weak in March 1880.

There is abundant evidence in the press reports that Land Leaguers or
Home Rulers were involved in most of the contests outside of Dublin. It
would be difficult to say, however, how many of them won their contests.
The results, like those of the national election, appear to have been mixed,
with nationalists making important inroads but by no means sweeping the
constituencies. In Castlebar, for example, nationalists competed for five
of six contested seats and won only two, one by a slim margin and the
other by a strong majority.[44] They lost three contests by wide margins.

In spite of a year of agitation the voters of Castlebar were still either reluctant to vote contrary to the wishes of their landlords, or unwilling to part with incumbents who had represented their divisions for years past.

In Westport, on the other hand, the league won a number of significant victories. Westport Leaguers won seven contests and lost three, though their cumulative vote of 709 votes was not much greater than the Conservatives' 650. The issue in these contests appears to have been clearly defined. All of the incumbents were candidates supported by the Marquess of Sligo; all of their opponents were Land Leaguers. The most noteworthy contest was that for the division of the town of Westport, in which one Leaguer and two nominees of the marquess fought for two seats. The Leaguer was the odd man out in this election, his 125 votes coming in third to 211 votes for James C. McDonnell, a middle-man landlord, and 175 votes for Patrick O'Dowd, a merchant. According to the *Connaught Telegraph*, Arthur O'Malley, the Leaguer, had had the majority of occupiers' votes but was defeated by proxies. As was mentioned in Chapter 1, it was customary for landowners to assign their proxies to a single agent, who would then concentrate them all in one or two electoral divisions where victory was deemed highly desirable by the landlords. This might have been done at Westport, and might account for the two landlord victories. If so, the Westport election proved the limitations of the proxy vote when confronted by a strong tenant opposition vote. Proxies were able to win two seats for landlords but were unable to salvage seven others.

There is no way of knowing whether the mixed Castlebar results or the one-sided Westport results were the more typical of nationalists' fortunes throughout the rest of the country. Press reports did not usually state party affiliations of the candidates at this early stage in the agitation. An indirect way of judging whether the nationalists increased their representation on the boards, however, would be to count the number of offices the tenant guardians were able to win in the officers' elections. This was done by using the same procedures as were used to determine the social composition of the officeholders in Chapter 1. The results are shown in Table 8, which gives the number and percentage of tenant-occupiers holding the various offices after both the 1877 and the 1880 officers' elections.

As Table 8 reveals, the tenants made substantial inroads on the landlords' monopoly of offices. Their total representation, which had been fifty-nine (12.1 percent) of the 489 offices in 1877, increased in 1880 to 101 (20.7 percent). Their sharpest gains were in the deputy vice-chairman's positions; in the chairmanships, however, they still occupied only four offices in 1880. The chairmanship was the coveted office, and the small

TABLE 8

Tenant-Occupiers Holding Board Offices in 1877 and 1880

Board Offices	1877		1880	
	Tenants	%	Tenants	%
Chairmen (163)	2	1.2	4	2.5
Vice-chairmen (163)	11	6.7	23	14.1
Deputy vice-chairmen (163)	46	28.2	74	45.4
Total (489)	59	12.1	101	20.7

number of tenants in that office indicates that the landlords were still in control of the situation in 1880. They were willing to make concessions to the tenants in the less-prestigious offices on many boards but were unwilling to relinquish the office that represented both the real and symbolic power. It is doubtful that they would have made even these minor concessions without a strong show of force from the elected guardians, so the increase in tenants in the lower offices probably indicates an expansion of nationalist representation among the elected membership. From these data and the data on electoral contests it is possible to draw three conclusions about the local government struggle in 1880.

First, there was a clear intensification of public interest in the elections, as was indicated by the overall increase in contested seats. Second, this intensification was connected with, if not directly a result of, Land League organization. This is exhibited in the regional distribution of the electoral contests, the number and increase of which were greater in the centers of agitation than in regions where the agitation was absent or positively resisted by the local leaders. Finally, the increased public interest was apparently unrelated to the fact that the local government struggle had been included in the new departure program. It occurred at a time when the local government question had been all but forgotten by the national leadership. In spite of a parliamentary election, which diverted the attention of both the national leadership and the national and local press, the local struggle went on and probably even intensified in 1880, suggesting that the momentum for the struggle emanated from local, rather than national sources, and was motivated by the electors themselves.

Parnell and the Poor Law Election of 1881

The unique feature of the Land League was its integration into a single movement, in unprecedented numbers, of elements that had not been included in earlier movements. The integration was both social and political. Politically, the league brought together not only the nationalist and land reform elements, but the moderate and radical elements within each. The characteristic these groups had in common was that they all stood to the left on the political spectrum. This was the reason for the early success of the agitation, in contrast to Butt's failure. Butt had tried to integrate the political left with the political right, and in Ireland this was a practical impossibility. However, the left had its own divisions and schisms, and, as Parnell later discovered, there was also a tendency among these groups to draw apart. Most conservative among this coalition were the Parnellite supporters in Parliament and their counterparts in the countryside. The parliamentary franchise in Ireland outside the boroughs was based on a £4 property qualification, the same as the poor law franchise. Thus, the working and artisan classes, who had always provided the support base of the more radical and violent movements, were excluded from the franchise. The remaining element who participated in elections—the more prosperous farmers and middle-class townsmen—supported the constitutional policies advocated by Parnell.[45] On the other extreme stood Devoy and those Fenians who normally advocated physical force policies but were willing for the time being to give constitutionalism a trial. The working and artisan classes, who were in this group, proved difficult to control, for their Fenian propensities resulted in their tending toward violence and outrage, rather than toward peaceable political action. In between there was Davitt and his supporters—probably mostly farmers, since Davitt represented the land reform element among the three nationalist leaders— who advocated nonviolence but supported hard-line policies such as nonpayment of rents as part of the tactics of agitation.

This spectrum had its counterpart among the local leadership. The organizers of the western meetings and the Land League were an amorphous group of farmers and townsmen of various political backgrounds. Most prominent in terms of numbers, by Davitt's account, were the Fenians, who were usually, but not always, men from the local towns or Dublin.[46] At the other end were the constitutionalists, recruited largely from the Home Rule and Tenant-Right movements of the seventies. They were less prominent in terms of numbers but probably more vital from an organizational standpoint because they supplied most of the speakers and assumed most of the responsibility for the leadership. Louden and Daly were representatives of this group, of whom there were a few in every community. In Roscommon, for example, T. A. P. Mapother, the landowning agitator on the Roscommon Board of guardians in 1872, spoke at an organizational meeting of the Roscommon branch of the league,[47] and in Limerick the first chairman of the Limerick Central Land League, which was for all practical purposes the Limerick Farmers' Club renamed, was Matthew O'Flaherty, a landowning farmer and former chairman of the Farmers' Club.[48] These four men, Daly, Louden, Mapother, and O'Flaherty—all relatively prosperous men, all active in the movements of the seventies, and all poor law guardians—helped organize the Land League agitation in their localities and assumed positions of leadership once it was organized. Not surprisingly, all four eventually became the chairmen of their respective boards of guardians, replacing the ex-officios who had monopolized the positions since the boards' founding. In this activity they were typical of nationalist guardians throughout the country, building up an organization outside of the boards, then rising on the support they received from the organization to positions of power on the boards.

Historians have tended to focus on the national leadership during this important period, leaving the impression that the agitation of 1879 was a direct product of plans drawn up and put into action by the creators of the new departure. There is no doubt some merit to this point of view, since the movement would probably not have achieved the focus it did without Davitt, Devoy, Parnell, and their colleagues' concentrating public attention on the issues with the widest appeal. Still, the new departure would have remained only an idea had the public not been made receptive to it by local leaders familiar enough with local conditions to translate the generalities formulated by the national figures into specific terms. The attack on Geoffrey Canon Burke by Daly and the others, and Louden's attack on Lord John Browne at Westport are instances of this kind of translation. Also, the local leaders were familiar and popular enough with the tenantry to bring them out to the meetings to hear the national figures, and to keep alive their messages when they were gone. In County Mayo, James Daly's influence was paramount, perhaps even decisive, to the success of the agitation. His newspaper publicized the events and the issues long before the national press took an interest in them, and his willingness to assume responsibility for the meetings by promoting them and chairing them at a time when few others could be found to perform these chores, established an example to the tenants that no outsider could have achieved so effectively.

As the leader of the agitation, Parnell's most important function was to hold together the various elements that made up the new departure coalition. This was a task for which he was marvelously suited, because although he personally preferred the strictly constitutional approach as the method safest and surest to bring results, he had a way of framing his rhetoric to give the outward appearance of being a revolutionary, while in his actions he took the course most likely to avoid violence and insurrection. Whenever the question of a rent strike was brought up, he avoided committing himself to it, because he knew that the government would react with a show of force, which would in turn generate rebellion in Ireland. He also tried to discourage acts of outrage against landlords and unfriendly tenants, advocating instead the use of the boycott, a form of ostracization in which shopkeepers and laborers refused to serve or sell goods to persons who were known to be unfriendly.

But in spite of his great personal abilities, Parnell was not always able to control the actions of his subordinates or of the league branches. In its organizational design the league was little more than a loose affiliation of units and members over whom no effective system of discipline was imposed.[49] The executive council formulated policies, but no mechanism existed for imposing the policies uniformly throughout the organization. Within the national body Home Rule M.P.'s representing the constitutional viewpoints competed against nonparliamentary Land Leaguers who urged radical programs. Many of these Leaguers held important administrative positions; Patrick Egan, the treasurer, and William Brennan, the secretary, were both ex-Fenians and advocates of hard-line policies. The league branches were self-supporting and therefore not dependent on the national body; consequently, the branches were not amenable to control from above. Given these conditions, Parnell could do little more than walk a tightrope between the dissentient factions and try to avoid falling entirely into the hands of one group or the other. He could hardly have done otherwise, because any attempt to enforce a uniform policy would have resulted in the breakup of the coalition.

Throughout 1880 these fundamental weaknesses in the organization remained concealed behind a genuine esprit de corps generated by initial enthusiasm and an extraordinary wave of expansion. By the end of the year the branches numbered in the hundreds—some estimates placed the number at close to a thousand.[50] Also, during the months following the general election, all eyes were focused on Parliament in the anticipation of conciliatory action by the new government. The Parnellites temporarily discontinued their obstruction policy so that the new chief secretary for Ireland, W. E. Forster, might have time to formulate a new Irish policy. Highest on the list of priorities both for the government and the Home

Rule party was some measure of land reform, for the Land Act of 1870 had not provided the "three F's" the tenants thought to be essential to any reform measure. Of these, the most urgently needed was a measure to halt the evictions that were taking place in increasing numbers in Ireland. As an act of good faith, the administration on June 18 brought in a Compensation for Disturbance bill, which reduced evictions by compelling landlords to pay certain categories of tenants compensation for removal. The bill passed all three readings in the House of Commons but was thrown out by the House of Lords on August 3. The Lords' action was a severe blow to Gladstone's program and also to the harmony that had been achieved between the administration and the Home Rule party in the anticipation of the bill's passage. In Ireland the action was met immediately by an increase in violent agitation, including, according to the *Annual Register*, "riots at evictions, assaults on land grabbers."[51] The Home Rule M.P.'s placed the responsibility squarely on the shoulders of the government, but maintained a cautious attitude in other respects—all of them, that is, except John Dillon, the most militant of the Parnellites, who made a speech warning of "bloodshed and massacre."[52]

Violence increased in the following months as the Land League expanded its activities. Parnell and Davitt tried to discourage the violence but nonetheless indirectly contributed to it by attempting to explain it away in terms of the tenants' insecurity. The government was willing to go part of the way in meeting the tenants' demands, and towards the end of 1880 began formulating a comprehensive land act to be introduced at the next session of Parliament. But the administration was also under pressure in both Ireland and England to bring in the military and suppress the violence; so also, towards the end of the year, Forster began hinting at the need for an arms bill to provide military power and a coercion bill to suspend temporarily the right of habeus corpus in Ireland.

Eager to demonstrate the need for coercion, the government began its attack by arresting five Irish M.P.'s, including Parnell, and a number of prominent Leaguers, including Patrick Egan and Thomas Brennan, on charges of conspiracy to prevent the payment of rent. The "state trials" that ensued had in Ireland the usual effect of closing the ranks of the nationalists. The trials ended in January with the government finding it impossible, also as usual, to secure convictions of the suspects. On January 7, 1881, while the trials were still in progress, Parliament opened, and Queen Victoria in her opening address called for the land reform measure and the two coercion measures. Parnell used the occasion to renew the obstructionist policy, and, together with the thirty Parnellites, succeeded in prolonging the debate over the Queen's speech for two weeks. On January 24, Forster brought in his coercion measure, the Protection of Person and Property (Ireland) bill, suspending habeus corpus. The Parnellites prolonged the next day's sitting to twenty-two hours. Finally, beginning on January 31, the obstructionists extended the sitting to forty-one hours, to which the government responded desperately by invoking a new cloture rule and terminating the debate. The coercion bill then passed its first reading. The next day the government announced the arrest of Michael Davitt. The Home Rulers, still in the House, rose to protest the arrest, using language insulting to Gladstone, to which the House again responded by ejecting and suspending thirty-six of the Irish members, including Parnell.[53]

The introduction of coercion presented the new departure coalition with the first real test of its solidarity. The state trials, the threat of coercion, and the renewal of obstruction, all coming within two months, had raised the spirit of defiance in Ireland to unprecedented heights. So confident were the left-wing elements represented by the Land League that many of them, including Davitt and Egan, had begun urging Parnell to take measures that were bound to lead to revolution. For some time, the radicals had been eager to try the method recommended by James Fintan Lalor— the rent strike—while others urged the more drastic move of secession from the British Parliament. Only a few days before Davitt's arrest, Davitt and a few other Leaguers proposed to Parnell that "on the day when coercion should become law the whole Irish party should rise and leave the House, cross to Ireland and carry out the no-rent campaign."[54] To many of Parnell's supporters on the left, the expulsion of the Irish members seemed the perfect opportunity to thrust this double-edged program into action, and they began urging Parnell to act on it. Parnell, however, was no revolutionary. He recognized the ultimate futility of the scheme and was prepared to resist it. His problem was how to do so without forfeiting the support he received from the left. As he so often did in cases when he was being urged to act against his better judgment, he cautiously removed himself from public view, and began a delaying action. He set out immediately for Paris, where the league had opened an office to keep the Land League funds out of the reach of the British government, and called a meeting of his council.

The council met several times in Paris to discuss the future direction of the league and the party. John Dillon and the league urged Parnell to go to America for support,[55] but Parnell preferred to stay out of the reach of the American extremists. He stayed in Paris throughout February and part of March, allowing himself to be seen in the company of Victor Hugo and the "notorious communard" Rochefort, probably so as to give the outward appearance of being a fellow revolutionary. At the same time he assured a Fenian from America that he meant "to go as far" as the Fenians. All the while the movement stood on the brink of disintegration, the spirit and cohesiveness built up over the previous few months threatening to dissolve. Clearly, some kind of action short of revolution was needed to keep the movement going forward. The course Parnell eventually settled on was to expand the league's activities in two new directions. The first of these was to England, and in an open letter to the *Freeman's Journal* on February 15 Parnell restated his opinion that parliamentary action was still the most sensible course for Ireland, but that he believed the Irish cause could be advanced by "widening the area of agitation" to include the English masses. The second new direction was in Irish local government, and on March 1, 1881, Parnell made his first and only statement on the local government nationalization issue. To understand how he arrived at it, it is necessary to go back a few months.

At a central Land League meeting the previous December, Michael Davitt had mentioned to the members that he had heard of a Land Leaguer who had been nominated for the office of clerk to the Thurles union and been defeated because five Land League guardians on the board voted against him. The guardians had done this, Davitt reported, because the Thurles branch of the Land League had not called a meeting to discuss the nomination, and the guardians understood from this that they were at liberty to vote against the gentleman in question. Davitt told the audience that he found this attitude appalling, adding, "I think it is right to state that the executive of the Land League is desirous of having these positions contested throughout the country, and that whenever a vacancy occurs in connection with the boards of guardians or town commissioners, or any of the boards in the country to possess influence, those who are friendly to this movement should be nominated, and supported, and elected." At this meeting Patrick Egan spoke on the same subject, saying that in the past the people had "too tamely submitted to the landlord conspiracy, especially in the matter of the boards of guardians." He thought that this was the "proper time—before the public mind was engaged with the approaching state trials, and with the proceedings in Parliament—to call upon the country to organize between the present and the time of the poor law elections in March next, and to see that no bailiff or agent or under-strapper or nominee of the landlords would be elected by the people as poor law guardians." If this were done, he concluded, the people would be able to return "honest tenant-farmers or traders who were friends of the tenants, and to expel from the position of chairmen and vice-chairmen the landlords and agents who had so long held them."[56]

Nothing more was mentioned on the subject until February 23, the week before the opening of the poor law nominations, when a third member of the league hierarchy, John Dillon, told a league meeting, referring to Davitt's speech of the previous December, that it was "necessary to strain every nerve to secure control of every board of guardians in the country," because the league should "meet the landlords everywhere." The few representative boards that were partly left to the people in the country, he said, ought to be occupied as "posts of vantage," and he trusted that "every poor law guardian returned by the people would be a Land Leaguer."[57] He gave this speech the day before the date on a letter Parnell wrote to the *Freeman's Journal* on the poor law elections. Eight days later (March 1) Parnell's letter appeared in the *Freeman's Journal:*

> The elections of poor law guardians are now close at hand, and it is of the highest importance that the people should be encouraged to wrest the local government of the country from the landlord classes. I trust, then, that the local branches of the League will everywhere see that all exertions are made to secure the return of Land League candidates as poor law guardians, and to drive from office the agents, bailiffs, and landlord nominees who have hitherto been allowed to fill these important positions.[58]

The following day John Dillon announced at a league meeting that he had circulated a letter to Land League branches the previous week, requesting that they convene special meetings to make arrangements to secure the return of Leaguers as poor law guardians.[59] Dillon's and Parnell's sudden interest in the local government question were too coincidental to be unplanned. Dillon had been in Paris with Parnell only the week before. Egan was also in Paris and, as we have seen, his concern about the poor law elections preceded Parnell's and Dillon's.

From these facts, and knowing Parnell's situation at the time, one may deduce the following progression of events. In February 1881 Parnell needed a solution to his immediate problems. He called his council together in Paris to develop such a policy. To be effective, the policy needed to have, if possible, four attributes: something that diverted the attention and energies of the Irish people away from the extreme no-rent and secession issues; something that appealed to the left-wing supporters of the movement; something that established the impression, if not the reality, of a forward movement against landlordism and British rule; and above all, something that emphasized constitutional, rather than violent or revolutionary, action. One of his colleagues in Paris, perhaps Egan, who had shown interest in the question, or Louden, a poor law guardian who had heard James Daly often mention the question during the western meetings, brought up the matter of the poor law elections, which were only six weeks away. The issue had all the necessary attributes: it was unrelated to the no-rent and secession issues; it had always appealed to left-wingers—Devoy, Davitt, and Egan, among others; the election of nationalists to the boards and board offices would demonstrate tangible and immediate gains against landlordism and British rule; and the entire activity was firmly within the limits of constitutional action. Because it was more immediate, it was even more ideal for Parnell's purposes than the English recruitment drive. Parnell, therefore, agreed to support an attack on the boards of guardians, assigning the mechanical details to John Dillon, the member of his party who was most respected by the left-wing elements in the league, while he himself wrote his letter of appeal to the press. Dillon circulated Parnell's letter to all league branches the week before the election. The language of the letter, urging that "all exertions are made . . . *to drive from office the agents, bailiffs, and landlord nominees,*" is reminiscent of the language used by Egan in his speech in December and by James Daly on a number of occasions. It was clearly designed to appeal to farmers, and also to Fenians, by dangling before them the carrot of victory over the hated oppressors. Parnell thus seized upon the coming poor law elections as a means of politicizing the agrarian agitation and steered the movement away from its revolution-bound course.

Parnell's letter had the desired effect. Within a few days the whole country was caught up in the poor law election with unprecedented interest. Land League branches everywhere held special meetings to nominate candidates, and the press covered the regional elections as though they were contests for parliamentary seats. Land Leaguers pursued the nominations, the campaigns, and even the contests for officerships, as the *Irish Times* observed, "with quite as much energy as if they were repealing the union."[60] Many of the preparations were reported to the press, and some of the reports attributed the activity to the Parnell letter. In Clare, for example, where partisan activity on both sides appeared to be even

116   THE REVOLT OF THE TENANTRY

more intense than elsewhere, the *Clare Independent* wrote of the Ennis union
elections, "Acting on the advice of their leader, Mr. Charles Stewart Parnell, the Land Leaguers are determined to effect a radical change in the
constitution of the board of guardians at the forthcoming election to be
determined on the 25th inst." The local league branch had received a copy
of the Parnell letter only a few days earlier.[61] In neighboring Kilrush, the
Kilrush Land League nominated eight names, publicly expressing "a determination to exclude bailiffs, agents, etc., in accordance with the rec-
ommendations laid down by Messrs. Parnell, Dillon & Co."[62] And after
the election, the *Freeman's Journal* reported that at Tullamore two guardians
were unseated by Land League nominees who had been supported by
"manifestos forwarded by the central branch."[63]

   The *Nation* and some provincial newspapers reported nominating meetings held in Mitchelstown (Cork), Manorhamilton (Leitrim), Tulsk (Roscommon), Dromore (Tyrone), Clonaslie (Queens), Knockerockery
(Roscommon), Drogheda (Meath), Tullamore (Kings), Cork city, and the
town of Roscommon.[64] The nominating technique used by the Roscommon branch was the most sophisticated of any reported. The branch called
a nominating convention consisting of two delegates from each electoral
division. Public meetings were then held in each division to choose the
delegates, and the delegates convened and chose a slate of candidates.[65]
The members of the Roscommon Land League were essentially the same
men who had challenged Lord Crofton in 1872. Their refined technique
no doubt derived from their long experience in managing poor law election
campaigns. Theirs was the only convention reported in 1881, but in subsequent years the convention method became popular in a number of other
unions as well. The need for unanimity in 1881, however, caused most
unions to shy away from democratic selection methods. Most branches
nominated their candidates in closed sessions and vehemently opposed any
attempts by members or others to challenge their choices. The Thradaree
Land League, for example, invoked the spectre of the boycott by declaring
in a resolution that "any tenant farmer who allows himself to be nominated
to contest the position of poor law guardianship in opposition to the nominee of the League is a supporter of landlordism."[66] The Kinsale branch
actually expelled a member who contested a seat against the branch
nominee.[67]

   The Land Leaguers carried out a serious campaign, advising the electorate about closing dates for nominations, canvassing the constituencies,
and showing the electors how to fill out ballots properly.[68] The election

was, for many, their first experience in conducting a campaign as representatives of a national party. The great question in 1881, as in earlier years, was still the question of whether the electorate could be induced to vote contrary to the wishes of their landlords. Some of the local leaders had high hopes that they would. One such leader, Austin O'Brien, Secretary of the Ennistymon (Clare) branch of the league, wrote to Thomas Brennan two weeks before the election:

> In the Ennistymon union we have initiated seven contests for guardianship of the poor. Every landlord man will have to walk if we can possibly manage it. I am myself contesting the principal division of the union, that of Ennistymon. My opponent is a solicitor and also a landlord. The spirit of the people is so thoroughly aroused that I am confident of licking him. In some of the other divisions we are sure of easy victories. What makes victory difficult in my case is that the bulk of the division is on the property of the McNamara minors and that the receiver, Tom Lucas, is dead against me. But with all of the landlord influences against me I am still confident of success.[69]

O'Brien's confidence proved to be premature. The Leaguers were defeated in all seven contests. O'Brien lost his own contest by a vote of 206 to 173, even with the league placing all its resources behind his candidacy. The nationalist *Clare Independent* blamed the league's defeat on that "certain class very numerous [undoubtedly farmers], who, however loud they may cheer and applaud at public meetings, are very backward when it comes to making a small sacrifice for their principles."[70]

The Conservatives did not remain silent in the election. In a letter to the *Irish Times* published twelve days after the appearance of Parnell's letter in the *Freeman's Journal*, a Clare inhabitant calling himself "Senex" wrote a rebuttal to Parnell that came to be the standard Conservative argument against nationalists controlling the boards of guardians:

> It is intended that at the approaching election of guardians on the 25th instant no one shall be elected to that office who is not a Land Leaguer. In many unions in County Clare this program has been put forth, many Land Leaguers having already been nominated for that important office.
>
> This is a move fraught with great danger to the administration of the poor laws, as many acts of jobbery are likely to be carried out, to the great injury of the poor and the cess payers. It is calculated on that the unions now represented by high-minded, honorable men, as chairmen, vice-chairmen, and deputy vice-chairmen, will be deposed, and that Land Leaguers of a very different type will be substituted. If so, we may expect boards that will be so constituted turning into regular pandemonium.[71]

Fears of nationalist "jobbery" were expressed commonly in Conservative electioneering propaganda in 1881 and later years. At the time of publication of the letter from "Senex," for example, a circular was being distributed in Dublin by a landlord group calling themselves the "Defence Association," urging the Dublin electorate to vote for two Protestant candidates, arguing that "there are so many matters of taxation and patronage now in the discretion of poor law Guardians that all voters should exert their influence to select the most honest and capable men for that distinction," and not the "most ignorant and bigoted of the Romish part in the country."[72] The Conservative fears were real, because the landlords were highly vulnerable in matters concerning the poor law. A nationalist board could, for example, augment the Land League fund for evictions by granting handsome relief payments to evicted tenants and charging the cost to the poor rates, five-eighths of which were paid by landlords. As will be shown later, this practice was used by many nationalist-dominated boards. On the whole, however, the landlords refrained from expressing their fears in public, preferring instead the tried and true methods of coercing their tenants to vote for Conservative candidates, or failing that, building up the ex-officios' strength at officers' election meetings to gain control of the all-important chairmanship. An ex-officio chairman was the best guarantee against nationalist "jobbery."

Landlord intimidation was still an important factor in some elections, especially in the impoverished regions along the western coast, where the tenants were poor and dependent on their landlords. A letter to the *Kerry Sentinel* by "an Old Inhabitant" of the Dingle Union tells of a particular election in that union, contested between a Land Leaguer and Captain de Moleyns, agent for Lord Ventry, in which "nothing was left undone" to secure the election of the agent. The letter charged that the clerk and the bailiff of the Ventry estate colluded to intimidate the tenant voters. "They knew when and where the relieving officer had determined on leaving the voting papers, and this was so well-timed that he had scarcely left when the clerk and the bailiff—the representatives of the ledger and the crowbar—appeared to ask, 'Will you vote for my masther?' What mockery! What farce! Freedom of election forsooth! The rent in the person of the clerk and the crowbar in the person of the bailiff, brought terror to the poor man's heart, and what could he say in reply but, with a curse on his lips and indignation in his heart, yield a reluctant consent."[73] However, in 1881 the landlords were not the only intimidators. The league had its own, equally effective weapons, to which a letter from a conservative candidate to the clerk of the Athy board of guardians stands as eloquent testimony:

Sir,

I beg to withdraw my candidature for the office of poor law guardian for the electoral division of Rathaspick, in the Athy Union, as I fear the parties who voted for me would be injured by the Land League, and I hereby caution you against showing the voting papers to any one, or disclosing to any person how any voter voted, as by this, my resignation, it will not be necessary for you to examine the voting papers.

Yours truly,
H. M. Redmond[74]

It was argued in Chapter 1 that the open ballot could continue to protect the landlords in elections only so long as the weapons of intimidation were solely in the landlord's hands. As Redmond's letter indicates, Captain Moonlight could indeed be as convincing an advocate as the minions of the ledger and the crowbar.

The methods employed during the campaign and the interest shown by the candidates, the electorate, and the press gave the election the tone of a parliamentary contest. One account of a Clare election even hinted at the use, long common in Parliamentary elections, of the ancient method of plying the voters with "poteen." "At Cree," reported the *Clare Advertiser*, "spiritualistic influence and the brightening beams of 'Three Star' persuasiveness carried the day. John Jameson was the umpire."[75] And after the election the winning parties in the same constituencies held victory celebrations similar to those that accompanied parliamentary victories. In the town of Navan (Meath) the counting of the ballots was accompanied by an interest that the *Belfast Newsletter* found to be unprecedented in that town, and that night "tar barrels were lighted in Scotch Street and other parts of the town" to celebrate a Conservative victory over the Land League in the divisional election.[76]

As a sign of the intensified public interest, the number of electoral contests increased sharply in 1881 over that in 1877. The election results of thirty-two unions were reported in the newspapers surveyed, of which twenty-two had been reported in 1877. Of the total number of elected seats in these unions, 8.8 percent had been contested in 1877 (see Table 9), whereas 19.0 percent were contested in 1881; this represented an approximate doubling of the number of contests and an increase of 10.2 percent in the ratio of actual contests to possible contests. The nine unions surveyed in 1880 (see Table 7, given earlier) showed a similar increase, from 8.4 to 17.9 percent of the possible contests between the two years, but it should be kept in mind that the 1880 increases were due largely to extraordinary increases in four unions, three of which were located in western unions. Had there been a higher proportion of eastern and northern unions shown in Table 7, as there is in Table 9, the overall increase would no doubt have been pulled down, since there was much less activity in eastern and northern regions in 1880. In 1881, as the provincial distribution in Table 9 demonstrates, the increases were general and not restricted to any one part of the country. The activity and increase in activity was still greatest in the west, with the two Mayo unions (Castlebar and Westport), the one Galway union (Galway) and two Clare unions (Kilrush and Ennis) occupying five of the top eight locations on the table. But some of the unions in the midland region, which had been least active in 1880, were heavily contested in 1881. The total contests in the unions of Donaghmore, Tullamore, Naas, and Carlow increased from six in 1877 to twenty in 1881. Other midland unions (Castlecomer, Limerick, Celbridge, Naas, Athy, and Edenderry) were either moderately active or quieter than in 1877. The Ulster unions of Lurgan and Lisburn also showed increases, though these were more moderate than the increases in most of the three other provinces, and a third Ulster union, the very Protestant union of Armagh, showed a decrease. On the other hand, Newtownards, a union in County Down with a larger-than-usual Catholic population in eastern Ulster, stood near the top of the list with five contests, an increase of five over 1877. The absence of any striking regional trends reveals clearly that the national increase in contests was about evenly distributed throughout the country, each region showing a spectrum of activity ranging from very active in some unions, to moderately active in others, to little or decreased activity in still others. The single exception was the area along the western coast, where the numbers of contests were uniformly higher than elsewhere. Even there, however, the differences were not as great as they had been in 1880. On the whole, therefore, one can say that in 1881 the tenants' movement to capture the boards of guardians developed into a struggle of national proportions.

The Land Leaguers won a number of significant victories in the election. The most striking victory was in Tralee, County Kerry (which is not shown on Table 9 because its elections were not reported in 1877). League-supported candidates contested seventeen of the Tralee union's forty-one

TABLE 9

Poor Law Contests Reported in Newspapers in 1877 and 1881

Union (Province)	No. Elected Seats	Seats Contested				Percentage Change
		1877	%	1881	%	
1. Castlebar (C)	18	0	0.0	7	38.9	+ 38.9
2. Drogheda (L)	25	1	4.0	10	40.0	+ 36.0
3. Ennis (M)	19	1	5.3	6	31.6	+ 26.3
4. Kilrush (M)	23	2	8.7	7	30.4	+ 21.7
5. Newtownards (U)	15	0	0.0	5	33.3	+ 33.3
6. Donaghmore (L)	15	4	26.7	7	46.7	+ 20.0
7. Galway (C)	37	1	2.7	7	18.9	+ 16.2
8. Westport (C)	21	0	0.0	3	14.3	+ 14.3
9. Tullamore (L)	32	0	0.0	4	12.5	+ 12.5
10. Naas (L)	33	0	0.0	4	12.1	+ 12.1
11. Carlow (L)	35	2	5.7	6	17.1	+ 11.4
12. Lurgan (U)	26	2	7.7	5	19.2	+ 11.5
13. Corofin (M)	9	1	11.1	2	22.2	+ 11.1
14. Castlecomer (L)	12	1	8.3	2	16.7	+ 8.4
15. Cork (M)	50	13	26.0	16	32.0	+ 6.0
16. Limerick (M)	46	3	6.5	5	10.9	+ 4.4
17. Lisburn (U)	30	2	6.7	3	10.0	+ 3.3
18. Celbridge (L)	19	1	5.3	1	5.3	0.0
19. Armagh (U)	38	4	10.5	3	7.9	− 2.6
20. Nenagh (M)	32	7	21.9	6	18.8	− 3.1
21. Athy (L)	29	2	6.9	1	3.4	− 3.5
22. Edenderry (L)	30	5	16.7	3	10.0	− 6.7
Total	594	52	8.8	113	19.0	+ 10.2

seats and won thirteen of the contests.[77] League successes were also reported in Westport, where they won all three contests, and in Parsonstown (Kings), where they won five of eight. Elsewhere their gains were mixed. They were successful in only three of the ten contests in Drogheda, four of fifteen in Boyle (Roscommon), one of four in Sligo and Clonmel, and two of seven in Galway.[78] Other reports were similarly mixed. Whether the election signified a victory for the league or for the landlords depends on whether one emphasized the inroads made by the league or the landlords' success in averting a decisive league victory. The Conservative *Irish Times* chose to emphasize the latter point of view. Pointing to the League's paltry showing in the Galway union, where Leaguers won only two of seven contests, the *Irish Times* declared that "it is enough to say that the effort to carry in Mr. Parnell's nominees universally and with a marked superiority was not successful."[79] The editor of the *Nation*, on the other hand, reviewing the results, settled on the conspicuous league victory in Tralee, and congratulated the Irish people for their "bold and successful fight," as a result of which "in many parts of Ireland the character of the boards had been changed completely." The *Nation* added, "in the South and West, the LL candidates have been very successful—indeed in Kerry the national organization has swept everything before it, showing pretty plainly what Kerry would do in a Parliamentary contest if only one arose."[80]

4

Organized Revolt, 1881–1882

Timothy Harrington and the North Kerry Land League

THE POOR LAW election of 1881 was the first test of the Land League's effectiveness in an election campaign. In 1880 the organization had not developed sufficiently in many parts of the country to be a decisive influence either in the poor law elections or the parliamentary campaign. As events were to prove, the 1881 election was also the last such test, because by the end of the year, as a result of the combined effects of coercion, internal discord, and structural weakness in the national organization, the Land League was all but defunct. Insofar as its role in the election was concerned, the League had met the challenge in 1881 with a moderate degree of success. Ten new elected guardians were installed in the chairmanships, bringing the national total of tenant chairmen to fourteen. Seventeen new tenants were added in the vice-chairman position and seven in the deputy vice-chairman position, bringing the national total in those offices up to forty and eighty-one respectively. After the election of 1881, therefore, the elected guardians controlled just under one-tenth of the chairmanships, just over one-fourth of the vice-chairmanships, and almost exactly one-half of the deputy vice-chairmanships in the country. The ex-officios who had been ejected from the high offices were for the most part the less powerful among the ex-officio chairmen. Apart from Lord Lucan, whom James Daly and his party had managed to unseat in Castlebar, and Lord Carew, whom the elected guardians had ejected in Enniscorthy, County Wexford, the defeated chairmen were all country gentlemen or lesser landowners whose influence was local.[1]

The key factor was electoral organization. Parnell's letter to the press provided the principal stimulus for action, but the stimulus was only as effective as the extent to which the local branches were willing and able to take advantage of it. Thus in Limerick, where a powerful group of moderate farmers and townsmen who had been active in the Limerick Farmer's Club had the controlling voice in the local organization, Parnell's letter and Dillon's instructions were met with extreme coolness, and virtually no changes were made that year either in the composition of the Limerick board of guardians or in its offices.[2] In Tralee, on the other hand, the North Kerry Land League under the direction of Timothy Harrington made a concerted effort to carry out the instructions from the central branch, with the result that thirteen seats on the Tralee board were won by Land Leaguers, raising the Land League total on the board to twenty-one; in the neighboring union of Listowel, which was also within the jurisdiction of the North Kerry branch, all the ex-officios were expelled from the offices.[3] The accomplishment in Kerry was significant not only for what it reveals about the relationship between organization and effectiveness, but also for what it reveals about the organizational talent of the principal figure there—Timothy Harrington. It would therefore be fruitful to examine the Tralee election in more detail.

Harrington, the president of the branch, would move eighteen months later to the center of Parnell's inner circle as one of the two secretaries of the National League. A former schoolteacher, who had left teaching in 1880 to become a publisher, Harrington had been a Home Rule supporter in the 1870s. In the spring of 1880 he helped to found the North Kerry branch of the league, assumed its presidency, and rapidly became one of the principal organizers in the southwest.[4] The *Kerry Sentinel*, which he founded with his brother Edward, was the voice of the Land League in the district.

Under Harrington's leadership the North Kerry Land League, headquartered in Tralee, had by 1881 extended its ambit northward in Kerry to the banks of the Shannon and southward to the borders of the Killarney union, roughly half the county. The Tralee union, which occupied the central portion of Kerry, had long been a scene of popular protest. The town itself had been the headquarters of an active Fenian organization in the 1860s[5] and of a Tenant-Right society in the 1870s. The county had been among the first to return a Home Ruler to Parliament[6] and had warmly received Isaac Butt on his visits there. The spirit of the Kerry voters was always high during elections. As Samuel Hussey, the well-known land agent to Lord Kenmare, once observed wryly, "An election in most places is an occasion for breaking heads, abusing opponents, and other demonstrations of ardent philanthropy. Such opportunities are never lost on Kerrymen, whose wits are sharper and whose heads are harder than the average run of humanity."[7] The Kerry poor law electorate, however, had never attempted to displace the ex-officio party that had governed the boards of guardians in the county since their inception. Harrington's accomplishment in the election of 1881 was to convert this raw material into a constitutional weapon for the reform of the Tralee board.

Before 1881 there were only seven Land Leaguers among the forty-one elected members of the board. In November 1880 the League had lost the opportunity to augment its strength by one, when a vacancy occurred through the death of an old member. In the ensuing by-election the landlords' candidate was victorious in spite of the league's effort to place one of its own men in the seat. Intimidation may have contributed to the outcome. The landlords, according to one account, "went in a body and brought their tenants to vote against the popular candidate."[8] The incident was not forgotten by the Leaguers, who eagerly seized the next opportunity to oust their enemies. Their principal target in 1881 was the board chairman, Major William Rowan, an ex-officio who was faultless in his attendance at its meetings and who never allowed a political resolution to be introduced by its members. As the chief obstacle to the Leaguers' ambition to win control of the board, Rowan clearly had to be removed. But before he could be driven from the chair, the League needed to expand greatly its strength on the board so as to neutralize the large ex-officio force that was bound to turn out for the election of officers. This expansion Harrington set as his first objective.

Before the Land League could hope to make any substantial electoral gains, however, the threat of reprisals by landlords had somehow to be countered. This could be done in two ways: by building up the voters' confidence through persuasion and instilling in them a readiness to set the landlords at defiance, and by threatening them with reprisals from the Land League's side. Harrington's strategy called for the use of both methods. During the two weeks before the election on March 21, Harrington organized a series of demonstrations in different parts of the Tralee union. In his speeches he emphasized the need for tenants to stand fast against landlord intimidation. The landlords, he told one audience, had sent out "whips" to canvass for their candidates. "But," he cried, "the people have at length learned to disregard such whips and such attempts at intimidation, and have determined to look after their own interests and the interests of their country in all future struggles."[9] At another meeting, repeating the imagery, he chided his listeners for their previous submission, declaring that the landlords' candidate for the division had been "so long playing the whip" on them that he believed they "would again be obedient to the lash." This feigned slur on his countrymen's courage brought cries of "No! No!" from the crowd.[10] Harrington's campaign, or at least the rhetorical portion of it, was really a mixture of taunts and words of encouragement designed to shock his auditors out of their tendency toward social deference.

The coercive portion of his strategy involved the use of his newspaper in an unusual way for reporting the election. In the 1881 election the most hotly contested electoral division was the town of Tralee, where eight candidates contended for four seats. Four of the aspirants were Land League nominees; the other four were landlords' candidates. At a meeting of the North Kerry Land League the week before the election, Harrington's chief aide, John Kelly (an elected member of the Tralee board),[11] secured the passage of a resolution that "any man who voted for candidates outside of those nominated by the League should be held up to opprobrium." The threat of reprisal was clearly implied in the motion, and to give it added force Harrington published the resolution in the next edition of the *Sentinel*.[12] But he did not stop there. In the following edition, which appeared after the election had taken place, he published a list of all voters and how they had cast their ballots. The open voting papers made such an action possible. There is no way of gauging the impact that publication of the poll made on the electors generally. But the next edition carried a letter from one alarmed voter begging in urgent tones to inform the *Sentinel* that it had misrecorded his votes, and that he had in fact cast all four of them for Land League candidates![13]

In the election two Land Leaguers and two Conservatives were returned for the Tralee divison. This represented an increase of two seats for the league in the division, since all the vacant seats had previously been held by Conservatives. In the other electoral divisions of the union the league secured eleven additional seats; after the election six more were gained by the apparent conversion of a number of guardians who had not run as Land League candidates. These additions raised the league's strength on the board to twenty-six elected guardians.[14] The league was now ready to confront Major Rowan in the officers' election at the first meeting of the new board.

It was to be, as the *Sentinel* described it, "the most exciting contest since the establishment of the workhouse." On March 28, one hour before the meeting was scheduled to begin, Harrington and twenty-five Land League guardians met in caucus at O'Sullivan's Hotel to nominate three candidates to oppose Rowan and the two other ex-officios currently occupying the board offices. The general feeling of this caucus, the *Sentinel* reported afterwards, was that Rowan should be opposed for the chairmanship by Patrick Kenny, a popular Land League guardian who had been a long-time spokesman for tenants' causes at the board. But Kenny was in prison, having been arrested only a few days earlier under the coercion act. The group decided that to nominate a "suspect" for chairman was unwise, since it would offer the ex-officios a pretext for calling on the local government board to invalidate the election. John Kelly was therefore selected to contest the chairmanship, Kenny the vice-chairmanship, and a third guardian who had also previously served on the board, the deputy vice-chairmanship.[15]

Full unity on the side of the Land League, however, was lacking at the board meeting. Major Rowan had been busy himself during the week gathering supporters for the contest. He was normally the only ex-officio who attended regularly, but for this particularly important meeting the erstwhile Major had been able to marshall twenty-six justices. A head count of the two parties yielded twenty-six for the ex-officios and twenty-five for the Land League. Four other guardians who were present were then uncommitted, and the future of the board seemed to hinge on their votes. The meeting opened, and each side nominated its candidate for chairman. In the ensuing poll three of the Leaguers who had attended the caucus bolted, while three of the four uncommitted guardians voted for Kelly. The major thus won the election by a vote of twenty-nine to twenty-six.[16] The defectors had cost the league control of the executive.

A less accomplished politician than Harrington might have sought reprisals against the renegades. Indeed, at the meeting of the North Kerry branch immediately following the election, one member did propose that they be expelled from the league. But Harrington halted the action. He argued that "while it is the duty of every member to urge his brothers to work and keep up the rules," he disapproved of "the system of bringing forward charges against members at meetings of the League very often on slight pretext."[17] The pretext, of course, was not slight. But Harrington perhaps had in mind the impression that dictation might leave among people not yet fully committed to the league—and the recent poor law election had shown clearly that there were numerous such people in the town. He might have calculated, moreover, that the league no longer needed the chairmanship, since it now possessed enough votes to control regular business meetings of the board. Major Rowan would never succeed in attracting ex-officios to regular meetings in numbers sufficient to overcome the new league majority.

Indeed, the major himself seems to have put that construction on the outcome. For at the next meeting of the board at which a Land League resolution was introduced, instead of refusing to entertain the motion, as he had done in the past, Rowan offered to step down from the chair after the board's usual business was concluded so that the resolution could be passed with someone else in charge. The Leaguers refused to accept this conciliatory gesture on the grounds that they had every right to introduce such resolutions as part of ordinary business.[18] Thus the struggle between Leaguers and landlords continued in Tralee until the elections of 1883, when the local branch of the National League finally won enough additional seats to evict the major from the chairmanship.[19]

The Tralee Election: An Analysis

It is normally difficult to make generalizations about voting behavior in poor law elections. Though local newspapers often gave the names of candidates, their party affiliations, and the total number of votes they received, the press almost never reprinted the actual polls or analyzed their content. None of the poll books themselves have been discovered. Consequently, there is no way to correlate the votes of individuals with social or occupational data.

The single known exception is the poll of the Tralee electoral division that Harrington published in the *Kerry Sentinel* to "inform the public who their friends and enemies" were. For a number of reasons historians could hardly have asked for a better record to have been preserved. The election took place in a predominantly urban electoral division rather than a rural one. Voters in rural divisions consisted almost entirely of farmers and landowners; urban divisions such as Tralee incorporated both the town and a portion of the farmland surrounding it. This circumstance permits the historian to study a broader range of social groups. The town of Tralee was also distinctive in size, large enough to provide a suitable sample for analysis (there were 568 names in the *Sentinel* poll), yet small enough not to be divided into wards, as were such larger towns and cities as Limerick, Dublin, and Cork. In towns having wards, each ward sent one candidate to the board of guardians. In Tralee the four seats were contested at large, with each voter casting four votes instead of one. The electors could vote entirely for candidates of one party, or could split their votes between the parties, thus providing the researcher with a measurable index of the strength of their commitment to either side. It is therefore fortunate that Harrington chose to use this particular method of electoral intimidation, and the opportunity to take advantage of his inadvertent contribution to scholarly research ought not to be missed.

The 568 names in the *Sentinel* poll[20] represented all enfranchised persons in the division of Tralee, in the order that their names appeared in the poll book and in the valuation records used to compile it. That is to say, they were listed in the order of their townland lot numbers or addresses. Next to each name on the list, four numbers between one and eight were assigned, each representing a different candidate for whom the elector voted. When an elector cast all four votes for the landlords' candidates (numbers 1 through 4), who for the sake of convenience are here called "Conservatives," the *Sentinel* listing stated "four old" rather than the numbers of the candidates. When an elector voted for all four Leaguers (numbers 5 through 8), the listing stated "four new" rather than the numbers. The designations "old" and "new" were used because all the Conservatives were incumbents and all the Leaguers were insurgents. When an elector split his votes between the parties or voted for fewer than four candidates, the actual numbers of the candidates for whom he voted were given. Finally, when an elector did not vote, the words "not vote" appeared, and when an elector committed a procedural error that caused his ballot to be invalidated, the word "informal" appeared. The election itself had been extremely close, with only 102 votes separating the most popular candidate (378 votes) from the least popular one (276 votes). Both were Land Leaguers. Two Conservatives and two Leaguers were elected.

For the analysis that follows, a variety of sources was used in an attempt to discover, for each voter on the list, the principal occupation from which the voter derived his income, and the valuation of the land and building he occupied or owned.[21] By these means a usable sample of 413 voters was compiled. These individuals were then assigned to six occupational categories: (1) landowners; (2) professionals, that is physicians, dentists, apothecaries, barristers, solicitors, teachers, journalists, and land or business agents; (3) clergymen; (4) manufacturers, including owners or operators of manufacturing firms, local distributors of goods produced by manufacturers outside the district, and builders; (5) tenant-farmers; and (6) shopkeepers, including merchants, publicans, and operators of shops in the town.[22] There were few artisans and no laborers on the list because members of these classes usually failed to meet the £4 property qualification required for the vote.

Table 10 shows the number and proportion of Tralee electors in each of the six occupational categories.

It is safe to assume that the great majority of voters in this election were aware of the central issue at stake. Whatever the long-term goals or ideological positions of the candidates, the single issue on which the election was fought was whether the "old" guardians who favored control of the board by the ex-officio party should be retained or be replaced by "new" guardians favoring control of the board by the Land League. It is therefore reasonable to conclude that persons who cast all four votes for Land League candidates were full supporters of the league, and that those who cast all four for Conservatives were full supporters of the ex-officio party. By the same logic those who cast three votes for Land Leaguers or three for Conservatives may be said to have demonstrated qualified support for that side, even if they cast their fourth vote for the other side or did not use it at all. Finally, those who divided their votes evenly between the two camps may be assumed to have been neutral in the contest, regardless of whether it was a consciously intended neutrality or the product of votes cast on the merits of the candidates. If one accepts these modest assumptions, it becomes possible to use the distribution of votes between parties as an index of a voter's commitment to the one party or the other, and to correlate the degree of commitment with the social data.

Table 11 summarizes the votes of the participating electors by occupation, with the electors placed in five voting categories. Category 0 contains those electors who cast no votes for Land League candidates. Category 1 signifies one vote for a Leaguer and the remainder for Conservatives—and

TABLE 10

Occupations of Eligible Voters in the Tralee Division

Occupation	No. in Sample	Percentage of Sample
Shopkeepers	236	57.1
Farmers	69	16.7
Landowners	48	11.6
Professionals	36	8.7
Manufacturers	16	3.9
Clergymen	8	1.9
Total	413	99.9%

Note: There were 150 additional voters whose occupations were not identified.

TABLE 11

Distribution of Votes by Occupation

Voting Category		Farmers No.	%	Shopkeepers No.	%	Manufacturers No.	%	Clergy No.	%	Professionals No.	%	Landowners No.	%	Total No.	%
Conservative	0	9	16	26	14	6	46	2	29	12	57	29	83	84	26
	1	7	13	22	12	1	8	2	29	4	19	5	14	41	13
Neutral	2	8	14	31	16	2	15	1	14	2	10	—	—	44	14
League	3	10	18	41	22	2	15	1	14	—	—	1	3	55	17
	4	22	39	67	36	2	15	1	14	3	14	—	—	95	30
Total		56	100	187	100	13	99	7	100	21	100	35	100	319	100

TABLE 12

Distribution of Shopkeepers' Votes by Valuation of Premises

Voting Category		Small Shopkeepers No.	%	Middling Shopkeepers No.	%	Large Shopkeepers No.	%	Total No.	%
Conservative	0	11	13	10	17	5	12	26	14
	1	10	11	8	14	4	10	22	12
Neutral	2	15	17	9	16	7	17	31	16
League	3	16	18	13	22	12	29	41	22
	4	36	41	18	31	13	32	67	36
Total		88	100	58	100	41	100	187	100

so on down to category 4, which signifies four votes for Leaguers and none for Conservatives. Those who did not vote, those whose ballots were (in a few cases) deemed informal, and those who cast only one or two votes were not included in the sample. Such votes were deemed insufficient to indicate either a party preference or neutrality. With these eliminated the sample of participating voters was reduced to 319.

Participation in the election was high: fully 82 percent of enfranchised persons voted. This turnout contrasts sharply with that of pre-Land League elections, when few seats were contested and voter apathy was prevalent throughout Ireland.

As Table 11 indicates, the voters were strongly motivated by partisan considerations. If voters had been concerned primarily with the personal merits of the candidates, one would expect to find a fairly arbitrary distribution among the five categories (0–4). But that was clearly not the case. Only a small minority of voters took a neutral stance (14 percent), while roughly the same numbers were partially Conservative (13 percent), or partially supportive of the League (17 percent). A majority of voters gave full backing to one or the other party, with Conservatives securing all the votes of 26 percent and the Leaguers receiving all the votes of 30 percent.

The voting preferences of some groups were predictable, and for them Table 11 simply confirms expectations. One would expect landowners to vote for the Conservative candidates, and so they did. The professional group might also be expected to have shown a preference for the ex-officio party, since their incomes and education placed most of them closer to the landed class than to the tenants. Again, this presumption is confirmed. Only three professional men, in fact, supported the league. One was Timothy Harrington, the second was his brother Edward, and the third was a solicitor who handled Land League litigation. Clearly, the league could not expect much endorsement from physicians, lawyers, and other professionals.

The manufacturers and clergy were small groups, together a mere 6 percent of the electorate. The seven clergymen in the sample represented only a fraction of the dozens of priests, nuns, and ministers in the union, most of whom lived and worked on church-owned land and were therefore ineligible to vote. Even if these two groups had acted in unison, they could not have had much impact on the outcome. As it happened, their votes were dispersed, the participating manufacturers leaning slightly towards the Conservative side, and the clergy following the dictates of their religious backgrounds. The four on the Conservative side were all Church of Ireland ministers; the two in the Land League camp were Catholic priests.

The groups mentioned thus far constituted only 24 percent of the electorate. The remaining 76 percent consisted of shopkeepers and tenant-farmers. The commitment of these two classes to the Land League is less impressive than might be expected. A slim majority of the farmers and of the shopkeepers registered qualified or full support for the league. In both cases those who gave full backing outnumbered those who gave partial endorsement. At the other end of the spectrum, however, a considerable number of farmers and shopkeepers voted against the Land League candidates.

The figures in Table 11 do not tell us anything about the kinds of farmers and shopkeepers who supported the league or opposed it. Did poorer farmers or shopkeepers vote any differently from prosperous ones? Did Catholics vote differently from Protestants? From which groups among the tenants and shopkeepers did the league and the landlords receive their principal support? To answer these questions it is necessary to focus on voting patterns within the farming and shopkeeping classes.

Tables 12 and 13 contain the same analysis for shopkeepers and farmers as did Table 11 for the entire electorate, except that the two classes are here divided according to the valuation of their holdings into "small," "middling," and "large." These designations were often used by contemporaries to describe their neighbors. I have attempted here to develop ranges of valuations for the subgroups that approximate contemporary definitions. The valuations for shops differ from those for farms, of course.

	Shopkeepers	*Farmers*
Small	£4–9	£4–19
Middling	£10–19	£20–49
Large	£20 or more	£50 or more

All three subgroups in Table 12 tend to exhibit the same general pattern of voting. A relatively small portion in each category cast all four votes for Conservatives, and a still smaller percentage cast three votes for Conservatives. Then the percentages rise in each category as one moves toward the Land League side, with between 31 and 41 percent providing four Land League votes. All groups, in other words, were decidedly pro-Land League and antilandlord. If there are any surprises in these figures, they relate not so much to the nature of the political commitment as to the degree of allegiance. More than half the voting shopkeepers were on the Land League side, and only slightly more than a quarter were in the Conservative camp. The Land League enjoyed a majority, but it was perhaps not so large as the rhetoric of Land League leaders would suggest. When neutral votes are included, it is clear that almost half the Tralee shopkeepers were not ready to throw their weight behind the league.

Within the three subgroups of shopkeepers there were some differences in the degree of commitment to each party, though these were marginal. Between 53 percent and 60 percent of each group voted on the Land League side, with the large and the small shopkeepers registering slightly more support than the middling ones. The most zealous supporters of the league were the small shopkeepers, of whom 41 percent gave all four of their votes to Leaguers. But these variations are inconclusive and do not establish any significant differences in the degree of support offered to the league by shopkeepers of varying size.

When we examine the farmers in Table 13, we note the small sample—it contains fifty-six voters. It is possible that this limited body of voters is not representative of all farmers in the region. Generalizations based on their voting behavior must therefore be approached with caution. As a body, the farmers tended to distribute their votes like the shopkeepers. The proportions given to the Leaguers and the Conservatives vary from the shopkeepers' by only two percent in each case. Substantial differences, however, appear in the voting patterns of the three subgroups. A slight majority of the small farmers voted in the two categories on the Land League side. A strong majority of the large farmers cast their votes this way. But only a minority of the middling group (41 percent) voted on the Land League side, while a larger section of the middling group gave three or four votes to Conservatives. In other words, middling farmers appear more Conservative in their voting preferences than either small farmers, whose commitment to the league was similar to that of shopkeepers, or large farmers, whose allegiance was exceptionally strong.

TABLE 13

Distribution of Farmers' Votes by Valuation of Holding

Voting Category		Small Farmers		Middling Farmers		Large Farmers		Total	
		No.	%	No.	%	No.	%	No.	%
Conserva-	0	4	17	3	18	2	13	9	16
tive	1	2	9	5	29	—	—	7	13
Neutral	2	4	17	2	12	2	12	8	14
League	3	5	22	1	6	4	25	10	18
	4	8	35	6	35	8	50	22	39
Total		23	100	17	100	16	100	56	100

This interesting contrast, particularly between middling and large farmers, might reflect an element of discord among farmers of varying wealth. But the sample is far too small to allow any such generalization without further investigation. The number of middling farmers who voted on the Conservative side was only eight, and the number of large farmers who voted on the Land League side was only twelve. There is always the possibility in such small groups that voting behavior was influenced by personal or other considerations not related to party. Recent research, however, has indicated a growing division of opinion between small and large farmers during the Land League years.[23] Moreover, this division broadened into an open schism during the later stages of the land war, when small farmers founded their own organization, the United Irish League.[24] Where did the middling farmers stand in this dispute? Were their loyalties divided between the two sides, or did they constitute a coherent faction among the tenantry? Further research into the relationships among farming groups will be needed before firm conclusions about the meaning of these data can be drawn.

Religious issues did not enter into the election campaign in Tralee. Nevertheless, it is common knowledge that the Land League was predominantly a Catholic-based organization, and that Protestants generally tended to shun or oppose it. Was this division reflected in the voting of the Tralee electors? With the assistance of Professor Maurice O'Connell, a Kerryman and historian who is familiar with the religious backgrounds of most families in the Tralee region, I was able to identify the probable religious affiliation of 120 Tralee voters.[25] There were sixty shopkeepers and sixty farmers in the sample, all chosen at random. An analysis of the sample showed that there were just eight Protestants among the sixty farmers, of whom only three supported the Conservatives. Three others did not vote, one was neutral, and one cast four votes for the Land League party. There were fourteen Protestant shopkeepers, of whom two were neutral, six did not vote, and six voted on the Land League side—not one of the Protestant shopkeepers backed the Conservative party! Perhaps as Protestants, they considered themselves exceptionally vulnerable to boycott and did not want to tempt the fates any more than was necessary. Clearly, religious affiliation was not a factor in the Tralee election.

For approximately one month during the agrarian agitation, the Leaguers in Tralee were absorbed in their exciting quest for control of the poor law board. Does their brief experience shed any light on the nature of the Land

League or on other broad themes relating to the period? Though this local event may not reflect conditions elsewhere, a few aspects of that experience, together with other data discussed in this study, lend themselves to generalization. The discovery that the middling farmers tended towards the Conservative side in their voting behavior, while the large farmers overwhelmingly supported the Land League, could be peculiar to Tralee alone or to only a few communities in Ireland. It is worth noting, however, that the deep commitment of the large farmers to the Land League cause is consistent with findings presented elsewhere in this study relative to large-farmer leadership in agrarian agitation. On the other hand, the finding that little more than half of the participating shopkeepers and farmers supported the Land League party, and that the other half either opposed it or remained neutral or uncommitted, almost certainly has national implications. It was shown that great emphasis was placed on the poor law elections by the league executive, and the Kerry contests were depicted by the nationalists themselves as the most extensive of the Land League incursions of 1881. The results therefore suggest that the Land League was not overwhelmingly effective in marshalling popular backing. The reasons for this deserve further exploration.

The study of the election campaign mounted by the North Kerry Land League provides insights into the operations of local political and agrarian bodies. Though the activities of other branches may have differed from those of the North Kerry branch in points of detail, the Tralee experience undoubtedly incorporated many features common to most branches in the poor law elections of the Land League period. It should be noted that the contests for the elected seats and board offices in Tralee were conducted largely by men who were newcomers to official politics. Apart from the few who held seats on boards of guardians or town councils before 1881, their previous political experience had been largely confined to such partisan organizations as farmers' clubs, Home Rule associations, and Land League branches. As previously noted, only seven members of the branch in Tralee had served on the board before 1881. Nineteen others were added as a result of the 1881 election. Although some of these nineteen may have worked for candidates in earlier parliamentary or local government elections, none had themselves stood as candidates. The poor law elections therefore provided most of them with their first opportunity to participate directly in constitutional politics.

That opportunity was a valuable one. In the 1881 contest the North Kerry branch served as a party machine. It nominated candidates for the elected seats, conducted the campaign, selected contestants for the board offices, and planned strategies to secure their return. These processes entailed the use of a number of techniques of modern electioneering, such as the canvass of voters, mass demonstrations, the party caucus, and different types of mass persuasion. These activities afforded members of the branch the chance to sharpen their skills in political maneuver. When the experience of the Tralee organization is multiplied by the hundreds of other poor law elections involving Land League branches, it becomes clear that the local elections of the early 1880s were a major instrument in the political education of the tenantry. Though it would be difficult to gauge their importance relative to other sources of politicization during the period, it is clear that the elections provided the branches with considerable independent experience in conducting political campaigns. Given the infrequency of parliamentary elections, one can hardly exaggerate the importance of the poor law elections in preparing the tenantry for their future role as voters and campaigners in the national contests.

The Disintegration of the Land League

By the time of the poor law election of 1881, the Land League had already begun to break down into its various factions, and the disintegration was greatly aggravated by the effects of the coercion act, which received the royal assent on February 28. The arrest of the local and national leaders after that date caused most of the branches to curtail their activities, and the big question in the minds of the leaders throughout the remainder of 1881 was whether the momentum that the league had achieved over the two previous years could continue in the absence of the organization that had set it in motion.

When the British government passed both a coercion act and a land act in 1881, it was pursuing a policy that dated perhaps from the beginning of the troubled relationship between the two countries. The exact terms of the "Irish Question" changed from generation to generation, but the constant factor that underlay all its variations was Irish resistance to British rule. For centuries, the first impulse of the British government was to crush the resistance with superior military force. This Britain had done on innumerable occasions in the past, only to discover that the force sooner or later was met in Ireland with increased resistance. Then, recognizing the cost and futility of the coercive policy, the government would attempt a conciliatory tack, offering concessions as a means of reestablishing good will between the two peoples. Inevitably, however, the Irish took these offerings as a sign of weakness and of the success of their agitation and were thus motivated to seek further concessions through a continued agitation. Once again frustrated and at a loss to explain the ingratitude of the Irish, the government reapplied the coercive policy. In any case this policy of "kicks and kindness" was certainly the principle behind the two acts of 1881.[26]

The Land Act received the royal assent on August 22. It was much more than a minor concession to the farmers' demands, for its provisions revolutionized the laws of land tenure in Ireland by finally granting the "three F's"—fixity of tenure, fair rent, and free sale. The act deprived the landlords of their right to decide arbitrarily upon rents, evictions, and sale. Tenants could not be evicted while their rents were paid, could sell their right to occupancy at the best market price, and could purchase their holdings with partial advances from the state. This last provision at first proved ineffective because most tenants were unable to pay their own portions of the purchase price, but this defect was remedied in 1885, when another act was passed providing for the advancement of the entire purchase price by the state, the loan to be paid back in installments over a forty-nine-year period at 4 percent interest per annum. In the short run, the most important provision in the 1881 act was one for judicially fixed "fair" rents, for which the act provided special land courts. These courts began operations in the autumn of 1881, and within months farmers were streaming into the courts to have their rents reduced. Over the next three years the courts fixed over 150,000 rents, with reductions averaging 20 percent. The overall effect of the act was to establish the principle of dual ownership of the land, by which the tenant was recognized as also having a legal right in the property, thus reducing the landlord, in effect, to little more than a collector of rent.[27]

Although the Land Act proved to be revolutionary, its benefits to the farmer are more apparent in retrospect than they were in prospect. In a sense, the act was the government's attempt to entice the Irish farmers away from the Land League, and the possibility of this happening was met by the national leaders with different reactions. Davitt and Devoy, representing the left wing of the movement, recognized the threat and urged Parnell to oppose the bill while it was still in Parliament. Their inclination was to go along with Patrick Ford, the *Clan na Gael* leader in America, and advocate an immediate general rent strike to ward off the disorganizing effects of the coercion act and pending land bill. Parnell viewed the Land Act as the great achievement of the Land League and refused to submit to the urgings of the left-wingers while the bill was being considered, until on May 2, while the bill was undergoing its second reading, the government forced his hand by arresting John Dillon under the coercion act. Dillon's arrest placed Parnell in the position of being unable to support the bill openly without losing his left-wing support, so he convinced his followers in Parliament to abstain from voting on the bill. Privately, he knew that the bill would pass without his support, and he continued to support it in committee, but his overt act brought the right wing of the movement down on him. The *Nation*, the *Freeman's Journal*, and the famous "Land League Archbishop," Thomas W. Croke of Cashel, all criticized him sharply for his role in the abstention.[28]

With the passage of the Land Act, the tendency toward disintegration within the national movement intensified. The agrarian agitation continued unabated, and American opinion was as militant as ever, yet the conservative church hierarchy hailed the act as a great benefit to Ireland. The radical extremists in the national movement did not bother to conceal their contempt for Parnell's moderation. As the pressures on Parnell mounted, the league, on September 11, held a conference in Dublin at which the question of whether the Land Act should be accepted was the leading matter of business. At this meeting Parnell introduced his famous formula: *test the act*. Instead of having tenants rush to the land courts to have their rents adjusted, the league in each area would submit only a few test cases. The intention was to force the land courts into bidding for the tenants' support. The members of the conference accepted the proposal unanimously, as they should have, since its alternative—the rent strike— could at that point have achieved little except the acceleration of the government's efforts at coercion. During the following weeks the testing program was put into effect and conducted skillfully under the Parnell formula. In spite of the serious divisions generated in the national movement by the Land Act, it is improbable that the act succeeded in 1881 in luring away many farmers from the League; during the early months of its operation there was too much uncertainty about the act's concrete benefits to farmers. Besides, any sense of gratitude the farmers might have felt was more than offset by their deep bitterness over the second portion of the government's program, coercion.

The coercion act posed a much more serious problem for the league, because it struck at the very core of the league's strength: its leadership. All together, 796 persons were arrested under the act, most of them leaders of local branches or important opinion leaders in the localities. The act provided for the arrest and internment, for an indefinite period and without trial, of any person who in the government's opinion contributed by his words or actions to lawlessness, violence, or disturbance of the peace. It gave the administration broad powers to intern not only perpetrators of illegal acts, but also persons who advocated resistance to the law or to paying rent, or who held a meeting for such a purpose. Of the 796 persons arrested under the act, 61 percent were arrested for non-violent acts including intimidation, holding illegal meetings, sending threatening letters or notices, and making seditious speeches or publishing seditious literature. Publicans and innkeepers were among the classes most victimized by the act, largely because many of the meetings that were judged to be seditious were held in their establishments. Journalists were also strongly represented, as were shopkeepers and farmers. Only clergymen escaped the arm of the law, the government judging wisely that the removal of the moderating clerical influence might prove more devastating than beneficial in its effects.[29] By mid-October, all national leaders of consequence were, or had been, in prison—Parnell, Sexton, Dillon, Davitt, and Brennan, among others (Egan was still in Paris).

Actual arrest and imprisonment were not in every case necessary to force the local leaders into submission. At the mere prospect of arrest, some of the more conservative ones speedily modified their behavior. Thus the leaders of the Limerick Central Land League refused to carry out Parnell's suggestion to attack the ex-officios on the board of guardians because "such an action on the eve of a Coercion Bill might be construed into dictation, perhaps intimidation."[30] But the coercion act was not the fundamental cause of malaise in the league. Like the Land Act, its pressures brought to the surface inadequacies and conflicts that had been built into the alliance from the start but had been masked during the earlier years because of the need of the members to maintain unity in the face of adversity. Eventually, the pressures from the extremists became so great that Parnell was put into the position of having to allow the league virtually to commit suicide.

By the fall of 1882 Parnell had been trying for months, with diminishing success, to appease both right and left wings. On October 7, Gladstone got Parnell out of most of his difficulties by denouncing and threatening both him and the Land League in a speech at Leeds. Parnell, at the time on a speaking tour in Ireland, answered Gladstone in the most insulting and violent language, which he must have realized would force Gladstone to order his arrest. He may even have been deliberately trying to get himself arrested in order to extricate himself from what had certainly become an impossible political situation. In any case, on October 13 he was arrested and sent to Kilmainham jail, where he was immediately confronted with renewed demands for a rent strike. He had previously rejected the rent strike as being not only unconstitutional, but useless during a period of coercion. His arrest, however, made the constitutional "testing" of the land act impossible, so he decided in prison to let the left-wingers have their way. On October 18 he issued the famous "no-rent manifesto" calling for a general strike against rent. He was accused by some of his contemporaries of issuing the document because he wanted to see the Land League destroyed. Conor Cruise O'Brien's explanation, which, in effect, appears to amount to the same thing, is that he calculated that the strike would fail and that his own hand would thereby be strengthened in effecting a future course of moderation.[31] In any event, that is exactly what happened. Not only did the government immediately suppress the Land League, but Archbishop Croke advised tenants to pay their rents and submit their claims to the land courts for rent adjustments. The no-rent manifesto only succeeded in accelerating the pace of violence and outrage, and the government redoubled its efforts at coercion. After October the Land League existed in name only, and though some of its functions were taken up by the Ladies' Land League, headed by Parnell's sister Anna, Parnell put a stop to that too, by cutting off the Ladies' League funds after his release from prison in May 1882.[32] In the nearly seven months Parnell remained in prison, he became in the eyes of many of his countrymen the symbol of the oppressed Irish nation, and in the eyes of the British government he became the only alternative to anarchy in Ireland.

One additional factor contributing to the disintegration of the league has been given little attention by historians. This was the uncooperative attitude of many locally influential nationalists toward the policies of the central branch. This uncooperativeness, which revealed itself at times in outspoken criticism, if not outright expressions of contempt for the national organization, came mostly from the constitutionalists in the localities. It derived partly from a continuation of old parochial attitudes: many of these constitutionalists had been active in politics in their localities long before the establishment of the national Land League, and they considered the instructions from the central branch to be an imposition on their local autonomy. The Limerick Central Branch's rejection of Parnell's letter on the poor law elections illustrated this parochial tendency. At the same meeting, when one of the less conservative members pointed out to the group that the attack on the ex-officios had been recommended by the central branch, the chairman of the meeting, Matthew O'Flaherty, who had been a member of the Limerick Farmers' Club, responded, "*They* have nothing to do with *our* elections."[33] But this tendency toward parochialism was further aggravated by ideological differences that existed between the local constitutionalists and the administrators of the national movement, most of whom were political extremists. The two administrators who were most conspicuous, because of their important positions and because their offices brought them into frequent contact with the local branches, were Egan, the treasurer, and Brennan, the secretary: both were ex-Fenians and both supported the rent strike. Egan in particular was suspect, not only because of his Fenian past but because he controlled the Land League finances. One of the recurring themes in the press throughout 1881 was the so-called Paris fund, controlled by Egan and often referred to sneeringly as "Egan's wages."

One local politician whose career between 1880 and 1882 typified the tendency toward political parochialism and moderate politicians' growing distrust of the national administration was James Daly of Castlebar. In his activities and his writings in the *Connaught Telegraph* during this period one finds all the elements that led to the deterioration of local confidence in the national movement among the constitutionalist supporters. Daly's enthusiasm for the Land League began to wane within months of the founding of the national organization. The first sign of his dissatisfaction appeared during the summer of 1880 over a minor incident involving the distribution of Land League relief funds. A relief committee had been established in Castlebar to distribute the funds, which were disbursed by means of vouchers redeemable for goods in local shops. Daly, a member of the Castlebar Land League, had been appointed to the committee, which was headed by Joseph B. Walsh, the branch treasurer. Sometime during the summer of 1880 Daly wrote a letter to Thomas Brennan complaining that Walsh was using the funds to fatten his own purse. Walsh was accomplishing this—so Daly claimed—by distributing the vouchers in his own establishment, the Old Harp Pub, for which the recipients would show their gratitude by spending a portion of the funds in the pub. Daly's letter has been lost, but the charges are mentioned in a letter from Walsh to Brennan in which Walsh refuted the claim, and launched a scurrilous counter-attack upon Daly, "this addle-pated fellow who became by acci-

dent proprietor of the *Connaught Telegraph*."[34] The incident does not appear
to have interfered with the two men's working relationship because the
following February they jointly conducted a mass demonstration in
Straide.[35] But from that time onward, Daly kept a sharp eye out for signs
of opportunism both in the national and local organizations.

As a political moderate, Daly was opposed to violence in any form.
Throughout the latter half of 1880, however, acts of violence and outrage
increased as the rhetoric of the Land League leaders grew more belligerent.
The leaders did not advocate violence, preferring instead the use of the
boycott, and there is good evidence that the parties who participated in
violent crimes were not Land Leaguers but rather discontented laborers
and adventuresome farmers' sons acting outside of Land League auspices.[36]
Nevertheless it was not difficult to see a causal relationship between belligerent rhetoric and violent acts, and Daly, who had once prided himself
on the fact that he "never quit a platform without first advising the people
to be peaceful in their endeavours to achieve their rights," began making
the connection. Although he had been among the first to advocate the
practice of shunning tenants who took the land of an evicted tenant (at the
Westport meeting in June 1879),[37] by January 1881 he began to advise
against the use of the boycott.[38]

In March 1881, Daly received a letter for publication from two tenants
of his old comrade-in-arms at the western meetings, John Louden. The
letter levelled serious charges against Louden as a landlord, saying that
Louden paid more rent to his own landlord, Lord Lucan, than the land
was valued (more than £500 rent as against £350 valuation), in spite of the
fact that the league urged tenants to pay no more than the valuation. Yet
Louden charged his own tenants double the valuation, making a handsome
profit as middleman. Louden's father, the letter charged further, had acquired the land originally by paying Lord Lucan £400 more than was
offered by Lucan's tenants, who had been given the opportunity to purchase their holdings at one-fourth of their valuation. And now Louden
had told one tenant not to sow any crops because he intended to evict the
tenant before the next harvest. Louden was, at the time, one of the leading
figures in the national movement. Since leaving the presidency of the Mayo
Land League in 1879 to become a member of the national executive, he
had been a member of the inner counsels of the league and had been present
when most of the important decisions were made. He had been the drafts-
man of the Land League version of the land bill, the provisions of which
provided the basis for much of the Land Act of 1881,[39] and he was also

present in Paris in February 1881 when Parnell decided to "widen the area of agitation."[40] Holding such an esteemed position in an organization that claimed to represent the interests of the tenants of Ireland, Louden might have been expected to conduct his personal affairs in such a way as to avoid casting the slightest shadow of a doubt upon his integrity. Yet the letter from his tenants, which Daly published in the *Telegraph*, depicted him as the model of a grasping middleman.

Throughout the month of March 1881, Louden was at his home in Kiltannon, where he had gone to await further developments regarding the coercion act, which had received the royal assent on February 28. In doing so he merely followed the lead of most of the other leaders of the national movement, who had determined to remain as silent and inconspicuous as possible until a new agrarian policy was formulated. It was during this time that Daly received the letter from Louden's tenants, and, his suspicions aroused, he began asking why Louden was in Mayo rather than in Dublin working to get the country out of its difficulties. At a mass meeting on April 2, Daly announced to the crowd that he, Daly, was "not there in the pay of the League, but was more disposed to be what is called a freelance, to show up and comment on acts of all parties, from the landlord to the sham patriot who some months ago preached patriotism by the yard, but who funked at the threat of coercion." Louden, who was on the speakers' stand, could hardly have missed the reference to himself, and when it came his turn to speak he derided Daly for placing "rather severe strictures on members of the League for their absence from their path of duty." It is unlikely that Louden would have used the phrase "absence from their path of duty" in a speech in which he was defending himself. One suspects that the quote was slightly distorted by Daly in his report of the meeting in the *Telegraph*.[41]

On April 14, Daly himself fell victim to the coercion act and found himself in Galway prison. A few days earlier at a meeting of the Castlebar board of guardians, he and his party at the board had engineered the overthrow of the ex-officio officers in the officers' election. They replaced the defeated chairman, Lord Lucan, with Charles O'Malley, giving the vice-chairmanship to James Daly in place of C. L. Fitzgerald, and leaving the ex-officios with only a vestige of their former power by electing Alex Larminie, Lucan's agent, to the deputy vice-chairmanship. Daly claimed that his arrest had been a result of his role in the coup.[42] The arrest appears to have completed his conversion to an anti-Land League position. Before that time his criticism of the League had been more suggestive than explicit and had been concentrated largely upon Louden. After his release on May 9, which had been brought about by his promise to the British authorities to conduct himself with "more propriety,"[43] he became an outspoken foe of the Land League and all that he believed it stood for. The main thrust of his arguments, which he published in his editorials in the *Connaught Telegraph* beginning in May, was against the league's leaders, whom he felt had misled the Irish people for the sake of their own political and financial aggrandizement. In an editorial on August 13 he asked: "Who are the executives of the so-called Irish National Land League?"

> They are not popularly elected and are, for the most part, unknown to the people save for the £2000 weekly which they receive from the people for rendering assistance to their suffering kinfolk. They are overpaid, and know as much about land as a crow does about Sunday.
> These mercenary patriots hold weekly meetings and lodge the funds they receive abroad, while those who are suffering for the cause of Ireland are allowed to pine or starve on prison fare in Galway and other Irish gaols. They give no legal assistance to prisoners, nor money nor food to evicted tenants in Mayo.[44]

In reaction to Daly's antileague activities during the summer and fall of 1881, the Castlebar branch of the league in late September expelled him from the branch;[45] Daly shrugged off the expulsion, saying that he had "long ago dissociated himself from this antinational ring . . . of near-relatives and connections of bailiffs, sheriffs, and rent office satraps."[46] By the beginning of November he had already begun to search for an alternative to the league, applauding in an editorial the efforts of two Mayo priests who had reestablished a Tenant-Right society in Westport. A letter of congratulations from the anti-Land League archbishop of Tuam, John McEvilly, which was read at the first meeting of the new organization, attests to the conservative character of the group. Daly felt that the priesthood everywhere—those "vigilant and faithful guides of the destinies of their people"—ought to follow the lead of these Westport priests.[47] The no-rent manifesto, issued on October 18, simply added fuel to the fire and convinced Daly more than ever that the Land League had fallen into the hands of unscrupulous opportunists. Significantly, however, he did not blame Parnell for the action, but simply viewed it as an act of desperation on Parnell's part, brought about by his need to appease the "mercenaries," "shameless swindlers," and "purchased bombasts," who for personal gain had "entered the movement and plunged their country into agitation and forced the government to pass the coercion act." These statements were contained in a letter to the *Telegraph* on October 28, 1881, from an anonymous correspondent calling himself "Connaughtman."[48] The style and content of the letter were so similar to Daly's that the letter could hardly have been written by anyone else. The fact that the letter contained a scurrilous and almost libelous attack upon John Louden adds further evidence of its authorship and also explains why Daly chose to use a nom de plume. Louden, the letter stated, was "the most untrustworthy of renegades and mercenaries . . . who, if he should raise his head in Mayo politics again, would be crushed as remorselessly as if he were an adder or a snake."

Finally, on March 18, 1882, Daly took the final step in his conversion by actually renouncing the role that he himself had played in creating the Land League. "Rassilas [*sic*]," he wrote, "dying from ennui envied all who had something to trouble them."

> Did we never know anything of him but this would it not prove clearly that he was not an Irishman, and that the Land League did not exist in his time. It does in ours. May God forgive us for permitting it.
> Time was when I had hopes that something good might come of it. I was young and inexperienced then, and I had as little idea of the wire pulling and trickery by which a few of the nineteenth century artful dodgers can deceive millions, as they have of the honesty or fair dealing between themselves and the same deluded millions.[49]

The pattern revealed in Daly's writings from the spring of 1881 to the spring of 1882 is that of a man growing increasingly dissatisfied with the violent direction that the agitation had taken, and increasingly contemptuous of the leaders whom he held responsible. Significantly, he did not find fault with Parnell or any of the other constitutionalists in the national movement, but placed the entire blame on the nonparliamentary Leaguers—those who were "not popularly elected"—who sat in their Dublin offices and set policies while Irishmen were left "to pine or starve on prison fare." His revived interest in Tenant-Right may have been motivated as much by his desire to take the agitation out of the hands of the national leaders and return it to local control, as to remove it from the dominating influence of Fenians and place it under the moderating influence of the clergy. For Daly, who was a man without any desire for national prominence and who was instinctively suspicious of any other man who harbored such designs, there was only one level at which the agitation could be safely governed, and that was the local. It is significant that the most scurrilous attack upon the Land League mercenaries published in the *Connaught Telegraph* came in the letter signed "Connaught-man." If indeed Daly was its author, then his choice of titles as well as his warning to Louden not to return to Mayo politics provided sufficient evidence of Daly's parochial preferences. The letter was Daly's way of saying, as the Limerick Central Land Leaguers had said a year earlier, "*They* have nothing to do with *our* election."

The reason for Daly's bitterness towards Louden is not entirely clear. Louden undoubtedly symbolized for Daly everything that was wrong with the Land League, particularly the opportunism and irresponsibility of its nonparliamentary leaders. But there were also personal elements that do not come through in Daly's writings except in the extreme contemptuousness of his language whenever he wrote about Louden. Whatever his motives, it seems that Daly had taken Louden's measure in singling him out for attack, because Louden's activities throughout 1881 brought him into disrepute with a large body of the membership of the national movement, and seemed to confirm Daly's charges of political opportunism. Louden's career deserves to be studied in its own right for what it reveals about the attitudes of contemporaries toward the politician of the day who "funked at coercion." On October 28, 1882, eleven days after the founding of the National League, the organization that Parnell erected to replace the Land League, two long letters appeared in the *Connaught Telegraph*, one written by John Louden, the other by Timothy Harrington, who had just been appointed co-secretary of the new organization. The subject of both letters was Louden's behavior during the period of coercion the year before. The letters had been prompted by an incident involving Louden which occurred at the National League's founding conference on October 17, in which Louden, appearing on the platform at the convention hall, was met by cries of "coward" and "renegade" not just from a few men but, in the words of an observer, "from men from several counties in the South, West, and North of Ireland."[50] After the conference, Louden wrote his letter to the *Connaught Telegraph* defending himself against the charges and claiming that his embarrassment before the conference crowd had been instigated by Harrington and John Sexton, a Home Rule M.P. Daly apparently showed Louden's letter to Harrington and offered Harrington an opportunity to reply, then he published both the defense and rebuttal side by side in the *Telegraph*.[51]

Louden, in his letter, stated that the charges of cowardice that had been raised against him at the conference were apparently based on certain of

his absences the previous year. The charges, he said, were entirely un-
founded, since "from the Irishtown meeting to the present . . . except for
a short summer tour, and a few trips on business to London" he had never
left Ireland. Harrington, in his letter, noted that Louden's business trips
happened conveniently to coincide with "certain acts of Mr. Forster." One
of the "so-called business trips," for example, was suggested by the arrest
of Thomas Brennan on May 23, 1881:

> Mr. Louden was then in Westport. Mr. Kettle, Dr. Kenny and I were the
> only members of the executive of the League then in Ireland. We knew that
> Mr. Brennan's arrest was the most severe stroke that had up to that time
> been inflicted on the organisation, and when a meeting was called to protest
> against it we fully expected that Mr. Louden would have come from his
> retreat at Westport to attend it. He did come, it appears, but in what garb
> or by what conveyance I cannot say, for the first news of his whereabouts
> that we had was a telegram from Holyhead asking us to imitate his example
> and cross the channel. Mr. Kettle soon followed Mr. Brennan to jail, and
> my turn came a few days after. . . . Mr. Brennan's arrest came on the 23rd
> of May. Mr. Louden's business trip must have been a long one, for he never
> put in an appearance at the Land League rooms until the 11th of October,
> by which time Mr. Forster had shown . . . that his high temper had subsided.[52]

October 11 was two days before Parnell's arrest. At the very moment
of the arrest Louden was making a speech to a crowd from a window of
the Land League offices on Sackville Street. In his own letter, Louden
pointed to this as a sign of his courage and fidelity to the League. Harrington verified Louden's whereabouts at the time, but then added that
Louden had forgotten to finish the story, for "ere his voice died out in
Sackville Street, he again decamped, leaving behind him a letter to the
Irish Times explaining away his speech." He continued, "A meeting was
convened in the Rotunda the next evening to protest the arrests, but Mr.
Louden was not there. . . . Then came the no-rent manifesto."

> Mr. Louden, the member of the executive of the League, the standard-bearer
> who lifted the banner at Irishtown, as he puts it, left to the ladies of Ireland
> the duty of trying to bring to the victims of oppression that aid which Mr.
> Louden had so freely promised ere the coercion act shook his nerves. He
> fled again to the Continent, this time to France, to study the peasant pro-
> prietary question on the banks of the Garonne for the comfort of the op-
> pressed and starving peasantry of Ireland.[53]

Harrington's letter also discussed certain other matters regarding Louden's
behavior, including his relationship with his tenants and the fact that for

several months he had been using his position as attorney to profit from the Land Act by charging a fee for representing tenants in the land courts. But his main concern, which, apparently he shared with many others at the conference, was Louden's behavior while under the threat of arrest.

Whatever Louden's real motives were, he was the only high-ranking member of the national movement, except for Egan in Paris, who was not arrested under the coercion act, and his contemporaries interpreted this as proof of his cowardice. The consequences to his previously promising political career were devastating. In February 1882 he sought nomination for a parliamentary seat in a by-election in Meath but was vetoed by the bishop of Meath, a nationalist who wielded a strong influence over elections in that county. He turned next to England, where a seat became vacant in March 1882 in Manchester, but he found the door closed to him there as well.[54] Then in October came the incident at the National League convention and Harrington's letter to the *Connaught Telegraph*. His unpopularity was clearly by that time general, but the most serious blow was Harrington's public denunciation of him. Next to Parnell, Harrington was the most powerful figure in the movement after 1882, and his opposition sealed Louden's fate in national politics. In 1885, when the National League held a number of local conventions to nominate the party's candidates for the upcoming parliamentary election, Louden placed his name before the Mayo convention to contest one of the seats for the county. This time he was buried by Parnell himself. There were four constituencies in the county and therefore four names to be selected by the convention. Five names, including Louden's, were proposed. Parnell, who was in the chair, put three of the names to the convention and asked for a show of hands. He then declared the three selected. He kept the strongest candidate, John Dillon, for the last and then told the convention that they would have to choose between Dillon and Louden. Naturally, Dillon was selected.[55] After this convention Louden abandoned hope of achieving national office and returned to the Westport board of guardians to salvage what he could of his political career.

The Poor Law Elections of 1882

In March 1882, while Parnell and most of the Land League leaders were still in prison, the time came around for the annual poor law elections. Though the times and circumstances in which the elections of 1882 were held did not appear to be propitious, they actually resulted in yet another substantial increase in the strength of the tenants at the boards of guardians. The 1881 campaign, for example, had been conducted by a fully geared national organization acting under direct instructions from Parnell. The instructions had been channeled through the central branch to the local units and had been widely publicized in the national and provincial press. This was done at a time when both the organization and the voters were being carried along by the momentum of almost three months of conflict between the parliamentary party and the British government. In 1881, in other words, conditions were optimal for a vigorously conducted and well-organized electoral campaign. The background in 1882 was quite the reverse. First of all, Parnell did not make any public statement about the election. From October 13, 1881, until May 2 the following year he remained in Kilmainham jail except for a brief parole in April to attend a nephew's funeral. At the time of the poor law elections he was not yet engaged in the negotiations with Gladstone that resulted in May in the landmark agreement known as the Kilmainham Treaty. These negotiations did not begin until Parnell's parole in April, a week after the board officers' elections had taken place. It is possible that he discussed the elections privately with William O'Brien, then editor of the party newspaper *United Ireland*, but if he did, O'Brien made no mention of it in his newspaper or his memoirs. If, therefore, Parnell had any part in the election campaign, it was an indirect part which did not involve the use of his name.

Second, the political organization that had been so active in organizing the campaign the previous year was completely nonexistent in 1882. Once the government pronounced the league anathema and declared illegal any meetings held under its auspices, the members simply stopped holding meetings and the league continued to exist in name only. Mass demonstrations continued to be held by the Ladies' Land League with prominent league men participating as organizers and speakers, but the women did not appear to be concerned with the poor law elections. In dozens of newspaper accounts of Ladies' Land League meetings, not one reference to the poor law elections was found. Thus, organization—the element that had been instrumental not only in 1881, but in a number of earlier elections—was not a factor in 1882. Without the formal organization to turn to for assistance, the candidates were left to their own devices in conducting their campaigns. Three Tipperary candidates, two of whom claimed the support of John Dillon, advertised their candidacies in the press, much the way parliamentary candidates did; elsewhere placards and handbills were distributed.[56] But these measures were hardly a suitable substitute for the canvassing and publicizing of candidacies that had taken place under league management in the past. The league's absence certainly had a dampening effect in some areas. In Tralee, for example, where election fever had reached its highest pitch the year before, the *Kerry Sentinel* reported: "This year they would have us believe that the old principles are defunct. Yet this is not so, for in the remote division of Baurtregaum an astounding revival of the popular vote was shown."[57] The very fact that the editor had to reach out to one remote division to find something to write about is suggestive in itself of the sluggishness of the election in the Tralee union.

Tralee, however, was clearly an exception, because all indications are that general interest in the election of 1882 was greater than it had been in 1881. The sample taken of contested elections revealed that in eighteen unions in which contests were reported for both 1881 and 1882, the number of contests increased from ninety-three in the former year to 104 in the latter. As Table 14 reveals, the increases in contests were no longer greatest in Connaught, as they had been the two previous years, but were distributed more evenly throughout the three southern provinces. Three of the five highest increases were in Leinster (Carlow, Castlecomer, and Athy), where little interest had been shown in poor law elections in the past. The decreases in contests were also widely distributed (four in Leinster, two in Munster, and one each in Connaught and Ulster), suggesting that local, rather than regional, factors had become more important. Another sign of increased public interest was a sharp acceleration in the tenants' drive to control the board offices. In 1881, tenants held 135 offices; after the 1882 elections they held 170, an increase of over 25 percent. Seven new deputy vice-chairmen were added, and twelve new vice-chairmen, but the sharpest increase of all was in the chairmanships, where fifteen ex-officios were replaced by elected tenants. The tenants emerged from the election controlling 55 percent of the deputy vice-chairmanships, 32 percent of the vice-chairmanships, and 18 percent of the chairmanships. The tenant chairmanships, which in 1882 numbered twenty-nine, were scattered throughout the four provinces, but the heaviest concentrations were in the two areas that had been organized even before the rise of the Land League. Five of the chairmanships were in contiguous unions in and around Kings and Queens Counties. These unions—Mullingar (Westmeath), Tullamore (Kings), Edenderry (Kings and Kildare), Mountmellick (Queens), and Athy (Queens and Kildare)—were located roughly within the spheres of influence of the old Queens County Independent and Edenderry Home Rule clubs. The other group—Tulla (Clare), Limerick and

TABLE 14

Poor Law Contests Reported in Newspapers in 1882 in Unions Also Reported in 1881 and 1877

Union	Province	Number Elected Seats	Seats Contested						Percentage Change, 1881 to 1882
			1877		1881		1882		
			No.	%	No.	%	No.	%	
1. Carlow	L	35	2	5.7	6	17.1	18	51.4	+ 34.3
2. Castlecomer	L	12	1	8.3	2	16.7	5	41.7	+ 25.0
3. Sligo	C	34	—	ᵃ	4	11.8	9	26.5	+ 14.7
4. Limerick	M	46	3	6.5	5	10.9	11	23.9	+ 13.0
5. Athy	L	29	2	6.9	1	3.4	4	13.8	+ 10.4
6. Westport	C	21	0	0.0	3	14.3	5	23.8	+ 9.5
7. Armagh	U	38	4	10.5	3	7.9	5	13.2	+ 5.3
8. Edenderry	L	30	6	20.0	3	10.0	5	13.3	+ 3.3
9. Galway	C	37	1	2.7	7	18.9	8	21.6	+ 2.7
10. Tullamore	L	32	0	0.0	4	12.5	3	9.4	− 3.1
11. Celbridge	L	19	1	5.3	1	5.3	0	0.0	− 5.3
12. Naas	L	33	0	0.0	4	12.1	2	6.1	− 6.0
13. Newtownards	U	15	0	0.0	5	33.3	2	13.3	− 20.0
14. Boyle	C	33	—	ᵃ	15	45.5	10	30.3	− 15.2
15. Ennis	M	19	1	5.3	6	31.6	4	21.1	− 10.5
16. Kilrush	M	23	2	8.7	7	30.4	4	17.4	− 13.0
17. Drogheda	L	25	1	4.0	10	40.0	6	24.0	− 16.0
18. Donaghmore	L	15	4	26.7	7	46.7	4	26.7	− 20.0
Total		496	28	5.6	93	18.8	104	21.0	+ 2.2

ᵃ Not reported in 1877.

Kilmallock (Limerick), Tipperary and Cashel (Tipperary), and Mitchelstown (Cork)—were contiguous unions centered in or bordering on the
region dominated by the Limerick Farmers' Club.[58] After two years of
Land League agitation, these older regions were still the best organized in
the country, and once the Land League had infected their inhabitants with
the desire to bring Home Rule into their communities, they proved themselves best capable of taking the necessary steps to secure it.

The vitality of the candidates and guardians was matched by a vigorous
coverage of the elections by the press. Newspapers that had given elaborate
coverage in the past, such as the *Freeman's Journal, Irish Times, Leinster
Express*, and *Connaught Telegraph*, continued the practice with undiminished
zeal, but were supplemented by other organs that had not shown much
interest previously. The *Roscommon Herald* (Boyle), *Limerick Reporter, Leinster Leader* (Maryborough), and *Kilkenny Journal* all devoted an unprecedented amount of editorial or news space to the local contests. The most
formidable addition, however, was the weekly *United Ireland*, Parnell's
own party newspaper, which had begun publication the previous summer
under the editorship of the most talented Irish journalist of the period,
William O'Brien. Parnell had established the paper in response to the
nagging criticism his policies had been receiving from the two other popular national organs, the *Freeman's Journal* and the *Nation*. He hit upon the
idea of establishing a Parnellite paper during the spring of 1881, and first
offered the editorship to John Dillon, who declined the offer. He next
approached William O'Brien, who accepted, though reluctantly, because
he had no publishing experience. The choice proved to be a happy one,
for O'Brien quickly demonstrated, through his selection of material and
his forceful use of the language, a natural talent as an editor. *United Ireland*
began publication on August 13, 1881, and rapidly reached a wide
audience.[59]

Prior to his becoming a journalist, O'Brien had exhibited no particular
interest in the local government struggle. Indeed, an examination of his
memoirs, speeches, and letters reveals no mention of the subject before
the poor law election of 1882. As a leading spokesman for the Home Rule
party, however, it was his responsibility to address himself to all matters
concerning the advancement of the party, and he soon educated himself
about the questions that were involved and the spoils that were at stake in
the local government struggle. In an editorial published a month before
the election of 1882 he demonstrated his command of the issues and their

significance for the broader struggle, employing the lively, metaphorical prose (with a touch of demagoguery) that typified most of his editorials:

> It is about time to be looking up good candidates for the Poor Law Boards, and to set about expelling both open enemies and white-livered friends. Don't be diverted from this duty by the intensity of the struggle we are in the thick of. It's all part of one struggle—the supremacy of the will of the Irish people. Every seat of power is ours by right. Up and seize it! Every post gained is a blow struck where the enemy most keenly feels it—a blow at his material power. . . .
>
> Ejected let them be all along the line, from the vampires in the Castle down to the creeping things that do the bidding of the *ex-officio* guardians at country poor law boards. It is of vital importance that good men go in and foes and sneaks go out at the approaching elections. It is the first rung of the ladder of national self-government. Win at the Poor Law Boards and we will presently win at the Castle! . . . if it were only a matter of out-door relief for evicted families, the Poor-law guardians about to be elected may be made to play a great and influential part in the death-grip with landlordism. Let not a landlord, nor a landlord's minion, show his head henceforth at a Poor Law Board, wherever the people have the power to crush him; and, wherever the people have any doubt that they have the power, let them try.[60]

Every year at election time O'Brien wrote similar editorials, and after the elections he summarized the recent struggle for his readers. His attention to the elections may explain why Parnell did not issue any public appeals concerning the elections after 1881. He left these tactical details to O'Brien, who was able to reach a wide audience through *United Ireland*, and left himself free to deal with questions of overall strategy. The increased participation of the press filled some of the void left by the dissolution of the Land League, but it could not account entirely for the passionate, almost fanatical (in some areas) zeal with which the population engaged in the electoral contests. The drive had to come from within, and a survey of the newspaper reports of the elections quickly reveals the source of that drive: without question it was the coercion act.

Coercion was clearly the issue in the union of Boyle, which overlapped the counties of Roscommon and Sligo in the region dominated by Col. Edward R. King-Harman, an early Home Ruler who severed his connection with the movement after its democratization in the mid-seventies. The struggle for supremacy on the Boyle board of guardians focused on a contest for the chairmanship between the old guard, whose leader and symbol was King-Harman, the present chairman, and the new guard, led and symbolized by James Cull, a Land Leaguer who had been arrested as a suspect under the coercion act and released from prison shortly before the election. Cull, who had not previously been a member of the board, contested a seat in the election of 1882 and quickly became the local symbol of Ireland's struggle against coercion. "A popular victory [in the election]," wrote the editor of the nationalist *Roscommon Herald*, "will mean far more than the return of a mere individual; it will be an emphatic protest against the system of coercion that prevails in this country."[61] It was the nationalists' intention first to secure the election of Cull and nine other Leaguers who were contesting seats, and then to challenge the erstwhile colonel for the chairmanship, hopefully using the victory as proof of the futility of coercion. In the event, only five of the ten Leaguers won, Cull among them, yet the jubilation of the electorate was so great that the Corrigeenroe fife and drum band came out to escort one of the victors home, while bonfires were lighted for another successful candidate who defeated a bailiff.[62]

King-Harman employed all his powerful influence, with some apparent success, to bring out the ex-officio vote for the officers' election. Reviewing those who appeared around the conference table at the election meeting, the reporter for the *Roscommon Herald* found present "the paralytic and the invalid, the toper and the bankrupt, . . . men from their sick couches and brandy bottles, . . . some from London, others from neighborhoods as distant as 20 to 40 miles away."[63] The nationalists were also well-represented, for their five electoral victories had raised their number on the board to twenty-two out of thirty-three elected seats. Cull was given the honor of nominating the league candidate for chairman, Patrick Martin, who had served as vice-chairman the preceding year. Just before the vote was taken, however, the union clerk announced that Cull, the controversial figure in the election, had recently lost a parcel of land, and that he therefore no longer qualified to sit as a guardian. Cull's disqualification cost the Land Leaguers the election, and Col. King-Harman left the boardroom the victor in Roscommon's struggle over coercion.[64]

Coercion was also the issue in Limerick. The town division of the union had been the headquarters of the defunct Limerick Central Land League, whose members had refused to engage in the poor law struggle the year before. One of the members of the branch who had favored supporting the national organization at the time was William Abraham, a merchant and guardian of the Limerick union for the town division. Though at the time an obscure figure, Abraham proceeded to gain a local reputation as a daring nationalist by speaking at public meetings and advising the people of the area to adhere to the no-rent manifesto. He was finally arrested and sent to prison in December 1881. He emerged from prison the following March 24, after having been reelected poor law guardian in absentia, and four days later he contested and won the chairmanship of the Limerick board, displacing Lord Emly.[65] Abraham was to the electorate of Limerick what Cull had been to the electorate of Boyle—the symbol of a coerced and oppressed Ireland. If this was not clear before the election, it became perfectly clear afterward in an incident that revealed the reason for Abraham's popularity.

On April 24, one month after his release, Abraham was arrested again for making a seditious speech at a Ladies' Land League meeting in Tulla, County Clare. He was brought up before Clifford Lloyd, the most hated of magistrates, who had imprisoned the only priest arrested under the coercion act, Father Eugene Sheehy of Kilmallock. Lloyd ordered Abraham to put up sureties amounting to £1,000 as a guarantee of his future good behavior. Abraham, declaring that the posting of such sureties would be tantamount to an admission of the legality of the coercion act, refused to comply and was returned to prison under a three-month sentence. Immediately upon his return to prison, his supporters in Limerick began taking collections and making preparations for a testimonial dinner in his honor to raise the bail money for his release. Abraham somehow received word of these preparations and sent a letter to the testimonial dinner committee stating that if his friends insisted on "buying" his way out of prison, he would leave Limerick within twenty-four hours of his release and never return.[66] On May 25, the Limerick board of guardians sent a petition to Gladstone requesting that their chairman be released from jail. By this time the Kilmainham Treaty had been made and Gladstone was eager to conciliate Ireland. He therefore ordered Abraham's release on June 7, and wrote to the Limerick board that the release had been ordered in response to the board's petition.[67] Abraham was subsequently rewarded for his heroism and popularity by being raised into national politics. In 1885 Parnell selected him to contest one of the parliamentary seats of the county, and he was returned without difficulty.

Abraham had had the good sense to know what Louden had not: that during periods of coercion there was no room in Irish politics for the fair-weather patriot. But there were many like Abraham in every community in 1882, and everywhere where they could be found the electorate rewarded them—and simultaneously registered their protest against coercion—by stamping next to their name the initials "P.L.G." Suspects were reported as winning contests in Athlone (Westmeath), Tullamore (Kings), Drogheda (Meath and Louth), Castlecomer (Kilkenny), Cashel (Kilkenny), Castlebar, and Tipperary.[68] William O'Brien, poring over the results of the election, reported:

> Ten Popular Party victories in Carlow; 13 in three divisions in Co. Down; in North Dublin scarcely a popular candidate was defeated; 24 in Naas; 16 in Manorhamilton; in Limerick the popular element is now supreme; all but one of the newly elected guardians in Meath; 23 in Boyle; 14 in Tyrone. . . . In Cashel, the Chairman, Vice-Chairman, and Deputy-Vice Chairman are suspects and ex-suspects; in Thurles the new chairman was Treasurer of the Land League, . . . and the *ex-officios* are practically extinguished; Tipperary union is now constituted chiefly of suspects and manifesto men; the Nenagh guardians can now do what they like; [in County Tipperary] only Clonmel, Carrick-on-Suir and Roscrea show any weakness.[69]

These victories made an impression on O'Brien, and in later years, when he recounted the developments of the period in his memoirs, he did not fail to draw the connection between the elections and the coercion act. "Secretary Forster," he wrote of these early months of 1882, "knew that the thanes were deserting him," and so "pleaded constantly that the rents were being paid up, and that all was coming right." All was not right, however, for "evictions, arrests, and imaginary crimes were multiplying." "The landlords, far from affording him any moral support, held a great meeting of 3,000 landowners . . . to cry anathema against the Land Commissioners for impiously reducing their rental. . . . Perhaps," he concluded, "the crowning blow of all was that, when the poor law elections took place in March, by one universal impulse the country rose, and, in spite of a sorely restricted franchise, swept the landlords from their old ascendancy at the Poor Law Boards, and put the most advanced of suspects in their places, thus tearing away the last rag of verisimilitude from the plea that the people were only pining to be delivered from the Parnell despotism."[70]

As the earlier analysis of board officerships demonstrated, the landlords were far from "swept from their old ascendancy" in 1882, though the phrase would certainly apply to most of the boards in the vicinity of counties Limerick, Tipperary, Queens, and Kings, and some of the boards in Mayo, Cork, Wexford, and Waterford. O'Brien's shrewd observation that the election reflected the weakened state of landlordism and British rule, however, was quite valid for two reasons. First, the election proved that whatever benefits the government had expected from the land act in terms of good will had been cancelled by the operations of the coercion act. The votes of the electorate were not those of a people grateful for concessions that had been granted. Rather, they were the votes of a deeply disgruntled electorate bent on humiliating the authorities by conferring the highest available honors on the most hard-bitten of the agitators. Second, though the electorate did not "sweep" the Ascendancy from their former positions of power, the election nevertheless foreshadowed their imminent decline and fall, by proving that the ratepayers no longer needed the stimulus of a letter from Parnell or the organizing effort of a Land League to express their discontent at the ballot box. The electors' votes were, as O'Brien so shrewdly observed, the result of a "universal impulse," provoked by nothing more than the voters' own desire to register their opinions about the imprisonment of their neighbors and political leaders. Thus coercion was a failure, and although it succeeded in dealing a death-blow to the Land League, it did not succeed in stifling the spirit that the league had awakened, and which Parnell now set about to harvest for the ends his own wisdom dictated were appropriate for Ireland.

5

⟪⟫ Constitutional Politics,
National and Local: 1882–1886

The Ascendancy of Parnell

ON MAY 1, 1882, Parnell was released from prison after concluding the agreement with Gladstone known as the Kilmainham Treaty. Under the terms of the treaty Gladstone agreed to release Parnell, relax coercion, and amend the Land Act to give protection to tenants in arrears of rent who had been excluded under the original act; in return Parnell agreed to use his influence to calm the country and secure a general acceptance for the Land Act in its amended form. During the summer of 1882 Gladstone fulfilled his part of the bargain by securing passage of an arrears bill, and although Parliament insisted on continuing the government's power to waive the right of habeas corpus by passing a new coercion measure, Gladstone removed most of the deleterious effects of the law by releasing the imprisoned suspects and enforcing the new law sparingly. Coercion had been a thorn in Parnell's side, for it had given the left-wing extremists an issue with which to justify their case for a continuation and escalation of the land agitation. With the issue of coercion temporarily removed, the land courts and arrears act in operation, and the economy by this time fully recovered from the distress of 1879–80, the way was cleared for Parnell to assume control of the situation in Ireland.[1] As the events of the next four years were to prove, this was a task to which he was more than equal.

The period between the Kilmainham Treaty and the first Home Rule bill of 1886 was one in which Irish national politics was completely dominated by the so-called Parnellites, and Parnell himself gained the unofficial, though perhaps properly bestowed, title of "uncrowned king of

Ireland." Beginning with the advantages he gained in the Kilmainham Treaty, which, in effect, gave him a free hand in Ireland, Parnell proceeded to convert the raw energy generated by the three preceding years of land agitation into a massive political force controlled by himself and his party and directed toward the single goal of Irish self-government. He began in 1882 by confiscating the Land League's funds, thus terminating the old organization, and in October of the same year, set up a new national organization, the National League, which excluded the most important nonparliamentary Land Leaguers and subordinated all other objectives to that of Home Rule. At the founding convention Parnell announced the reordering of priorities: self-government for Ireland, land reform, local self-government, extension of the franchise to agricultural laborers, and the improvement of Irish manufacture and commerce—in that order.[2] To ensure that the organization would not fall into the hands of extremists, he structured it so that the Irish Parliamentary party with him at its head would control its finances, administration, and policies. The party was to have the nomination of sixteen members out of a council of forty-eight, the remaining thirty-two to be elected by county conventions composed of delegates from the local branches. This council was, in fact, never elected, and the league was governed by its "organizing committee," a supposedly temporary body set up pending the election of the council. Of the thirty members of the committee, twelve were, at the time of its establishment, already members of Parliament. Seven others were later elected to Parliament. The committee's chairman was Parnell; two of its three secretaries were Timothy Harrington and Timothy Healy, both at the time devoted followers of Parnell.[3]

Under the Land League no provision had been made for the selection of candidates to contest parliamentary constituencies, with the result that local candidates were often favored over national nominees. In the new organization Parnell rectified this oversight by delegating the nomination of candidates to ad hoc county conventions made up of local branch delegates and priests, the latter being included partly to win clerical support and partly to act as a moderating influence over nominations. In fact, the proceedings of the conventions were tightly governed by steering committees on which there were always at least two influential members of the parliamentary party, often including Parnell himself. The committees presented the conventions with carefully selected candidates, whose nominations were then simply ratified by the delegates.[4] In 1882 the party membership numbered about thirty, a number insufficient to influence the balance between the two major parties in the lower House. The party's power of obstruction had moreover been severely curtailed by the new cloture rule. There was little the party could do but attend to its business quietly and prepare the way for the next general election, when it might increase its membership sufficiently to become a force to be reckoned with. From 1882 to 1884, therefore, the parliamentary party was relatively inactive in the House of Commons, and the issues it brought up were less sensational than those of the period immediately preceding. Nevertheless, certain events during the period pointed to a great victory for the Parnellites whenever that election should be called.

In a series of by-elections the party membership was expanded by ten to about forty members. Seven of the contests occurred in 1883; all but one, that in Dublin, took place in counties having populations with large Catholic majorities. Parnellites were elected everywhere except in Dublin, demonstrating the strength of the party in the Catholic areas.[5] Because of the expansion of the party membership, and in anticipation of further expansion to come, the National League in 1884 decided to tighten the discipline within the party itself, and introduced a pledge by which parliamentary candidates bound themselves, if elected, to "sit, act and vote with the Irish parliamentary party," and to resign their seats if the party should decide that they had failed to fulfill this undertaking. In October 1884 the Irish bishops, who since Cardinal Cullen's death in 1878 had been moving gradually toward a rapprochement with the nationalist forces, lent their support to the movement by formally entrusting Parnell and the Irish Parliamentary party with the responsibility for pressing their educational claims in Parliament.[6] Then, in the parliamentary session of 1884, a franchise law was enacted which improved the party's electoral outlook. The household franchise, which gave the vote to the ratepayers in the towns, had existed in the British boroughs since 1867. In passing the law, Parliament extended the franchise to the British and Irish counties as well. In Ireland the act had the effect of expanding the electorate from about 200,000 to over 600,000, virtually handing over the counties outside of eastern Ulster to the Home Rulers.[7] A further development, more difficult to trace than the others mentioned, signaled the growing strength of the party machine during the first two years. National League branches, most of them Land League branches reconstituted under the new name, were formed in a great many Irish localities. By July 1885, according to police records, there were 818 branches;[8] unfortunately, no timetable showing the progress of their expansion is available, but branch meetings in many localities were reported in the press from the time of the National League's founding.

In the spring of 1885, Parnell's efforts began to bear fruit. In Britain, both Liberals and Conservatives, sensing that a general election could not be far off and recognizing that with the extension of the franchise Parnell's following in the House of Commons would be greatly expanded, became increasingly eager for his support. Parnell, believing that he might be able to exact a few concessions from a Conservative government and at the same time prove to the Liberals that his support could not be taken for granted, decided for the time being to throw in his lot with the Conservatives. When in May Joseph Chamberlain, the leader of the Radical faction in the Liberal party, submitted his resignation of his cabinet post, the Parnellites and Conservatives took advantage of the weakened condition of the government and combined, a few weeks later, to bring down the government on a minor budget point. For the next six months, from June through November, the Conservatives took office under Lord Salisbury, courted tentatively by Parnell while in turn courting Parnell with measures favorable to Ireland. Coercion was finally terminated, and a comprehensive land purchase scheme was introduced under the Ashbourne Act. In Ireland during these months the party machine went into action, holding conventions in all counties to select the Home Rule party's candidates. Efforts were made to extend the league's influence into every locality; the success of these efforts was revealed in the rapid expansion of league branches: between July 1885 and January 1886 the number of branches increased by about 50 percent from 868 to 1,261.[9]

The election, held at the beginning of December, revealed for the first time Parnell's full impact on Irish politics. Parnellite candidates selected at county conventions and bound by the party pledge were elected in 85 of the 103 Irish constituencies. Another Parnellite, T. P. O'Connor, was elected for Liverpool, increasing the party's strength to 86. In Ireland Parnellites captured almost every constituency in the three southern provinces and also in Ulster, outside the Protestant east. Conservatives were victorious only in sixteen constituencies in counties Antrim and Londonderry and in the northern portions of Down, Armagh, and Tyrone—all heavily Protestant and traditionally loyalist districts. Even there the boroughs of Londonderry and West Belfast missed falling to the Parnellites by, in both cases, fewer than a hundred votes. In the south Conservatives won only the two Trinity College seats. The average national ratio of Parnellite to Conservative votes was about 4,000 to 650. Not one Liberal was elected in Ireland.[10]

Another aspect of Parnell's impact was revealed in the election campaign, which was conducted on the single issue of Home Rule. At the time, agricultural distress was again serious in Ireland, caused not by crop failure but by declining agricultural prices. As usual the distress fell hardest on the West, where evictions, accompanied often by violence, were increasing. In years past, conditions such as these usually resulted in a revival of land agitation, but in 1885 Parnell appealed to the farmers to remain calm and trust that Home Rule, now within reach, would solve the land problem. The land agitation did not revive, and Home Rule continued to be the issue of the hour.[11]

The election results had far-reaching effects on the balance of power in Parliament. The number of Liberals returned in the election was 335; the number of Conservatives, 249. The difference, which was 86, exactly equalled the Irish party's strength. Parnell was therefore in a position to keep either party out of office, but he could put in only the Liberals. Gladstone, even before the election, had decided that the granting of Home Rule was inevitable, but he believed that the time was not yet ripe to announce his new position. But in mid-December his son Herbert leaked the news without authorization to the London press, forcing his father's hand. The alliance between the Liberals and Parnellites followed soon after, and in January 1886 Gladstone became prime minister again, committed in fact, if not formally, to a policy of Home Rule.

Gladstone's resumption of office, and the anticipation of his formal announcement about his conversion to Home Rule, bring the present narrative down to the poor law elections of March 1886, the last such election to be examined in detail in this study. The events that followed—the introduction of the first Home Rule bill in April, the cautious political machinations of Gladstone and Parnell during the discussions of the bill in May and June, and the disappointing defeat of the bill on June 8, resulting from the last-minute defection of a combination of English Whigs and Radicals on the bill's second reading—all occurred after the poor law elections took place and need only be mentioned here to complete the story of the Home Rule movement during the period of Parnell's most effective leadership. It was a period in which the political climate was highly favorable for the development of constitutional attitudes and modes of action. All the significant political developments—the deemphasis of the land war in favor of the struggle for self-government, the reformulation of local organization as part of a vast, efficient political machine centered around the parliamentary party, and the bold, imaginative leadership of Parnell, who never missed an opportunity to teach the Irish people, by example

and precept, respect for political power and its uses—all these contributed
to the developing political consciousness of the population, as was revealed
in the election of 1885. It was within this context that the movement to
nationalize the boards of guardians took place and worked itself to its
conclusion from 1882 to 1886.

Local Politics and the National Movement

Before embarking on an analysis of the developments on the poor law
boards, it is necessary to say a word about the extent to which the local
movement was influenced by the national developments just described.
Parnell's influence on Irish politics, and the strength of his party machine,
which has often been thought of as exercising de facto government in
Ireland, were so effective in determining the course of events on the national scene, that one is compelled to ask whether local political events
such as the board nationalization movement also came within the sphere
of the national movement either by direct intervention of Parnell and the
league or by the reflected energy radiated by their activities. The board
nationalization movement was so broad, the motivations of its participants
so varied, and the existing evidence relating to national-local relations so
scanty and diffuse, that it would not be possible to offer more than a few
impressions gathered from the evidence that is available. The question is
important, however. It has been argued in earlier chapters that the motivation for board nationalization derived largely from local sources and only
gained its direction and impetus from national events. This hypothesis
would be seriously impugned if it could be shown that the entire local
movement became a contrivance of national policy.

By all indications, board nationalization, and indeed local politics generally, remained outside of the sphere of jurisdiction of the national movement, although, to be sure, the activities of the local political groups were
influenced by events on the national scene or by the general political environment created by Parnell and his aides. Given Parnell's personal popularity and the universal acceptance of his Home Rule program during
these years, it would be surprising if most of the elected guardians were
not Parnellite nationalists, regardless of whatever else they might have
been. Indeed, there are signs enough of Parnell's influence in press reports
of boards of guardians' activities. The most striking example to come to
my attention was an editorial in the *Kilkenny Journal* in 1885, commenting
on a resolution passed a few days earlier by the Thomastown board of

guardians concerning the Labourers' Act of 1884, and addressed to "Mr. Charles Stewart Parnell, our national leader."

> The action on the part of the Thomastown guardians indicates the great and beneficial change that has taken place in almost all parts of Ireland. A time there was when a public body like the Thomastown board of guardians would apply to the Lord Lieutenant for the time being if they sought the redress of any grievance, or wanted to have any concession granted. The times are changed now, and we find our corporate bodies and public boards addressing their memorials, *not* to the Lord Lieutenant, but to the recognized leader of the Irish people. We trust that the spirit of self-reliance that has been infused into the people during the past few years by the exertions of Mr. Parnell and his colleagues, will teach all Irishmen that they must look for support to the National Party and not to the representatives of foreign rule.[12]

The editor's comments reveal the deep devotion to Parnell felt by most of the Irish people by the time of the editorial's publication, and the action of the Thomastown board supplies evidence to support the argument for the existence of a de facto Parnellite state. If public confidence may be taken as a sign of recognition of sovereignty, then clearly Parnell, to whom the resolution was sent, and not the Lord Lieutenant, who would have received such a resolution in years past, held the sovereign power in the eyes of the Thomastown guardians.

An incident in 1883 involving another resolution revealed not so much Parnell's influence as the influence of nationalism as a force in Ireland. On January 30, 1883, a meeting of delegates from various poor law unions took place in Belfast. The meeting was called to consider certain proposals for poor law reform that had been discussed among guardians in all parts of the country for several years. The poor rates had been rising for several decades for reasons nobody seemed fully to be able to explain. Guardians' functions had been proliferating, out of control it seemed to many, because of new assignments that were continually being given them under various acts of Parliament. One of the reasons for the increases in the poor rates was that these new programs required the hiring of additional personnel and new expenditures, the cost of which Parliament had inevitably tagged on to the local rates. To make matters worse, most of the programs had little to do with the original purpose of the poor law but dealt rather with education, health and animal inspection, vaccination, dog catching, factory inspection, and other matters irrelevant to poor relief per se. The salaries of the union officials had been rising over the years, and superannuation laws had established a system of pensions, for which the officials were pressing for increases through a newly formed professional organization called the Poor Law Association. Finally, workhouses built to accommodate the hordes of Irish poor before the Great Famine were operating, in a more prosperous and depopulated Ireland, at only one-fourth of their capacity, yet staffs of doctors, nurses, chaplains, custodians, and clerks needed to be maintained at full salary. These were the questions to which the Belfast delegates addressed themselves.

The delegates who attended the meeting were members of boards in eastern Ulster unions: Belfast, Larne, Ballymoney, Lurgan, Lisburn, and Ballymena. All these unions had voted Conservative in the election of 1885. The number who were present was not given in the press report of the meeting.[13] Most of those whose names were mentioned were J.P.'s and most (if their names are any guide) were Protestants. The chairman of the meeting was Lord Waveny. The group represented a fair cross-section of the power establishment in the poor law administration in eastern Ulster. The *Freeman's Journal* described the group as a "phalanx of J.P.'s and D.L.'s."[14] This was apparently not by design, for according to the press report invitations had been sent to all boards of guardians in Ireland. After a day's deliberation, the group arrived at a list of demands, drawn up as a petition to be presented to the lord lieutenant. These included: (1) an amalgamation of workhouses wherever they were being operated at far less than their capacity; (2) the transfer to the Exchequer of charges paid out of the poor rate for purposes of the Parliamentary Voters' Act, the Jurors' Act, Contagious Diseases Act, "and other measures for imperial purposes"; (3) the rejection by the government of attempts by the Poor Law Association to deprive guardians of their right to give or withhold superannuation allowances as they saw fit; and (4) "that the power to manage, reform, amalgamate or abolish workhouses should be voted by the provincial boards, elected by the people by ballot." The introduction of the secret ballot was the closest the delegates came to politics at the meeting.

Before the meeting adjourned, one of the delegates remarked to the group that the petition would be strengthened immeasurably if it could claim the support of boards throughout the country, rather than the few represented at the meeting. The question was taken up by the delegates, who decided that another meeting would be held one month later to ratify the petition; in the interim, the secretary would advise all of the boards in Ireland of the proceedings and request that they support the propositions either by sending delegates to the second meeting or passing supporting resolutions. The second meeting was held on March 2, with a larger group attending.[15] Only two new unions, however, were represented—Newtownards and Banbridge, both of which were in County Down in eastern Ulster. The secretary announced to the group that supporting resolutions had been sent in by eight boards: Omagh, Lurgan, Banbridge, Oldcastle, Kells, Parsonstown, Edenderry, and Scariff. The first three were eastern Ulster unions; the next four were in Meath and Kings counties in northern Leinster; and Scariff, the only representative from the west, was in County Clare. Of these unions only two, Kells and Scariff, had elected guardian chairmen at the time. The delegates then appended one more demand to the petition—the demand for union rating (rather than the existing system of rating by electoral division). They ratified the petition and forwarded it to the lord lieutenant.

There is no obvious reason why the boards in the south should not have displayed more interest in the Belfast proceedings than they did. Most of the guardians north and south had at some time complained about the onerous rates, the burdensome duties, and the imposition of charges that they believed rightfully belonged to the imperial treasury. Furthermore, the one proposition that contained any political content at all—that the guardians themselves, elected by ballot, should enact the reforms—was well in line with the demands for local autonomy being made by the Home Rule party. Why then did only a few boards in the south respond, and why did the support come largely from eastern Ulster? The answer goes back to the principle of public confidence, inferred from the *Kilkenny Journal*'s observation about the sending of petitions to Parnell. If indeed a resolution reflected a certain confidence on the part of those who passed it that the demands stated would be heeded, then the Belfast resolution—being a list of demands for reform made to the government—would naturally have received the greatest support from those who held the highest confidence in the government. These were the guardians of eastern Ulster. By the same line of reasoning, the indifference to the resolution in the south could be interpreted as a lack of confidence in Britain's ability or willingness to enact the reforms, and if that were the case, one might presume that the reason for this lack of confidence was that the majority of the controlling membership in the southern boards were nationalists.

We cannot be certain that this was indeed the case, but an editorial in the *Freeman's Journal* published the day after the second Belfast meeting adds to the credibility of this explanation. "Some of the points on the

platform adopted at Belfast may give rise to controversy, but all showed
a real desire to grapple honestly with pressing difficulties," the *Freeman's
Journal* wrote.

> The great end to be aimed at is how best to unite the two ends which are
> to be pursued in this country—how best to secure on the one hand the
> greatest possible economy in managing the moneys of the ratepayers; on the
> other, the largest possible measure of relief for the suffering poor. . . . We
> do not believe that a question like this will make much progress until local
> self-government is, in some shape or other, conceded. The reform of the
> Irish poor laws is a matter with which the Imperial Parliament, staggering
> under the load of business and hating the very name of Ireland, can never
> effectively deal. It can only be disposed of by an assembly or assemblies
> sitting in Ireland, having time to deal with Irish questions effectively, and
> such knowledge and interest in these questions that they would be ap-
> proached in a proper spirit and placed on a satisfactory footing.[16]

The viewpoint that it was useless to speak of reform so long as the decision-
making power resided in a British parliament was a fundamental tenet of
the Home Rule movement. Isaac Butt had used the same argument with
regard to land reform in 1874 when answering those of his followers who
had been pressing him to introduce a land bill. If the attitude of the *Freeman's Journal* may be taken as representative of nationalist opinion in Ireland—and during this period the newspaper was notable for keeping its
ear to the ground in this respect—then its argument with regard to the
Belfast proceedings probably explains the indifference of the guardians in
the south: most of them were Home Rulers.

To say that most of the elected guardians were Home Rulers, is not,
however, to say that their actions were directed by the national movement.
In fact, a scanning of hundreds of documents and press reports of National
League and boards of guardians meetings turned up surprisingly little
evidence of any interference whatsoever in the operations of local government by any of the major national leaders, with the exception of William
O'Brien, who reported poor law elections in *United Ireland*. Parnell did not
publicly address the attack on ex-officio leadership after his initial intervention in 1881; neither did Harrington, nor, apparently, did the central
branch of the league sitting corporately. Occasionally, individual members
of the party intervened in poor law elections within the counties they
represented. In 1886, for example, William Abraham and John Finucane,
newly elected members for Limerick and officers of the Limerick board of
guardians, attended the officers' election meeting and agreed to retain their

offices in absentia in order to avoid a power struggle for their seats that seemed to be developing within the nationalist camp.[17] But their case was exceptional, and their interest undoubtedly stemmed from their long familiarity with the board in the past.

The local branches of the league, on the other hand, were often intensely interested in poor law elections and boards' proceedings. Their relationship to the boards of guardians was similar to the National League's relationship to Parliament: they considered it their responsibility to support the nationalist party at the boards and to formulate strategies and organize voters at election time. Often they emulated the central branch by holding nominating conventions and party caucuses to pick slates of candidates for the general elections and officer positions. But again, the branches carried out these functions without any supervision from the central branch. Representatives of the national movement were never present at the meetings (except in the case of Limerick and one or two other unions whose M.P.'s were also poor law guardians); often the most influential persons present were local priests, who usually participated actively in poor law election campaigns. The national movement ordinarily refrained from dictating to branches on questions of purely local concern, though occasionally, when the actions of a branch seemed to endanger the league's program, the organizing committee would threaten the branch with dissolution (in at least one case, the threat was carried out).[18] So, though the branches played an important role in board nationalization, it cannot be said that they did so on the orders or in the interest of the national movement. Their participation, like that of the guardians who sent petitions to Parnell, was purely voluntary and locally motivated.

The failure of the national leadership to take notice of the local government movement might have stemmed from sheer indifference on their part toward local politics or ignorance of the vast movement that was taking place, but more likely it was, for them, a question of priorities. First, as members or representatives of a parliamentary party, their inclination was to seek reforms in Parliament rather than in the countryside. Bills to reform the boards of guardians were introduced by the Home Rule party in every year of the eighties except 1889.[19] The most sweeping measure was introduced in the session of 1884; it would have abolished the ex-officio office, eliminated the proxy vote, and installed the secret ballot in poor law elections. The bill passed successfully through the House of Commons but was killed on the second reading by the Lords. Second, the national leaders were interested in reforming all local government in Ireland, not just the boards of guardians, and their principal targets were the grand jury system and other appointive boards that were not amenable to reform by any other means than parliamentary action. Thus, at the founding conference of the National League in 1882, Parnell, in enumerating the objectives of the league, gave local self-government as the third of five objectives, and then proceeded to outline a three-point program including (1) the establishment of county boards and the transfer to those boards of the fiscal and administrative powers of the grand juries; (2) the election of boards on a representative system; and (3) the abolition of appointment by government to boards such as the Local Government Board, Board of Works, and Board of National Education. No mention was made of the boards of guardians.[20]

But perhaps the most important reason for the leaders' neglect was the same one that caused them to deemphasize other important questions such as land reform—their overriding concern for an independent legislature, against which all other issues took second place. As Parnell told the voters during the agricultural distress of 1885, there would be plenty of time to deal effectively with the land question once Home Rule was achieved. His attitude toward local self-government appears to have been the same, as shown by his actions during the episode known as the central board scheme negotiations of 1884–85.

During the early part of the 1880s many English politicians and others concerned with the Irish question began to consider local government reform in Ireland as a possible concession to meet Ireland's demands for self-government half-way. One plan that was proposed often was the elimination of the existing system of grand juries and boards of guardians, and their replacement by a system of elective county councils to assume all the responsibility for the administration of local government. As early as 1881 Gladstone had begun to show an interest in the county councils plan, and that year his administration introduced a county councils bill which, probably because of the great concessions that had already been made under the Land Act, never reached the floor.[21] Further advances were for a time tabled, but writers and politicians continued to show an interest in the subject over the next few years. In 1882 Richard O'Shaughnessy, an Irish M.P. affiliated with the Shaw faction, published a scholarly article outlining the principal faults of the existing system of Irish local government, arguing that a more representative system would not only improve the administration but also act as a school to prepare the Irish people for a time when Ireland would be granted independent status.[22] That same year, Parnell indicated his own interest by his speech to the founding convention of the National League. Then, in an article published in *Macmillan's Magazine* in 1883, William O'Connor Morris, an Irish judge and historian, introduced a novel idea which he believed might serve to fulfill Ireland's demands for Home Rule without establishing a separate parliament. A system of elective county councils would be established, headed by a supervisory board known as the central board, which would administer Ireland's internal affairs. The central board would have a president and a staff, and its members would be elected by the county councils.[23]

In 1884 Gladstone, who—like many of his English colleagues—was not yet fully aware of Parnell's intransigence on the question of Home Rule, deputed Joseph Chamberlain, then secretary of the Board of Trade, to investigate possible avenues for local government reform in Ireland and to report his findings to the cabinet. Chamberlain was considered an expert on local government questions by virtue of his former position as mayor of Birmingham. Possibly influenced by the Morris article of the year before, Chamberlain was convinced that a central board scheme might be acceptable to the nationalists if, in addition to administrative powers, the board also had powers of legislation over land questions and a few other specified areas of policy. Having worked out the details of his central board scheme, Chamberlain approached Parnell's intermediary, Captain William O'Shea. A protracted series of negotiations followed, beginning in November 1884 and continuing until May 1885, when Chamberlain, unable to get a positive commitment from Parnell, brought his proposal before the cabinet, which proceeded to reject it. It was at this point that Chamberlain, frustrated at having his idea rejected by both Parnell and the government, offered Gladstone his resignation and set in motion the series of events leading to the fall of the government.[24]

Chamberlain's frustration had been caused in part by Captain O'Shea's duplicity throughout the negotiations. For reasons known only to himself, O'Shea contrived to keep the fruitless negotiations going by misleading Chamberlain into believing that Parnell might be amenable to the central board scheme. In fact, Parnell's position, which he made clear to O'Shea early in the negotiations and maintained steadfastly throughout, was that he was willing to consider any proposal which would lead to an improvement of local government in Ireland, but that local government reform was under no circumstances to be considered a substitute for the restitution of an Irish parliament. With that in mind, he would not support any local government proposal that conferred legislative powers to the administrative body.[25] Had Chamberlain been made fully aware of Parnell's position earlier, he might not have tried to force the proposal on the cabinet, and events might have turned out differently. However, as the central board negotiations demonstrated, there was only one issue on which Parnell was completely intransigent—Home Rule under a separate Irish parliament. Toward questions of local self-government, as toward land reform and all other matters, his position was entirely different: it was, to put it simply, negotiable.[26]

Considering board nationalization as a movement for local self-government, one can find a number of reasons why the national party did not attempt to use its influence to promote it: it did not fall within the scope of subjects the leaders considered to be most urgent; it was outside of the realm of legislative politics; and it was a matter best handled by the local branches, in whose affairs the national party did not care to interfere so long as questions concerning the national movement were not involved. There were, however, certain practical advantages to be gained by the party from board nationalization, as William O'Brien, more than any other national figure, seemed to recognize. In a *United Ireland* editorial published in February 1885 O'Brien enumerated these advantages, referring both to the impending poor law elections and to the recent defeat by the House of Lords of the poor law reform bill that would have abolished the ex-officios.

1. [The Irish boards of guardians] disburse annually over £1,200,000 and it is highly important that the ratepayers should be sufficiently represented to watch the manner in which this great sum is spent.

2. A large portion of this amount goes in patronage, i.e., salaries of officials. This patronage has been hitherto dispensed by the "true-blue" element.

3. Without any legislation . . . the people can themselves effect considerable reforms in these bodies. Dispensary Committees, for example, which are elected by the guardians, appoint doctors. The tendency has been for guardians to elect landlords to these committees.

4. The best way to prove to the Lords the fruitlessness of obstructing reform is to show them what the people by a vigorous rally can do with the system as it now exists.[27]

Without stating the argument in these terms, O'Brien was advocating the conversion of the entire poor law machinery into a wing of the de facto nationalist state, and the use of its revenues for patronage, its offices for the political advancement of the tenantry, and its elections for demonstrating to the British government the extent of nationalist support in the country. If the editorial represented not just O'Brien's but the entire national party's view on the subject, then it is clear that the board nationalization movement, and the benefits derived from it by the national movement, did not go unnoticed by the party leadership. However, the fact remains that the party did not attempt to use its formal authority or its machinery to promote the movement; in fact, its participation was limited to a few occasional remarks in *United Ireland* and to the intervention of a few individual members in elections in their constituencies. The logical conclusion is that the local movement was a separate movement, locally motivated though influenced indirectly by events on the national scene.

The Boards of Guardians, 1882–1886

Though the Parnellite period of Irish history is acknowledged to be important, little is known about public opinion during the developmental years between the parliamentary elections of 1880 and 1885. We know that the Home Rule party led by Parnell won about thirty seats in the 1880 election, that it picked up about ten other supporters in by-elections between 1880 and 1885, and that in the election of 1885 it swept the entire country outside eastern Ulster. From these developments it can be deduced that somewhere between 1880 and 1885 the Irish became "politicized"— that is to say, they became aware of the uses of political forms of expression. But because there were no general elections between 1880 and 1885, it is difficult to ascertain just when this politicization occurred—whether it took place during the Land League period, during the Parnellite period, or gradually over the course of both periods. Researchers have adopted different views on the question, depending on the emphasis of their studies and the kinds of evidence used. Conor Cruise O'Brien, for example, studied the period from the standpoint of the parliamentary party and came to the conclusion that the conversion of the movement from one based on land agitation to one based on political agitation was primarily Parnell's contribution, and that the conversion took place largely after the Kilmainham Treaty.[28] In another study, Samuel D. Clark, studying the land war through police records in combination with social statistics, concluded that the politicization occurred during the Land League years, and that it was accomplished not by Parnell or the national movement, but by the inhabitants of the provincial towns, who brought the rural population into politics.[29]

Leaving aside the merits of these respective points of view, it may be said that, given the absence of other kinds of quantitative evidence, the poor law elections can provide a few important clues about the progress of the developing political consciousness of the Irish people. The elections occurred annually, and their results are to some extent measurable by the method that has been employed in this study—namely, examining the changes in board officerships from year to year. As I have shown, the poor law electorate as well as the elected members of the boards responded to events on the national scene, and their responses took the form of votes for nationalist or "popular" candidates over the candidates of landlords. It may be possible, by examining the changes in the officer composition from 1880 through 1886, to construct a barometer of political activity and to draw some conclusions about the rate of politicization.

We saw that from 1877 to 1882 the number of tenant-occupiers holding board offices increased from fifty-nine to 170, representing an increase in tenant representation from 12 percent to 35 percent of all offices. During the four years following the Kilmainham Treaty the number rose from 170 in 1882 to 244 in 1886, representing an increase from 35 percent to 50 percent. The annual changes were as follows:

Year	Number of Tenants	Percentage of Offices	Change
1877	59	12%	—
1880	101	21%	+ 8.7%
1881	135	28%	+ 8.7%
1882	170	35%	+ 9.9%
1883	174	36%	+ 1.2%
1884	188	38%	+ 4.4%
1885	216	44%	+ 8.6%
1886	244	50%	+10.3%

The last column shows the increase in each year over the previous year, based on the ratio between new tenant offices and the number of available offices in each year. Since the principal question here is one of increase or decrease in activity from year to year rather than absolute change, it is necessary to discount offices that were already occupied by tenants at the beginning of a year.

The increases were continual, but we can see two major periods of progress: one up to and including 1882, the other from 1884 to 1886. The annual changes can be partly but not completely explained by national developments at the time of the elections. The 1881 and 1882 elections were influenced by the developing Land League organization and the coercion act. In 1883 the political environment was considerably subdued because of Parnell's attempts to calm the land agitation and redirect the focus of the national movement. That year only 1.2 percent of the available offices fell to the tenants, reflecting the general decline in political activity. Then, from 1884–86, activity increased again at a steady rate until 1886, when a high of 10.3 percent increase was attained. What factors might be adduced to explain these latter increases? The political environment was still relatively calm in March 1884, when the poor law elections took place. Although the parliamentary party was somewhat more active, mainly because of the introduction of the franchise bill in February, the major debates over the bill did not occur until later in the year, and the bill itself was not enacted until December. No other single event occurred around the time of the poor law elections that would account for a significant renewal of local political activity.

By March 1885, the pace of national politics was again in full stride; the franchise act had been enacted, the Irish bishops the previous October had announced their support for the Irish Parliamentary party, and the entire country was stimulated by the knowledge that a general election could not be far off. The eager expectation of the election was heightened by speculation in the press and elsewhere as to the possible effects of the franchise act upon Parnellite fortunes in the election. Could this excitement have accounted for the 8.6 percent increase in new tenant offices that year? Or was it the establishment of more than 800 local National League branches by then? It is possible that a direct correlation existed between the increase in branches and the increase in board activity over time; if that were true, it might also explain the smaller increase in 1884. Unfortunately, there are no data available with which to test this hypothesis.

Between March 1885 and March 1886 there was continual and increasing excitement in Ireland. The attention of the whole country was focused on Parliament, as Parnell's machinations with the Tories, the existing electoral campaign, the astounding Parnellite victory in the election, and Gladstone's expected conversion to Home Rule all seemed to point to the final achievement of self-government for Ireland. As was to be expected, the new tenant advances in the board offices reached their zenith in 1886 with a 10.3 percent increase in new offices. But is the increase to be attributed to national developments or, rather, to the increase in the number of National League branches by almost half (to 1,200)? Certainly both factors must have played a part, and because the increase in national activity and the increase in branches were related, it would be futile to try to ascribe a fixed amount of influence to either one. There was, of course, a third possible factor in 1886—the agricultural distress, which reached its point of greatest severity during the winter of that year. But though the economic factor might have contributed to the pitch of the boards of guardians' agitation in 1886, it cannot be used to explain the fluctuations of 1882–85, since these were all relatively prosperous years.

It is difficult to account for the annual changes with any one circumstance. The fact that the tenants' greatest advances were made when activity in the national movements was high, and that gains were smallest in the one year when the national movement was least active, suggests the existence of some relationship between the general political environment and the movement to nationalize the boards. Specific developments such as the influence of Parnellite constitutional politics, the development of branch organizations, or the onset and decline of agricultural distress, however, appear to have had no consistent effect on the progress of nationalization. Except for the one year 1883, the progress of the movement was continual and not apparently dependent on any given event. If, therefore, the changes in the offices may be taken to represent a general index to politicization in the Irish localities, the conclusion one might draw would be that, except for 1883, politicization progressed at a fairly even rate under both the Land League and the Parnellite organization, and that different factors accounted for its development at different times: the Land League in 1881, coercion in 1882, and an undefined combination of factors in 1884–86. To put the argument in another way, once the pattern of politicization took hold in 1879, practically every event that occurred afterward helped to promote it. Neither Parnell and his party nor the Land League alone should be given full credit for the electoral victories of 1885. Though this analysis terminates with the election of 1886, there are good reasons to believe that the changes that occurred in the board offices after 1886 were slight. For the most part, the 244 offices won by the tenants by 1886 represented practically the sum total of changes in the poor law boards' leadership.

The national statistics listed above may serve as a general guide to board nationalization at that time, but they do not begin to reveal the full extent of the local movement. Figure 1 breaks down the statistics by province, showing the annual percentages of board offices occupied by tenants between 1877 and 1886. There was a substantial difference between the progress of the movement in Ulster and its progress in the three southern provinces. Beginning at approximately the same point in 1877 (about 10 percent in Ulster, Leinster, and Connaught and 21 percent in Munster), the Munster, Leinster, and Connaught percentages veered sharply upward and away from Ulster's, reaching a peak in 1882, declining slightly in 1883 (and also in 1884 in Munster), then rising again away from Ulster from 1884 to 1886. In Ulster the total increase of tenants was from 10 percent to 24 percent, most of this increase occurring before 1882; in the south the increases were much greater: Munster (21 percent to 68 percent), Leinster (11 percent to 53 percent), and Connaught (9 percent to 53 percent). Therefore, board nationalization, like the Parnellite victory in the election of 1885, was least successful in Ulster; it was most effective within Ulster in

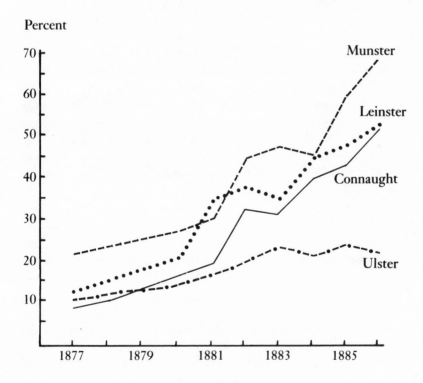

Fig. 1.   Percentage of board offices held by tenants, 1877–1886.

the districts where the Parnellites were also strong. Not all of the board offices in the south were captured by tenants, however, though Parnellite candidates made a clean sweep of the three southern provinces in the parliamentary election.

A pattern similar to that shown in Figure 1 may be found in the statistics on outdoor relief expenditures for the same period. Of all of the administrative powers the guardians possessed, the power to grant outdoor relief (rather than relief in the workhouse) was the one with the broadest political implications. The founders of the poor law had provided for the granting of outdoor relief only for the sick, aged, and disabled, but during the Great Famine this stricture proved impossible to uphold, and in 1847 the law was amended with a new clause added, the controversial "quarter-acre clause," which provided for outdoor relief to be given, at the guardians' discretion, only to occupiers of less than a quarter-acre of land.[30] During the 1850s, 1860s, and 1870s, a tendency developed among guardians north and south to interpret the clause liberally and grant outdoor relief, mostly in the form of seed and provisions, to increasing numbers of able-bodied paupers. The tendency was unrelated to politics, but grew rather out of a liberalization of attitudes toward pauperism which developed throughout the United Kingdom during these decades. In 1881 the power was expanded by an amendment providing for outdoor relief to the families of imprisoned suspects.[31] No legal maximum was fixed for the amount to be granted in individual cases, but the Local Government Board appears to have set an informal limit of £1 per family per week, beyond which guardians who granted higher payments were subject to fines for malfeasance in office.

Needless to say, the power to grant outdoor relief was a boon to the nationalist guardians. Relief in the workhouse was considered a burden, not a prize, and by granting a high cash sum to evicted tenants and suspects' families, the nationalists could both reward the martyred families and exhibit their contempt for coercion or the landlord system, while revealing themselves as staunch supporters of the popular cause. The attractive features of the relief payments for nationalists were discussed in an article published in the *Fortnightly Review* in 1886, by Robert Staples, J.P., an ex-officio guardian of the Abbeyleix union who believed he saw "a trend among rural boards of guardians [in Ireland] to use their legal powers with a view rather to the injury of political opponents than to the furtherance of public ends."

Outdoor relief has been lavishly distributed to persons evicted on account of their obedience to the no-rent manifesto, whose support would otherwise have devolved on the National League's evicted tenants' fund. Contracts are given to tradesmen and others remarkable for their Nationalist sympathies, quite regardless of the interests of the ratepayers. As to the incidence of the union rate, it must be remembered that since in Ireland the owner pays half of the poor rate on land in the occupation of his tenants besides the whole where it is in his own hands or occupied by tenants rated at below £4—a large class—at least five-eighths of the total poor rates are paid by the owners. It is evident, therefore, that on the imposition of a very small rate upon themselves a combination among the small occupiers could effectively mulct to a considerable extent any large landowner or occupier with whom they had reason to be displeased. Indeed, to remonstrances sometimes made to guardians concerning the great increase in the amount granted as outdoor relief, the answer is given, "Sure doesn't the landlord pay half your poor rates and his own as well?"[32]

The best evidence for the use of the rates for political purposes was, however, in the relief statistics themselves. Figure 2 shows the percentage of total relief spent on outdoor relief in the four provinces between 1875 and 1890. With a few minor variations, the figure bears a striking resemblance to Figure 1 giving the board officer changes. In 1879 the percentages expended in Munster and Connaught were almost the same as that expended in Ulster. Leinster's statistics are distorted somewhat by the inclusion of Dublin, where outdoor relief was granted much more liberally than elsewhere, chiefly because of the impracticability of interning hordes of seasonally unemployed urban laborers in already overcrowded workhouses. After 1879, however, something clearly happened in the relief-giving policies in Connaught and Munster. The figures increase sharply, away from Ulster's, to a peak at about 1881. This increase might be attributed to the distress of 1879–81, which struck the south and west harder than the rest of Ireland. However, the distress ended by 1882, yet the Connaught and Munster expenditures did not return to the Ulster level but maintained an approximately parallel course thereafter. The changes were smaller in Ulster and Leinster. Leinster remained about 6 to 8 percentage points higher than Ulster throughout the period, but the fluctuations in the Leinster graph during periods when the graphs of the two other southern provinces were also fluctuating suggests that Leinster was also influenced by the political trends after 1879.

The outdoor relief statistics provide yet another view of the growing politicization of the boards of guardians, demonstrating essentially the same trends as were revealed in Figure 1: two periods of rising political activity separated by a slow period around 1882–83, a wide gap between Ulster and the south, and a similar ordering of the provinces at the end (Munster at the top, Ulster at the bottom, Leinster and Connaught almost equal and slightly below Munster). But the two graphs measure activities that occurred at different times. Figure 1 reflects conditions as they existed on one day a year—the day on which the elections were held. Election meetings, as it has been shown, were far from normal meetings, since both sides put out an extra effort to bring their supporters in for the elections. Relief allocations were part of the regular business of the boards, and the relief statistics reflect conditions during the other fifty-one weeks of the year. But the differences in the evidence only make the conclusion more convincing. Clearly, the progress of board nationalizations, as well as the end result, was marked by distinct regional differences.

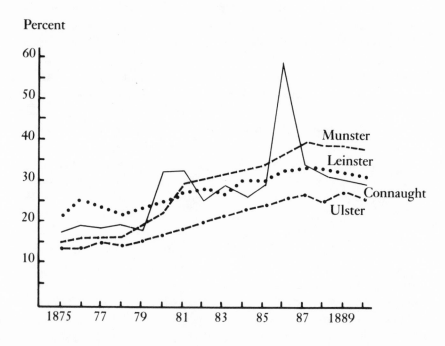

Fig. 2.   Percentage of total relief spent on outdoor relief, 1875–1890.

Local Motivations for Board Nationalization

The discovery of regional variations in the pattern of local politics might come as a surprise to those who, like me, believed that all political activity in Ireland from the Kilmainham Treaty to the Home Rule bill centered around the activities of Parnell and his party machine. Indeed, the general election of 1885 seemed to give the impression that only one issue, Home Rule, had any real potency, and that the Irish public could be divided politically into two groups—those who supported Home Rule and those who opposed it. While this may have been true with regard to national issues, it was by no means true in questions of local concern. The fundamental difference between the national and local movements for self-government was that each was directed against a different "enemy." The national movement recognized the British government as its enemy. Any reforms that might be won by the nationalists could be exacted only from the British government within the British Parliament. The local movement had two enemies—the British government as represented by the Local Government Board, and the landlord sitting as ex-officio guardian. The nationalist guardians' position on the Local Government Board was clear: as the representative of British rule, the board's authority was to be opposed and obstructed whenever possible. Henry A. Robinson, a local government official who spent more than forty years dealing daily with Irish boards of guardians, noted this tendency in his memoirs when discussing the difference between the guardians of Ulster and those of the south:

> The truth is that there were never any difficulties in Ulster from the hostility of local bodies to the central authority. Ulster prided itself on its loyal support of the British Government, and recognized the status and powers of the public departments responsible to Parliament, and submitted to their rulings as a matter of course.
>
> In the rest of Ireland, on the other hand, opposition to the Irish government and the executive in and out of Parliament was the first principle of political life, and the determination to obstruct and make the government troublesome could in great measure be effected by constant resistance to the Local Government Board. The Board had therefore pitfalls to avoid in the South which were unknown in the North, and as their decisions in the South were daily the subject of numerous questions in the House of Commons, they had constantly to be on the *qui vive*, whereas their administration in the North was rarely, if ever, challenged.
>
> Moreover the chief characteristic of northern administration was rigid economy. The members of the local bodies were mostly business people

with the Scottish instinct to get value for their money fully developed, and they kept the rates down and seldom fell foul of the auditor; while the southerners were characterized by a greater open-handedness and a more high-spirited contempt for the restrictions of English Acts of Parliament, and had to be more closely shepherded.

It will thus be understood that in the story of the vicissitudes of local government in Ireland Ulster plays a small but honourable part.[33]

The position of the ex-officios was much more complicated because of the two roles—political and socio-economic—that they filled in Irish society. Politically, their position as magistrates, as members of the class that occupied the highest positions in government, and as Conservatives who openly supported the British connection, placed them in opposition to the nationalists, who regarded them as symbols of British rule in Ireland. Socially and economically, their position as landlords placed them in opposition to the tenantry. It was in this distinction between the political and economic roles that the confusion was rooted. Not all elected guardians were both nationalists and doctrinaire opponents of landlordism. There were boards whose entire elected membership were radically nationalistic and antilandlord, and others whose members were neither; in between were boards whose members supported nationalism but were not necessarily against landlords, or were perhaps even friendly toward them. The decision of a board to elect or not to elect an ex-officio to office was determined largely by the corporate attitude of its members toward both nationalism and landlordism. A few examples will illustrate the point.

One of the most radical boards of guardians in Ireland was the board of the Tulla union in County Clare. Its members held the most extreme views on both the national and the land questions. Contemptuous of British authority in any form, the board in 1883 passed a resolution and published it in the *Limerick Chronicle* as a warning to two of the union's officials who had carried out a Local Government Board order against the wishes of the Tulla board. The exact issue that provoked the resolution was not stated, but the intentions of the guardians are obvious.

> We know we have no power to remove the clerk or [workhouse] master for carrying out the instructions of the L.G.B., but we have power to punish them socially and pecuniarily in a number of ways, of which, perhaps, the Local Gov't Board are unaware, and once and for all we tell those officers that the Local Government Board reside over one hundred miles away, while we, with the "resources of civilization" at our backs live on the spot, and those resources will be unsparingly exercised for their punishment, in case there is the smallest attempt to disobey our orders. We must decline to reply

to any further communication which the L.G.B. . . . may make on this silly matter.[34]

Obviously, no doubt existed in the minds of the authors as to which authority, theirs or the government's, was supreme in County Clare.

For the Tulla guardians the issues of nationalism and landlordism were one issue, inseparable and indistinguishable. The board chairman from 1881 to 1885, whose name was Matthew Clune, had been president of the Tulla branch of the Land League, and had once been described by no less a personage than Chief Secretary W. E. Forster as a "village tyrant." Both Clune and the vice-chairman, Patrick Frost, had been arrested and imprisoned as suspects under the 1881 coercion act.[35] Deeply involved in the land agitation, Clune and Frost made life so miserable for the ex-officios on the board that not one ex-officio could be found at a meeting after 1881.[36]

The union neighboring Tulla to the south was Ennis, whose chairman until 1885 was Lord Inchiquin, a Catholic Whig member of the House of Lords. In December 1883, the Ennis board passed a resolution at a meeting from which Inchiquin was absent, condemning a land court decision that had approved increases in the rents of a number of Clare laborers. The resolution was strongly worded, denouncing the establishment of rackrent by the court and calling upon the other boards of guardians in Clare to protest to the appeals court for a reversal of the decision. The guardians circulated this resolution among the other boards in the county, including Tulla.[37]

The Tulla guardians received the Ennis resolution coldly, and instead of following the suggestion to protest to the appellate court, the board passed its own resolution revealing in no uncertain terms the contempt its members held for the members of the more conservative union to the south.

We are neither displeased nor disappointed at the action of the Land Court at Ennis in raising rents, and because of which some members of the Ennis board call for their condemnation we decline to do so. We believe that the higher rents are kept up by means of the machinery of Mr. Gladstone's late Land Act the sooner will this huge humbug come to an end. We cannot besides co-operate with a Board of Guardians who have helped to depopulate our country, and who have thrown overboard the labourers.[38]

The mention of depopulation referred to Ennis's voluntary participation in the emigration clauses of the Arrears Act, which provided for government loans for unions to assist resident paupers to emigrate.[39] The counter-resolution reveals the Tulla guardians as hard-bitten extremists, possibly revolutionists, who were contemptuous not only of landlords and the British government, but also of other nationalists less radical than they. Their extreme disposition made it a certainty that they would elect no ex-officio to a board office, and they never did after 1881.[40]

One degree to the right on the political spectrum were boards whose elected members were ardently nationalistic but not averse to dealing with landowners who were nationalists, or were at least willing to support a nationalist for chairman. During the early years of the land agitation not many such landowners were to be found. But after the subduing of the land agitation and the re-emphasis on Home Rule under Parnell's leadership after 1882, a few landlords began to appear here and there who were ready to swallow their pride, admit defeat, and resume their places at the boards as nationalist supporters. This was probably a difficult transition for a supporter of the Conservative party to make, but Liberals could justify their change of heart by pointing to the close association that had been struck between the Liberal party and the Parnellites in the Kilmainham Treaty.

Two boards that fit into this category were the boards of Limerick and Kilkenny. Before the opening of hostilities in 1879 most of the elected and ex-officio members of the Limerick board had been Liberals. The old board chairman, Lord Emly, a Catholic Whig, was popular with the elected guardians whose Liberalism dated back to the Tenant-Right movement of the 1850s. As we saw in the last chapter, the elected guardians and ex-officios of the Limerick board parted ways in 1882, and William Abraham replaced Emly as chairman. In the general election of 1885 Abraham contested and won one of the Limerick parliamentary constituencies running as a Parnellite. The board's vice-chairman, John Finucane, won the other constituency. Upon their election to Parliament, Abraham and Finucane tendered their resignations from their board offices, giving the reason that their new duties would not permit them to attend board meetings; but when it appeared that their vacancies would open the way for a power struggle within the nationalist camp, they both agreed to stay on in absentia, provided they could choose the deputy vice-chairman who would manage the board in their absence. The man they chose was John McInerny, who had been associated with Finucane in the Limerick Farmers' Club of the seventies.[41]

In the officers' election of 1886, Abraham and Finucane put in an appearance to accept their honorary offices. Seven ex-officios were present at the meeting. McInerny opened the proceedings by welcoming the members and giving special thanks to the young recruits who were present, as well as to the "few ex-officio members who came . . . to support the National Party." He observed that although in 1882 the board had been made up of twenty-two Whigs, eighteen Conservatives, and sixteen Nationalists, there was at this meeting "not one Conservative present." He then nominated William Abraham for chairman. As a gesture of good will, the nationalists conferred the honor of nominating Finucane on one of the ex-officios, a Dr. O'Shaughnessy. O'Shaughnessy began his speech by complimenting the present leadership for the fine manner in which they had carried out their duties during the preceding year; then, before he could catch himself, he betrayed his awkwardness in his new role by saying, "The Liberal Party at this board—," when an elected guardian interrupted him, saying, "—We are not Liberal at all." O'Shaughnessy corrected himself: "The *National* Party may be proud of the management of the union for many years." After a few more words he nominated Finucane for vice-chairman.[42] It was apparent that the accord was of recent origin, and from McInerny's comment about the Conservatives it might be inferred that the ex-officios were still Liberals.

The participation of some landowners in the nationalist movement created for some guardians a hazy area in the distinction between the landlord as an economic foe and the landlord as a political foe. This confusion created a minor crisis at a nationalist convention held in Kilkenny city in 1887 to nominate a slate of candidates for the officerships of the Kilkenny board that year. The nationalists had attempted twice, in 1885 and 1886, to rid the board of its aristocratic chairman, the Marquess of Ormonde.[43] These attempts had failed because the nationalists could not capture a number of seats sufficient to overcome the combined force of the ex-officios and the moderate elected guardians at the officers' election meetings. By 1887 the level of frustration had risen among the nationalists, and the National League branches of the area called a convention on February 9 to organize the branches for a concerted attack on the seats occupied by the moderates. They called a second convention on March 28, after the poor law election, to pick the candidates to oppose the marquess and the two other officers, who were elected guardians but not nationalists.

At the first convention the mayor of Kilkenny, P. M. Egan, who chaired the meeting, made a speech in which he revealed that Ormonde was not an unpopular chairman, but that so far as the nationalists' goals were concerned, the personal qualities of the chairman were of little account.

> Some, perhaps, think that a position of this kind should not be competed for on political grounds; but in every country where there is anything like political life, every position which is regarded as one of honour is made a gift bestowed by reason of the man's political faith who receives it, and I don't see why Kilkenny should not be equal to the occasion, nor why it should be dormant when all other unions of this country have pronounced upon this question so plainly and have elected a nationalist chairman. . . . No doubt it may be said that the Marquis of Ormonde never offended any political party during his chairmanship, and I am free to admit that the assertion is true; but it is entirely beside the question . . . which involves the national principle which at present, and I hope will forever, actuate the people of Ireland.[44]

Three days after the meeting the *Kilkenny Journal* published a letter from a nationalist priest, Father N. Murphy of Ballycallan, which addressed the mayor's comment about Kilkenny being an anomaly among boards of guardians: "I am certain that Mr. Kelly [the nationalist spokesman at the board] will do his part in order to remove from the 'City of the Confederation' the disgrace of having any longer as chairman of the board of guardians a bitter anti-nationalist."[45]

Leaving aside the question of Ormonde's true political character, the statements of Mayor Egan and Father Murphy reveal a great deal about the attitudes of the Kilkenny nationalists toward the board nationalization movement. It was important to them that the board chairman be a nationalist, but it was perhaps even more important from the standpoint of local pride that Kilkenny should not be the last board in the country to have a nationalist chairman. This attitude might explain why, as was shown in the analysis of changes in the board chairmanships (Figure 1, given earlier), the resurgence of the tenants into the offices began again in 1884 without any apparent stimulus from external sources, and continued thereafter at a steady rate without relation to major political events. It might well have been that by 1884 a bandwagon effect had begun to develop, in which elected guardians began to challenge the ex-officio chairmen for no other reason than to "keep up with the Joneses." The further possibilities of this explanation will be explored in the next chapter.

The second Kilkenny convention, at which a slate of officer candidates was to be chosen, took place just after the poor law elections. All the delegates at the second convention agreed that the officers of the board should be nationalists. Ormonde clearly did not fall into that category. But what of the other landowners? Were they too to be rejected out-of-hand because of their ex-officio status, even though some among them possibly were nationalist supporters? What indeed was the definition of a nationalist? This question arose at the meeting, when a delegate introduced an amendment to a resolution calling for the election of nationalists, which added the following condition: "it will not only be essential to elect thorough nationalist guardians to these [officer] positions, but they must also be elected guardians." The amendment was immediately opposed by two other delegates, one of whom said he thought the amendment went too far, adding that "some magistrates are as good nationalists as elected guardians." The second delegate supported the first by offering as an example a certain magistrate who had supported the nationalist candidate in the previous year's election. Much bickering followed, until the dispute was finally resolved by a clear-headed priest who proposed that the amendment be altered to read simply that "the Chairman, Vice-Chairman and Deputy Vice-Chairman be members of the National League."[46] In the election, the nationalists defeated the ex-officios and replaced the Marquess of Ormonde and his colleagues with three elected guardians, all Leaguers, none landowners.[47]

Further to the right of the Kilkenny and Limerick boards in the political spectrum were a highly diverse group of boards dominated by nationalist majorities but having nonnationalist ex-officios in one or two of the offices. In some cases, as at Mountmellick in Queens County and Boyle in Roscommon, the ex-officios retained their offices only by overpowering the nationalists numerically at officers' election meetings.[48] During the rest of the year the nationalists held the controlling majorities. More often, however, the ex-officios retained their offices with the consent of the nationalists and were able to do so only by relaxing their opposition to political discussions and generally allowing the nationalists a free hand in the management of affairs. Usually the ex-officios who held the offices were also good landlords who were respected by the tenants in the community. An example of such a board was the Naas board in County Kildare. The chairman of the board from 1882 to 1888 was an ex-officio named Major R. H. Borrowes, an owner of a fair-sized estate valued at £1,340 whom Finlay Dun had met on his tour of Ireland and described as "an improving landlord who has built houses, farm premises and cottages, and has placed his tenants, like himself, in the fair way of farming profitably."[49] The vice-

chairman from 1879 to 1888 (and afterwards chairman) was Edward Fenelon, an active member of the National League in Naas whom I mentioned
earlier in connection with his activities in the Queens County Independent
Club in the seventies.[50] Fenelon had been an early advocate of board nationalization, having begun his agitation for a fairer voice for the elected
guardians in the management of the board as early as 1877. In 1884 he
appeared before a House of Lords select committee on the Irish boards of
guardians to argue in favor of the case for abolishing the office of ex-officio
guardian. The deputy vice-chairman from 1882 to 1888 (and afterwards
vice-chairman) was another nationalist-elected guardian named Patrick
Driver. Both Fenelon and Driver were farmers, although Fenelon was a
tenant-farmer whereas Driver held a small farm of £37 value in fee.[51]
Driver was also a nationalist, but was generally more moderate in his
rhetoric and behavior than Fenelon was.

The manner in which the Naas board elected a nonnationalist ex-officio
for the first office and two nationalist-elected guardians for the second and
third offices presents an interesting study in corporate psychology. Between
1878 and 1881 the board developed a custom of allowing the ex-officios to
choose the first two officers, and the elected guardians to choose the third
officer of the board. This arrangement had been a concession made by the
ex-officios to Fenelon's demands for a greater voice for elected guardians
in the management of the board.[52] In conducting the elections, the board
used the usual procedure of nominating and voting for each candidate in
turn. This had always been the method on every board of guardians, and
there would have been no reason for any of the guardians to question it.
By 1881, however, the warfare between the ex-officios and elected guardians was evident everywhere, and at the Naas officers' election one of the
ex-officio regulars of the board, Baron de Roebuck, perhaps suspicious
that the elected guardians might try to emulate their colleagues on other
boards and attempt to take over all the offices, suggested that the election
that year be carried out *en globe*.[53] By the *en globe* procedure, all candidates
were nominated and elected corporately by a single vote of the board. De
Roebuck's intention was to avoid a contest over the offices by presenting
the members with a previously arranged slate of candidates, a fait accom-
pli. Fenelon, who was then deputy vice-chairman, denounced the baron's
suggestion as a sign of bad faith and an insidious attempt to overthrow the
custom "whereby the deputy vice-chairmanship went to an elected guardian who was chosen by the elected guardians." Nevertheless, Fenelon gave
in and agreed to the *en globe* procedure. The officers elected that year were

John Latouche, the old chairman, R. H. Borrowes, the old vice-chairman, and Edward Fenelon again.

The next year the board employed the *en globe* procedure again, but with a slight twist. Latouche retired and Borrowes was raised to the chairmanship, Fenelon was raised to the vice-chairmanship, and Patrick Driver joined the officers in the deputy vice-chairman position. Baron de Roebuck had moved the nomination of the new slate, so it can be assumed that the two nationalists had been installed with the assent of the ex-officios. This time Fenelon did not object, but on the contrary praised the new arrangement, which he said reflected "the kindly feelings" that existed on the board between the elected and ex-officio guardians.[54] Borrowes, Fenelon, and Driver continued to hold these same offices until 1888 when Borrowes retired. Then Fenelon and Driver each moved up a notch, and another ex-officio became deputy vice-chairman. In this way a new officer selection system was worked out based on seniority rather than land holdings. The new system had grown up out of fear and distrust. There was, however, a desire for political stability that resulted in a spirit of compromise not present on the three other boards discussed earlier.

No member of the Naas board symbolized this spirit of compromise better than the chairman, R. H. Borrowes. As vice-chairman during the latter part of the 1870s, he held the traditional ex-officios' attitude towards political discussions at board meetings and consistently refused to allow the introduction of political resolutions when he was in the chair. These refusals were the main source of friction on the board, since the Naas nationalists considered the right to discuss politics as the most fundamental of their rights as guardians. Its importance was revealed by Fenelon during his testimony to the House of Lords' select committee in 1884. He was being questioned at the time by Viscount Powerscourt, who had had personal experience with nationalist agitation as chairman of the Rathdown union in counties Dublin and Wicklow. Fenelon, who had come before the committee to argue in favor of the then-pending bill, to abolish the office of ex-officio guardian in Ireland, told Powerscourt that the ex-officios tended to monopolize the board offices wherever they were powerful enough to do so, and the following dialogue ensued:

Powerscourt: I am the chairman of the Rathdown union, and I do not think that is the case there.

Fenelon: I would ask your Lordship if there has been any elected guardian chairman of the union?

Powerscourt: The Vice-Chairman is an elected guardian.

Fenelon: In Baltinglass, in Carlow, and Edenderry and South Dublin they
are all *ex-officios*; and they were all *ex-officios* at Naas until two or three
years ago.

Powerscourt: There was no feeling against them till two or three years ago,
on the ground that they were *ex-officios*, was there?

Fenelon: None; but what caused the feeling at the commencement was
this; that they would not allow one word to be said except about indoor
and outdoor relief; some six or eight years ago I gave notice to have
certain questions discussed; fixity of tenure, fair rent, and so on, and
the result was that the three chairmen walked out of the board; they
would not have it discussed. . . .

Powerscourt: Then you think that one of the great advantages of getting
rid of the *ex-officios* as chairmen will be that you will be able to bring
in political questions, and to have them discussed at the Poor Law
Board?

Fenelon: Not so much that, as that the people would not be sat upon,
whenever they wished to express themselves.[55]

Borrowes must have been one of the officers who "walked out," since
he had been vice-chairman of the board at least from 1872. Had Borrowes
continued to hold his intransigent position on political resolutions, it is
doubtful that Fenelon and the other nationalists on the board would have
agreed to any compromise which included Borrowes as chairman. But
during the opening years of the 1880s he dropped his restrictions against
political resolutions. On at least two occasions in 1881 the board passed
anti-eviction resolutions with Borrowes in the chair.[56] By 1886 Borrowes
was not only admitting such resolutions but actively supporting them. At
a meeting that year Fenelon moved "that the board ask the Members of
Parliament to request the Chief Sec'y to use all means in his power to put
a stop to evictions." Borrowes responded from the chair, "We passed a
similar resolution about four months ago. Will we pass it now?" Only
three of the thirty-six members present dissented. Borrowes voted in the
affirmative.[57]

Borrowes' willingness to meet the elected guardians more than halfway
preserved his influence at the board, just as the ex-officios' willingness to
give more than half a loaf in allocating the board offices retained for them
at least some of the respect and authority they had possessed before the
new departure. There were other boards like Naas, where durable arrangements were worked out for sharing power between the elected and
ex-officio guardians. At Castlebar, for example, James Daly and his col-

leagues forced out Lord Lucan and C. L. Fitzgerald in 1881 but placed Lucan's land agent, Alex Larminie, in the deputy vice-chairmanship. The three new officers, Charles O'Malley (chairman), James Daly (vice-chairman), and Larminie held their respective positions until 1890, when O'Malley died. From 1890 until 1898, when the board was subsumed under the newly formed Urban District Council created by the Local Government Act of 1898, Daly was chairman and another elected guardian was vice-chairman, and Larminie retained his position as deputy vice-chairman. After 1898 Daly and Larminie became elected members of the Urban District Council, although not as officers. In 1910 Larminie was elected chairman of the council (Daly died the next year), and he held this position until 1928, when, after nearly fifty years of public service, he resigned the office over an argument with one of the council members.[58]

Larminie was undoubtedly an excellent administrator, and he was almost always present when meetings were held. This may account in part for his durability. But land agents were usually competent administrators and punctual attenders; these features were implicit in their occupation. Yet these characteristics had not kept most other land agents from summary dismissal at the hands of nationalist guardians. An author writing in 1892, under the pen name "A Guardian of the Poor," noticed how far the land agent's stock had sunk in the new Ireland: "Of late years the agent has lost much of his dignity. 'Popular' appointments to the commission of the peace have crowded him off the bench of justice. And the farmers, being independent since the passing of the Land Acts, elect men of their own class as chairmen of Boards of Guardians."[59] To understand Larminie's durability, one must look to his employer, Lord Lucan. In 1886, the old Lord Lucan, who had been notorious for his absenteeism and summary treatment of his tenants, died and was succeeded by his son, an amiable and progressive young man who lived on the estate and was popular with the tenants of the region. Under his influence, which was already present in his father's dealings during the last few years of the old man's life, a new relationship of respect and confidence was built up between the Lucan family and the tenantry. In 1882 the old Lord Lucan instructed Larminie to give the tenants on the estate every facility to obtain the benefits of the Arrears Act, and in subsequent years the son divested the estate of 6,000 acres of land which he gave to the tenants outright. He was the first landlord in the county to sell the remainder of his estates under the Wyndham Act of 1903.[60] This generosity of his employer was probably the reason for Larminie's remaining in office while other land agents were forced out of public positions. Once again, as at Naas, the tenantry were willing to reciprocate when a landowner treated them generously. But it should be added that at both Naas and Castlebar, the *tendency* to reciprocate was already present. One cannot imagine the guardians of Tulla making the same kinds of concessions, no matter how agreeable a particular land-lord or a group of them might have been.

The boards of Tulla, Limerick, Kilkenny, Naas, and Castlebar all stood to the left, left-center, and center of the political spectrum; all were na-tionalist-dominated boards having, in the different instances, a progres-sively conservative view on the question of landlord-tenant relations. Between these boards and those on the right a wide gap existed. Boards on which the loyalists retained their majorities usually followed the older pattern of choosing their officers on the basis of land ownership. Since we have already explored these values, we shall not need to discuss them here except to say that on these conservative boards, which were characteristic of Ulster and some unions in the south (of which several were mentioned by Fenelon), the guardians continued to elect aristocrats, gentry, and large landowners to all three board offices, on occasion reserving the deputy vice-chairmanship for an elected, usually loyalist, guardian. It can be taken as a general rule that if a board has two or more tenant chairmen, a majority of its members were supporters of the popular movements, and if it had two or more landowning officers, a majority were loyalists and anti-Lea-guers. This is not to say that all landowners were loyalists and all tenants nationalists. The chairmen of the boards of Lismore and Waterford in 1886 were landowners and also Parnellite Members of Parliament. At Lismore the vice-chairman was also a landowning nationalist, which gave the board the appearance of being conservative, whereas in reality it was radical.[61] However, these were exceptions, for it was in the nature of the struggle that most landowners were loyalists and most tenants nationalists, and it became a point of local pride for boards having nationalist majorities to place tenant guardians in at least two of the offices, just as it was a matter of principle for loyalists to demonstrate their superiority by retain-ing ex-officios in their offices.

6

Social Aspects of Board Nationalization

Patterns of Radicalism and Conservatism

UP TO THIS point, we have focused on the more general aspects of the board nationalization movement. Regional or particular differences have been introduced only to demonstrate that differences existed. The differences themselves will now be the subject of study, for two reasons. First, it is clear from the analysis in the last chapter that the impact of the movement varied not only from Ulster to the southern provinces but also from one southern province to the next. We want to know whether similar variations existed within each province, and whether they reveal any regional patterns. Second, if discernible regional patterns existed, we will want to know whether these political patterns were related in some way to social or other conditions in those regions. It might be possible by these means to identify the social origins of board nationalization, and to draw some general conclusions about landlord-tenant political relations in Ireland as a whole. With these broader aims in mind, we shall proceed first to attempt to identify, in some measurable form, shadings within the spectrum of radicalism and conservatism that was described at the end of the last chapter.

One way to measure political differences between boards, short of the impractical if not impossible method of analyzing their entire membership, would be to measure the extent of the nationalization of their board offices. For example, we may assume that three tenant officers on a board signified a high degree of radicalism in its membership, two tenants and one landowner less radicalism, one tenant and two landowners still less radicalism and three landowners an absence of radicalism (which we might designate as "conservatism"). The provincial distributions break down as shown in Table 15.

In Munster the number of boards in each category decreased significantly with each decrease in the radicalism of the category. In Ulster the exact reverse was true. Leinster and Connaught presented no consistent pattern either way. The consistencies in the table seem to verify the validity of the classification method used. If the guardians had been arbitrary in their selection of officers, one should expect to find an arbitrary distribution pattern, with the percentage rising and falling between and within the provinces and the categories with no discernible consistency. But in Table 15 there is a clear pattern of strong radicalism in Munster, less and almost equal radicalism in Leinster and Connaught, and strong conservatism in Ulster, whether the figures are viewed from the standpoint of the distribution of categories within the separate provinces, or the distribution within each category from one province to the next. These regional consistencies suggest that the boards' choices were not random: it was significant whether a board chose two landowners instead of one, or one landowner instead of none.

The provincial distributions are useful for making general geographic comparisons, but they are of little value in isolating finer regional distinctions. For this we need to see the distributions of offices by union, as is shown in the maps that follow, which give the same information as Table 15 on a union-by-union basis for the years 1877, 1882, and 1886. Concentrating on the map for 1886, we again find proof of the validity of the radical-conservative continuum. The unions sharing similar officer characteristics are not strewn helter-skelter throughout each province but are

TABLE 15

Boards of Guardians in 1886, Grouped by Province from Radical to Conservative

	0		1		2		3		Total
Province	No.	%	No.	%	No.	%	No.	%	No.
Munster	23	46	13	26	9	18	5	10	50
Leinster	11	27	9	23	11	27	9	23	40
Connaught	7	25	7	25	10	36	4	14	28
Ulster	2	5	4	9	16	36	22	50	44
Total/Avg. %	43	27	33	20	46	28	40	25	162

0 = radical; 1 = moderate-radical; 2 = moderate-conservative; 3 = conservative

concentrated in contiguous groups. Ignoring the isolated exceptions—such as the conservative unions of Mallow (Cork) and Clifden (Galway) standing amid groups of radical and moderate-radical unions, and the three isolated radical unions scattered along the coasts of Ulster—it is possible to discern three important centers of conservatism: Ulster, the Leinster midlands, and the southern coast of Cork. There are also three centers of radicalism: one incorporating all the south except for southern Cork, another extending over the two counties of Meath and Westmeath into Longford, and the third occupying the western half of Connaught and excluding the eastern portions of Mayo, Sligo, and Galway. Standing between the radical and conservative centers in most areas are buffer zones of moderate unions, which also tend to cluster together. These clusterings are probably not accidental; they reflect distinct regional differences which fade gradually as one moves from one center to the next.

A comparison of 1877 and 1886 reveals the dramatic changes that occurred during this nine-year period. In 1877 there were only six boards on the radical half of the spectrum. Five of these were in Munster (Castletown, Macroom, Kilmallock, Ballyvaughan, and Corofin); the other was at the northernmost tip of Ulster (Inishowen). The majority of the boards in all provinces except Munster had three landowning officers. By 1886 Ulster and the area to the immediate south and west of Dublin had not changed much, but elsewhere a massive radicalization had occurred. A highly interesting fact revealed in the 1877 map is that the moderate-conservative boards were most heavily concentrated in the areas that later became radical centers. Kilmallock, which had already been nationalized by 1877 and which stood at the approximate geographical center of the southern radical area in 1886, was surrounded by boards having one tenant officer. Again, there was a long band of one-tenant unions stretching westward through Meath, Westmeath, and Longford, and another large cluster in northwest Connaught. Of the sizeable groups of moderate-conservative unions in 1877, only one—that which wandered through south Wicklow, Carlow, and part of Kildare and Wexford counties—was not in an area that was in the radical half of the spectrum in 1886. This pattern reveals, significantly, that the major changes that occurred later had already begun to take place in a modified form even before the Land League.

The progress of radicalization between 1877 and 1886, though not shown in these maps, reveals another distinct pattern common to these regions. In each of the three centers dominated by tenants the changeover from landowner control to tenant control began in one or two unions and then

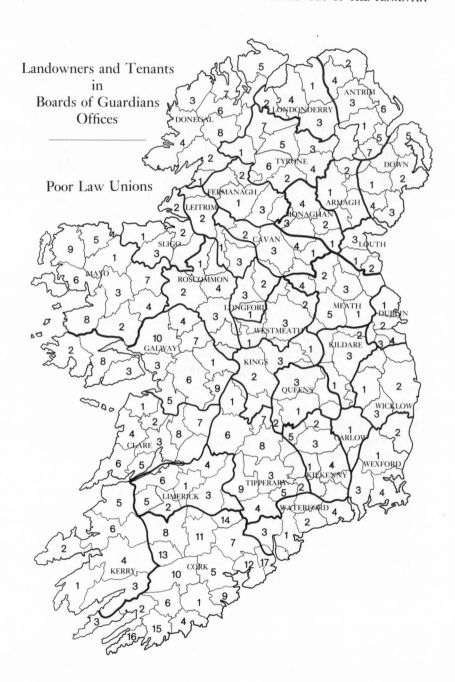

Landowners and Tenants
in
Boards of Guardians
Offices

Poor Law Unions

Irish Poor Law Unions
(by county)

ANTRIM	1. Antrim; 2. Ballycastle; 3. Ballymena; 4. Ballymoney; 5. Belfast; 6. Larne; 7. Lisburn
ARMAGH	1. Armagh; 2. Lurgan
CAVAN	1. Bailieborough; 2. Bawnboy; 3. Cavan; 4. Cootehill
DONEGAL	1. Ballyshannon; 2. Donegal; 3. Dunfanaghy; 4. Glenties; 5. Inishowen; 6. Letterkenny; 7. Milford; 8. Stranolar
DOWN	1. Banbridge; 2. Downpatrick; 3. Kilkeel; 4. Newry; 5. Newtownards
FERMANAGH	1. Enniskillen; 2. Irvinestown; 3. Lisnaskea
LONDONDERRY	1. Coleraine; 2. Londonderry; 3. Magherafelt; 4. Newtown Limavady
MONAGHAN	1. Carrickmacross; 2. Castleblaney; 3. Clones; 4. Monaghan
TYRONE	1. Castlederg; 2. Clogher; 3. Cookstown; 4. Dungannon; 5. Gortin; 6. Omagh; 7. Strabane
CLARE	1. Ballyvaughan; 2. Corofin; 3. Ennis; 4. Ennistymon; 5. Killadysert; 6. Kilrush; 7. Scariff; 8. Tulla
CORK	1. Bandon; 2. Bantry; 3. Castletown; 4. Clonakilty; 5. Cork; 6. Dunmanway; 7. Fermoy; 8. Kanturk; 9. Kinsale; 10. Macroom; 11. Mallow; 12. Midleton; 13. Millstreet; 14. Mitchelstown; 15. Skibbereen; 16. Skull; 17. Youghal
KERRY	1. Cahirciveen; 2. Dingle; 3. Kenmare; 4. Killarney; 5. Listowel; 6. Tralee
LIMERICK	1. Croom; 2. Glin; 3. Kilmallock; 4. Limerick; 5. Newcastle; 6. Rathkeale
TIPPERARY	1. Borrisokane; 2. Carrick-on-Suir; 3. Cashel; 4. Clogheen; 5. Clonmel; 6. Nenagh; 7. Roscrea; 8. Thurles; 9. Tipperary
WATERFORD	1. Dungarvan; 2. Kilmacthomas; 3. Lismore; 4. Waterford
CARLOW	1. Carlow
DUBLIN	1. Balrothery; 2. Dublin North; 3. Dublin South; 4. Rathdown
KILDARE	1. Athy; 2. Celbridge; 3. Naas
KILKENNY	1. Callan; 2. Castlecomer; 3. Kilkenny; 4. Thomastown; 5. Urlingford
KINGS COUNTY	1. Edenderry; 2. Parsonstown-Birr; 3. Tullamore
LONGFORD	1. Ballymahon; 2. Granard; 3. Longford
LOUTH	1. Ardee; 2. Drogheda; 3. Dundalk
MEATH	1. Dunshaughlin; 2. Kells; 3. Navan; 4. Oldcastle; 5. Trim
QUEENS COUNTY	1. Abbeyleix; 2. Donaghmore; 3. Mountmellick
WESTMEATH	1. Athlone; 2. Delvin; 3. Mullingar
WEXFORD	1. Enniscorthy; 2. Gorey; 3. New Ross; 4. Wexford
WICKLOW	1. Baltinglass; 2. Rathdrum; 3. Shillelagh
GALWAY	1. Ballinasloe; 2. Clifden; 3. Galway; 4. Glenamaddy; 5. Gort; 6. Loughrea; 7. Mount Bellew; 8. Oughterard; 9. Portumna; 10. Tuam
LEITRIM	1. Carrick-on-Shannon; 2. Manorhamilton; 3. Mohill
MAYO	1. Ballina; 2. Ballinrobe; 3. Castlebar; 4. Claremorris; 5. Killala; 6. Newport; 7. Swinford; 8. Westport; 9. Belmullet
ROSCOMMON	1. Boyle; 2. Castlerea; 3. Roscommon; 4. Stokestown
SLIGO	1. Dromore West; 2. Sligo; 3. Tobercurry

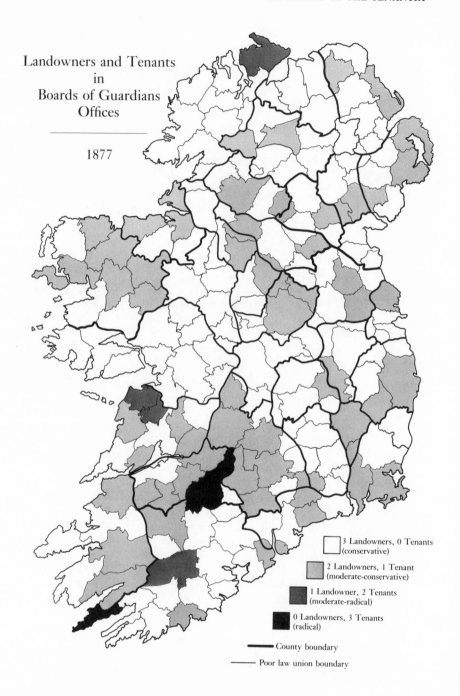

Landowners and Tenants
in
Boards of Guardians
Offices

1877

☐ 3 Landowners, 0 Tenants
(conservative)

▨ 2 Landowners, 1 Tenant
(moderate-conservative)

▩ 1 Landowner, 2 Tenants
(moderate-radical)

■ 0 Landowners, 3 Tenants
(radical)

——— County boundary

——— Poor law union boundary

Landowners and Tenants
in
Boards of Guardians
Offices

1882

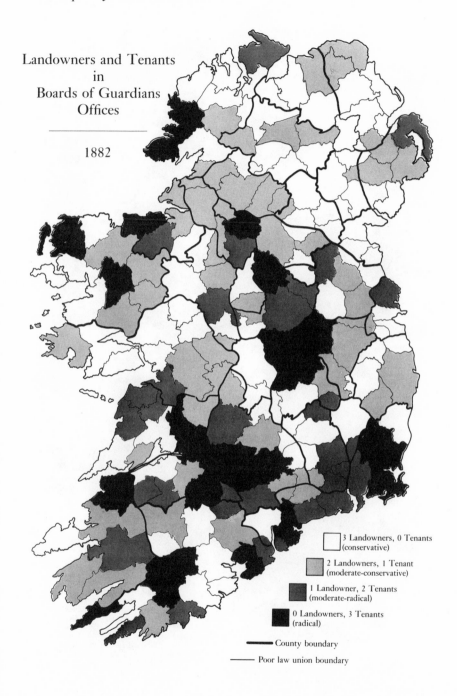

3 Landowners, 0 Tenants
(conservative)

2 Landowners, 1 Tenant
(moderate-conservative)

1 Landowner, 2 Tenants
(moderate-radical)

0 Landowners, 3 Tenants
(radical)

County boundary

Poor law union boundary

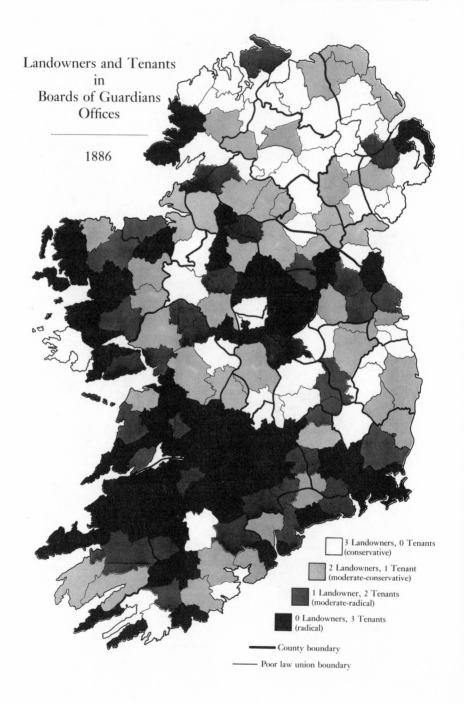

Landowners and Tenants
in
Boards of Guardians
Offices

1886

3 Landowners, 0 Tenants
(conservative)

2 Landowners, 1 Tenant
(moderate-conservative)

1 Landowner, 2 Tenants
(moderate-radical)

0 Landowners, 3 Tenants
(radical)

County boundary

Poor law union boundary

spread outward to neighboring unions. In North Munster the process began in Kilmallock in 1872. In the 1877 map Kilmallock was still the only completely nationalized union in the area; by 1882 it had been joined by other unions to the northwest, while unions still further on the periphery had begun to indicate signs of change. By 1886 practically all of Munster (except for the southern rim of Cork) was either fully radical or moderate-radical. Similarly, in Connaught the changeover began first in Castlebar in 1881 (joined by Belmullet and Dromore West in 1882), and spread to the entire western coast (except for Clifden and Killala) by 1886. The North Leinster region exhibited the same tendency with a slight variation. There, several unions in Queens, Kings, Westmeath, and Longford counties were nationalized in 1882. The north-south direction of the pattern suggests that this area might have linked up with the radical regions in the south. But this never occurred; instead, Mountmellick and Edenderry reverted to the ex-officios in 1884, while the nationalization spread on an east-west axis to the coast of Dublin and Meath in one direction and to Longford in the other (see the 1886 map). The landlord resurgence in Edenderry and Mountmellick confirms the impression given by the 1886 map about the entire section of territory from Dublin and Wicklow to East Galway—it was basically conservative. In the two unions where a radical change occurred, the tenants had not been able to sustain their hold. The conservative resurgence was not, incidentally, only temporary: in 1890 three J.P.'s were still in the offices of Mountmellick and Edenderry and also Carlow, Dublin South, and Rathdown. Baltinglass, Rathdrum, Shillelagh, and Gorey still had two J.P.'s. Thus in the south Leinster midlands, landlord power continued to survive long after it had collapsed elsewhere in the south. In Ulster, it apparently was never questioned.

Social Factors in Nationalization

Having identified the regional variations within the radical-conservative spectrum, it is now possible to search for social patterns that might account for the differences. Why did some regions turn radical and others not, and why were there large regions between the radical and conservative centers where change did not occur or was not completed? In order to compare the similarities and differences between politically similar regions, it will be necessary both to expand the area of survey and to simplify the political rating method. For determining broader regional variations, the county rather than the poor law union provides a more suitable and manageable area, since most statistics were gathered by county, and most counties were fairly homogeneous in their social makeup. The designations "radical," "moderate-radical," "moderate-conservative," and "conservative" were useful for determining fine gradations between unions; we are now interested not in fine gradations but in clear differences between radical and conservative areas. Therefore, counties whose union offices in 1886 were filled by more than 60 percent tenants will be rated as "radical," and those whose offices were filled by more than 60 percent landowners will be designated "conservative." Those counties with union offices fairly evenly distributed between tenants and landowners will be included but not rated politically. The counties break down as follows:

RADICAL (60 percent tenants)	CONSERVATIVE (60 percent owners)	OTHER
Clare	Louth	Galway
Kerry	Kings	Roscommon
Mayo	Queens	Sligo
Kilkenny	Kildare	Cork
Limerick	Carlow	Leitrim
Waterford	Dublin	Cavan
Meath	Donegal	
Tipperary	Monaghan	
Westmeath	Wicklow	
Longford	Fermanagh	
Wexford	Tyrone	
	Armagh	
	Londonderry	
	Down	
	Antrim	

Are there significant social differences between the counties in the first two columns?

Religion

The first difference one would expect to find would be a difference in the religious composition of the populations. The struggle that took place in the 1880s was not a religious war in the sense that one party wanted to impose its religious views on the other, although, to be sure, one of the most important issues from the Catholics' viewpoint was the Protestants' imposition of their views on Catholics through the education system. Nevertheless, the contestants in the larger political struggle were divided along religious lines, and one would look for a similar division on the boards of guardians. Comparing the various counties, therefore, we expect that counties with high Catholic ratios will be on the radical side and those with high Protestant ratios will be on the conservative side. Such a pattern is revealed in Table 16, which gives the political distribution and percentage of Catholic inhabitants by county.

TABLE 16

Radicalism and Conservatism Within the Counties in 1886 by Religious Distribution

County	Percent Catholic	Conservative	Radical	Other
Clare	98		x	
Kerry	97		x	
Galway	97			x
Mayo	97		x	
Roscommon	97			x
Kilkenny	95		x	
Limerick	95		x	
Waterford	95		x	
Louth	94	x		
Meath	94		x	
Tipperary	94		x	
Westmeath	92		x	
Longford	92		x	
Sligo	92			x
Cork	91			x
Leitrim	91			x
Kings	90	x		
Wexford	90		x	
Carlow	89	x		
Queens	87	x		
Kildare	86	x		
Cavan	80			x
Dublin	76	x		
Donegal	76	x		
Monaghan	75	x		
Wicklow	66	x		
Fermanagh	55	x		
Tyrone	55	x		
Armagh	46	x		
Londonderry	45	x		
Down	30	x		
Antrim	26	x		

Source: United Kingdom, Parliament, *Parliamentary Papers*, 1881, vol. 96 (*Reports*), C. 2931, "Census of Ireland, 1881: Preliminary Report," p. 12.

Note: No attempt was made to distinguish between the various Protestant denominations.

As the table indicates, only four counties consisted of a majority of Protestants: Armagh, Londonderry, Down, and Antrim. These were the only counties where the Parnellite party experienced losses in 1885. Above them on the list were Fermanagh and Tyrone, where Catholics had a slight majority; taken together with the other four counties they composed what is today Northern Ireland. The other counties all had strong Catholic majorities. But interestingly, conservatism was not confined only to counties with Catholic minorities. In fact, the only counties where board nationalization was extensive enough to be considered radical were counties in which more than 90 percent of the population were Catholic. Some counties in the 90 to 100 percent bracket were evenly split between conservatism and radicalism (Galway, Roscommon, Cork, and Sligo), and others just below it were fully conservative (Kings, Carlow, Queens, and Kildare). One explanation for this pattern might be that the tendency toward conservatism was so strong, or the landlords so powerful, that either could be overcome only in areas where the opposition was overwhelming—the areas whose populations were almost entirely Catholic. This explanation is reasonable but almost impossible to test. Another explanation involves a theory of political elites, and will be discussed below. For the time being, it is sufficient to say that religion, though a factor in board nationalization, was not the determinant: there were almost as many unions with high Catholic populations on the conservative side of the ledger (nine), as there were on the radical side (ten).

Poverty

The argument was made by many contemporary figures—Davitt and others who sympathized with the popular movement—that the impoverishment of the Irish people was the principal source of antagonism between landlords and tenants in Ireland. The fact that the Land League took hold first and was strongest in the "congested districts" of the west coast (districts with large populations living on lands whose soil was unproductive) seems to lend credence to this point of view. The board nationalization movement offers an excellent means of testing the theory, since the movement was one of tenants against landlords, and its results are measurable. If indeed poverty was an important factor, then one would expect to find a direct correlation between poverty in a region and a tendency for its boards of guardians to become radicalized. Poverty is, of course, difficult to measure, because it involves so many different elements—overcrowding, scanty means of subsistence, unproductive land. However, a handy index to poverty in Ireland appears in a table devised by T. W. Grimshaw in 1885, which Grimshaw intended as a means of comparing the economic and social backwardness in the various Irish counties. His method was rudimentary, but it is no less serviceable than others that might be devised for combining a multitude of factors into one. He simply took four measurable factors—density of population, productivity of land, means of subsistence (which unfortunately he did not define), and standard of education—and for each he placed all counties in the order in which they fell statistically from the lowest to the highest (poorest to wealthiest, least educated to most educated, etc.). Thus he had four columns of counties, each numbered from one to thirty-two. He then added together the position number of each county in the four columns, and rearranged the counties in order of their combined numbers. This gave him a list indicating the relative positions of the counties with all four factors taken into account. Grimshaw's list, together with the political designations of the counties, is shown in Table 17.

The briefest glance at the table reveals not the slightest relationship whatsoever between poverty, or economic and social "backwardness" as defined by Grimshaw, and either radicalism or conservatism. It is possible, of course, that Grimshaw's index is not reliable; for example, his method of giving equal emphasis to all four factors might in some way have distorted the picture so as to make some counties seem more or less impoverished than was actually the case. If so, the distortion could not have been great: persons with even the slightest familiarity with conditions in nineteenth-century Ireland know that poverty was most widespread along the western coast, particularly in the first five counties on the list, while the five counties at the bottom were among the most prosperous in Ireland. Further statistical evidence of this will be given in Table 18. Poverty, then, was not a factor in landlord-tenant relations at the level of the boards of guardians. If anything, it was a restraining factor in board nationalization, since, as the table shows, only four of the eleven radical counties were in the upper half of the poverty index, while eight of the fifteen conservative counties were in that half.

Landholding Size

The poverty index rates the counties only in relation to each other but does not reveal differences between the counties. Also the index says noth-

TABLE 17

Radicalism and Conservatism within the Counties, Arranged by Relative Poverty

County	Position in Poverty Index	Conservative	Radical
Mayo	1		x
Sligo	2		
Donegal	3	x	
Galway	4		
Leitrim	5		
Roscommon	6		
Kerry	7		x
Cavan	8		
Tyrone	9	x	
Armagh	10	x	
Longford	11		x
Clare	12		x
Monaghan	13	x	
Louth	14	x	
Fermanagh	15	x	
Londonderry	16	x	
Cork	17		
Wexford	18		x
Waterford	19		x
Down	20	x	
Limerick	21		x
Kilkenny	22		x
Kings	23	x	
Westmeath	24		x
Antrim	25	x	
Tipperary	26		x
Dublin	27	x	
Kildare	28	x	
Queens	29	x	
Wicklow	30	x	
Meath	31		x
Carlow	32	x	

Source: T. W. Grimshaw, "On Some Comparative Statistics of Irish Counties, compiled from the Returns obtained during the late Census and the Census of 1841, and other publications issued by the General Register Office of Ireland," *Journal of the Statistical and Social Inquiry Society of Ireland* 8 (1879–85), p. 457.

Note: 1 denotes the poorest, 32 the most prosperous.

ing about the kinds of agriculture carried on in the counties. It might be that board nationalization had nothing at all to do with population density or education, and that it was related not to poverty but to wealth, or to a particular kind of farming. In this respect, farm sizes are a better guide,

TABLE 18

Radicalism and Conservatism within the Counties, Arranged by Percentage of Farms over Thirty Acres

County	Percentage of Farms above 30 Acres	Conservative	Radical
Cork	56		
Wicklow	50	x	
Kerry	50		x
Waterford	50		x
Limerick	48		x
Carlow	47	x	
Tipperary	45		x
Clare	45		x
Kilkenny	44		x
Wexford	44		x
Meath	35		x
Kildare	35	x	
Queens	33	x	
Kings	33	x	
Antrim	32	x	
Westmeath	31		x
Fermanagh	30	x	
Dublin	28	x	
Donegal	28	x	
Tyrone	27	x	
Londonderry	26	x	
Longford	24		x
Down	21	x	
Louth	21	x	
Galway	21		
Cavan	19		
Leitrim	18		
Sligo	17		
Roscommon	15		
Mayo	15		x
Monaghan	13	x	
Armagh	12	x	

Source: T. W. Grimshaw, "On Some Comparative Statistics of Irish Counties, compiled from the Returns obtained during the late Census . . . ," *Journal of the Statistical and Social Inquiry Society of Ireland* 8 (August 1883), Table 1.

because they provide a statistically measurable index of land distribution, and thus some idea of whether the farmers of a county generally were large or small farmers, and whether they engaged principally in cattle grazing or arable farming. Table 18 rates the counties by their radical or conservative tendencies, arranging the counties in order of the percentage of farms in the county above thirty acres.

As the table indicates, farm sizes varied widely (12 percent above thirty acres in Armagh to 56 percent in Cork), and fell into regional groupings. The first ten counties, which were all above 44 percent, included every county in Munster and south Leinster. The remaining counties ranged gradually downward from 35 percent. The midland counties of Leinster (Meath, Kildare, Queens, Kings, and Westmeath) were in the upper portions of this group; the Ulster counties of Antrim, Fermanagh, Donegal, Tyrone, Londonderry, and Down were generally below the midland group; and at the bottom with the smallest farms in Ireland stood the five Connaught counties of Galway, Leitrim, Sligo, Roscommon, and Mayo, and three counties along the southern border of Ulster—Cavan, Monaghan, and Armagh. In terms of their political composition, the counties with the highest prevalence of large farms showed the strongest tendency towards radicalism. There were some conspicuous exceptions: Cork, with the largest farms, was politically mixed; Wicklow and Carlow, also in the large-farm group, were conservative; Meath, Westmeath, and Longford in the middle-ranging group were radical; and Mayo, near the bottom of the list, was radical. These exceptions will be dealt with shortly.

The most confusing group were the Connaught counties, for were it not for this partly radical group standing below the middle-ranging conservative group, it would be possible to make the generalization that on the whole, the tendency toward radical change increased in proportion to increases in farm sizes. It could be that the findings in Table 18 are distorted by the use of the county standard, rather than some standard of smaller size. As the 1886 map indicated, radicalism in Connaught tended not to conform to county boundaries: the coastal portions of Sligo, Mayo, and Galway were generally more radical than the inland portions, and in Roscommon, the radical unions (Carrick-on-Shannon, Stokestown, and Athlone) were adjacent to the radical group in the midlands. The opposite condition existed in Cork, where radicalism was weakest along the southern coast but very strong inland. To get a clearer idea of the relationship between radicalism and farm sizes, it is necessary to use a smaller geographical unit such as the poor law union in correlating the two factors. The results are shown in Table 19. To distinguish more accurately between farm sizes within different unions, the unions were classified in six categories of mean farm sizes. The calculations included only those boards that were radical (that is, had three tenant officers) in 1886.

TABLE 19

Correlation of Farm Sizes with Radicalism on Boards of Guardians, by Union

Mean Farm Size of Union	Correlation Coefficient[a] (The probability that the board would have three tenant officers, on a scale of + 1.000 to − 1.000)
less than 1 acre	.088
2 to 5 acres	.072
6 to 15 acres	−.225
16 to 30 acres	−.226
31 to 50 acres	.113
over 50 acres	.226

Source: United Kingdom, Parliament, *Parliamentary Papers*, 1882, vol. 74 (*Accounts and Papers*), C. 3332, "Agricultural Statistics of Ireland . . . 1881."

[a] Mean square contingency (0) analysis.

A coefficient of 1.000, had it appeared, would have signified that every single union having the acreage mentioned had a board with three tenant officers; and conversely, a coefficient of − 1.000 would have signified that not one of the boards in such unions had three tenant officers. A coefficient of .000 would have signified that exactly half the boards in a category had three tenant officers. Thus we observe that there was no correlation between mean acreage and office takeovers by tenants where the landholding sizes were small (under 5 acres), since the coefficients in these classes approached .000. This finding is in accord with the county comparisons in Table 18. These two classes include most of the predominantly urban unions where there were few farms but many residences and shops, and also some unions on the west coast. Most rural unions were in the next four classes. In unions where mean farm sizes were small or medium sized (between six and thirty acres), the correlation was negative. Boards in these unions tended not to have three tenant-officers. Again, this supports the findings in Table 18. In the next highest class the correlation was positive (.113), but not significantly so. Knowing the acreage, one could not really predict a particular union's radicalness. Most of the unions in the midlands counties were in this class. However, in the over-fifty-acre class, which included most of Munster, south Leinster, and the eastern seaboard south of Dublin, the correlation was distinctly positive (.226).

How significant is this data? Few statisticians would say that a positive correlation of .226 out of a possible 1.000 represented a strong correlation between land sizes and office holdings, or that − .226 represented a convincing negative correlation. Taken in relation to each other, however, the figures .226 and − .226 are significant, for they reveal a distinct positive tendency in the first instance and a distinct negative tendency in the second. The fact that the small and medium farm unions showed a tendency not to be radical, and that the tendency toward radicalism increased with each step up in farm sizes, suggests that radicalism was in some way related to large farms. What the .226 figure means is that farm sizes were not the *only* factor, and that other elements need to be taken into account.

One of these factors, religion, has already been suggested. The religious factor helps to account for almost all the exceptions in Table 18 (farm sizes by county). Wicklow and Carlow were among the large farm counties but, unlike the others, were conservative. Yet, reverting to Table 16 (religions by county), we see that the Roman Catholic populations of both of these counties were under 90 percent (Wicklow, 66 percent; Carlow, 89 percent), whereas all of the other large-farm counties were in the over-90 percent Catholic bracket. Indeed, Carlow at 89 percent, which would appear to be a marginal case, is most important in proving the rule that 90 percent was the significant breaking point. In other words, if the Protestants made up anything more than 10 percent, that, in conjunction with the county being a large farm area, was enough to tip the balance in favor of conservative boards of guardians in that county. Again, among the middle-ranging group in Table 18, all the counties were conservative except Meath, Westmeath, and Longford. In Table 16 these three counties appear in the over-90 percent Catholic bracket, while all of the other conservative counties were under 90 percent—some of them, the Ulster counties, considerably under. Interpreting these findings in social terms, one might say that the tendency for unions to be radicalized increased wherever there was a conspicuous large-farmer class and where the overall population was overwhelmingly (more than 90 percent) Catholic. Where the large farmer was less the norm, or the population had a higher proportion of Protestants (more than 10 percent), the tendency toward radicalization decreased. Where there were few large farmers, as in Connaught, neither farm sizes nor religion seemed to have any influence. In spite of the uniformly small farms and the uniformly large Catholic populations in Connaught, the region was neither uniformly radical nor conservative, but was divided between radicalism and conservatism from west to east. Apparently, in Connaught other forces were in operation.

County Cork remains a problem. There the farms were the largest in Ireland and the Catholic population was above 90 percent, yet conservatism remained entrenched in portions of the county. The combination both of farm sizes and of uneven religious distribution probably also accounts for the differences in Cork, but the fact that religious data was not given by union but only by parish and county makes it difficult to correlate religion with farm size. There was a high Protestant concentration in the city of Cork and its environs, and the parochial statistics confirm that Protestantism was generally strong along the entire southern coast.[1] Although farms were generally large everywhere but on the southwest coast, the largest farms in the county were in the dairylands of the north in the unions of Mitchelstown, Kanturk, Mallow, Fermoy, and Millstreet. Since the Protestants were concentrated in the south of the county, and the county as a whole was 91 percent Catholic, the large-farm region of the north must have been strongly Catholic. It would not be too risky to say that the radical unions of north Cork were, like those to the immediate north of them, unions of predominantly large Catholic farmers. In the far southwest, farms were small and unproductive, and landlord power in some districts remained strong (Bantry and Skibbereen, for example, remained conservative). Around Cork city the Protestant population was larger, and again conservatism continued to be the rule. The size and diversity of Cork was such that no single factor can explain the political variations within the county.

Other Factors

The argument that board nationalization was most likely to occur in unions where large farmers and high proportions of Catholics coincided does not, of course, account for all the conditions observed in the maps of the board office distributions. It does not account for the fact that some groups of adjacent boards chose to elect two tenant officers or two landlord officers rather than three. This was the case, for example, in the area that incorporated the unions of Fermoy, Clogheen, Clonmel, and Callan, which were two-tenant unions strung out along the southwestern border of Tipperary. It was also the case in the two-landlord unions of Enniskillen, Lisnaskea, Clones, Cavan, Bailieborough, Carrickmacross, and Dundalk, which ringed virtually the entire southern boarder of Ulster. The argument also does not account for conspicuous regional exceptions such as Clifden (Galway), a three-landlord union in the center of a three-tenant region. Most of all, it does not account for the radicalism along the coast of Mayo and Galway, which were counties with large Catholic populations but relatively few large farms. In most of these cases we need other factors to account for the patterns. Descriptions of the more significant possibilities follow.

Geographical Proximity. The two-tenant and two-landlord unions on the 1886 map tend to congregate alongside and in between large areas of three-tenant and three-landlord unions. This suggests that geographical proximity to radical or conservative centers was a factor determining the voting behavior on some boards. We observed in the Kilkenny nationalists' convention of 1887 that the nationalists were not so much concerned with the politics of the Marquess of Ormonde as chairman, as they were concerned that Kilkenny should not be the last union in Ireland to cast out its ex-officio chairman. From their point of view their concern was well-founded. By 1887 Kilkenny was the only board between Clare and Wexford to have an ex-officio chairman. Things were changing so rapidly that they could not have known that other boards further north would not follow suit, leaving Kilkenny as the only board in the south with an aristocratic chairman. In Kilkenny's case, therefore, the unseating of the Marquess of Ormonde contained an element of keeping up with the Joneses. Kilkenny was probably not unusual. Once a few boards in an area became nationalized, the pressure on adjacent boards to do the same must have been strong. In this way, a bandwagon effect developed, carrying the enthusiasm for ejecting the landlords farther and farther afield until it reached districts where antilandlord opinion was diluted and insufficient to motivate a sustained attack on the ex-officios. Boards in these marginal areas tended to compromise by putting both ex-officios and elected guardians in office. This would explain the graduations of radicalism as one moved out of the large-farm or heavily Catholic regions into smaller-farm or Protestant regions.

Local Factors. In some instances local factors accounted for divergences from a regional pattern. For example, not one landlord was to be found in any of the board offices along the west coast of Mayo and Connemara, save for Clifden and Killala, which had three landlords and two landlords respectively. Killala and Clifden were exceedingly poor unions populated almost entirely by subsistence and marginal farmers, almost all Catholics, who, because of their precarious economic position, were dependent on their landlords. On the other hand, these unions were not as impoverished as Belmullet, the most barren of unions in Ireland, yet all three of the ex-officios who had occupied Belmullet's offices in 1877 were removed by

1886. Economic factors, then, cannot explain the differences, and it is necessary to know more about the particular political situations in the unions. An examination of the minute books of Killala, for example, reveals that the Gore and Kirkwood families attended board meetings regularly and generally kept close rein over the affairs of the union.[2] A similar situation may have existed in Clifden, although this would be difficult to discover because of the absence of minute books, and because local politics in Clifden received very little coverage in the Galway press. Clifden and Killala simply prove the limitations of the quantitative method in describing particular political phenomena.

Urban Influences. In an article in *Irish Historical Studies*,[3] Samuel Clark offered a well-documented argument in support of his view that the land war of 1879–81 was organized largely by inhabitants of the rural towns and Dublin. He based this view on extensive data gathered from police and valuation records and from newspaper reports of organizational meetings in the west during 1879, which revealed that townsmen, particularly publicans and commercial traders, were evident during the organizational stages of the land war in numbers far greater than their proportions in society would lead one to expect. The article is an early version of a chapter in Clark's doctoral dissertation, since published as a book.[4] In the larger study he makes the general argument, drawing from a wider variety of data over a longer period, that the land war was largely a product of the development of social communication among the tenant classes during the post-Famine period, which enabled the potentially rebellious Irish tenantry to organize for rebellion. Central to this system of social communication was a newly developed class of urban bourgeoisie, made up largely of traders, publicans, and shopkeepers, whose urban environment and continual contact with the farmer placed them in an excellent position to provide leadership, disseminate information, and organize the farmers for agitation. Insofar as the farmers were brought into the nationalist political movement during the land war, it was these townsmen who accomplished the rural politicization.

Clark's study is an important contribution to Irish studies because it fills in part of the wide gap in our knowledge of local political organization and of the role of the rural towns in the politicizing process. However, his findings may have been biased by his time and geographical concentrations. His study did not go beyond the Land League, and his most forceful conclusions lean heavily upon conditions in Connaught. As I have attempted to demonstrate, the politicizing process occurred unevenly in different parts of the country, and much of it took place after the termination of the Land League. Furthermore, by selecting Connaught as the focus of his study, Clark inadvertently chose the region in which his generalizations were most applicable. This, at any rate, is my impression after studying the boards of guardians. The nationalization movement in Connaught supports Clark's thesis to the letter. The farmers on the Connaught boards, though mostly nationalist, were among the most passive in Ireland. Most of the agitation at board meetings was carried on by townsmen. Townsmen usually organized the overthrow of ex-officio officers, and once the landlords were out of office, most of their seats were taken by townsmen.

Townsmen were active everywhere in the board nationalization movement either as direct participants or as outside organizers and publicists. However, their proportion among the agitating body as a whole was exceptionally strong in Connaught—particularly in Mayo and a few coastal unions outside Mayo. For obvious reasons, it was also strong in the cities and larger town unions. But outside these areas the leadership was provided for the most part by large farmers. Where there were not many large farmers to supply leadership, the movement was generally weak.

The Tenant Officers of 1886

The question of who accomplished the board nationalization movement and who benefitted from it are admittedly not necessarily the same question; nevertheless, an examination of the beneficiaries—those who took over the instruments of power from the landlords—should provide some idea of the classes who dominated the movement after it began. And, if this examination is extended over different points in time, it should be possible to trace the involvement of the various classes during the earlier and later stages of change. For these purposes, it will be necessary to abandon the simple distinctions "landlord" and "tenant," which so far have been used advantageously, and break down the tenant officer group into its various social components. Table 20 gives, for 1877, 1882, and 1886, the percentages of the total body of officers that fell into ten occupational categories. The method of defining the categories and deciding which individuals belonged in which was the same as was used in the Tralee election analysis, as were the sources for identifying the occupations (see the Methodological Appendix). For purposes of contrast, 1886 is shown twice: once for all of Ireland and once with Ulster excluded.

TABLE 20

Occupations of All Boards of Guardians' Officers, by Percentage of the Total Group, in 1877, 1882, and 1886; and of All Officers Outside Ulster in 1886

Occupation	1877 (n = 489)	1882 (n = 489)	1886 (n = 486)	1886[a] (n = 354)
Landowners	87.9%	65.3%	49.8%	38.9%
Farmers	6.7	18.8	26.2	34.5
Shopkeepers	1.0	6.1	8.8	8.2
Publicans & innkeepers	.4	1.0	1.4	2.0
Professionals	.6	1.0	1.2	1.7
Merchants & manufacturers	1.0	1.2	1.2	.8
Members of Parliament	.2	.2	.2	.6
Land agents	.6	.6	.4	.2
Business agents	.4	.2	.2	.2
Civil servants	.2	—	.2	.2
Unidentified	1.9	5.5	9.9	12.2
Total	100.9%	99.9%	99.5%	99.5%

[a]Excluding Ulster.

Table 20 indicates that the changes were greatest between the two largest occupational classes—the landowners and farmers. The landowners declined by 1886 while the farmers increased. The change was most pronounced in the three southern provinces, where at the end of the period the landowners exceeded the farmers by only 4.4 percentage points (38.9 against 34.5 percent). Shopkeepers increased by more than eight times over the period. This was a faster rate of increase than the farmers', who approximately quadrupled their representation; however, shopkeepers still held less than 10 percent of the offices in 1886. Furthermore, as we can see by comparing the changes in the two groups during the 1877–82 and 1883–86 periods, the farmers continued to increase at a high rate during the later period, whereas the shopkeepers tapered off. There were minor changes in other occupational categories, but none of these groups was at any time numerically significant enough to influence the overall pattern. Perhaps the most interesting feature of the smaller groups was the increase in publicans and innkeepers and professionals, and the decrease in land agents and business agents, which signified the changing importance of these groups in the power structure.

The shopkeepers, though not a large group, were distributed throughout the unions in such a way as to make them influential in the regions where they held office. In 1886 shopkeepers made up 8.8 percent of the total in all of Ireland and 8.2 percent in the southern provinces alone. Interestingly, of eighteen shopkeepers in the forty-four unions of Ulster, seven were in the unions of County Donegal. Among the nine tenant officers in that county (which had the highest number of tenant officers of any Ulster county), there were two bakers, four grocers, one farmer, and two unidentified persons, one of whom had an address in the town of Glenties and was therefore probably a shopkeeper. Thus the election of shopkeepers as officers in Ulster was not a tendency typical of the entire province, but was largely confined to one of the most Catholic of the Ulster counties. When we move to the south of Ireland, we find a similarly disproportionate distribution of shopkeepers. Of twenty-nine shopkeepers in the three southern provinces, ten were in one county, Mayo, while the rest were distributed throughout the other counties. In fact, if all town occupations are taken into consideration, we find that Mayo had thirteen (20 percent) of the sixty-six townsmen in the southern unions, although it had only nine (6 percent) of the unions. The thirteen fell into four of the town occupational categories: shopkeepers (6), publicans and innkeepers (1), professionals (4), and commercial agents (1), with one additional townsman of unidentified occupation. Mayo also had two of the three land agents in the sample. In having a preponderance of townsmen among its officers Mayo differed from Galway, its neighbor to the south, where not one of the fifteen tenant officers was identified as having a town occupation.[5] Sligo, to the north, had one grocer and one publican among its five tenant officers (the third was a farmer and two others were unidentified), and Roscommon had a grocer and a solicitor among its three tenants, the third being a farmer. Taking into account County Donegal, one can say, as a rule, that insofar as townsmen were elected to offices they tended to concentrate in the Catholic counties along the northwestern coast. These were counties where the large-farmer class was weaker than elsewhere and where, as Samuel Clark has argued, the leadership devolved upon the town classes.

In the regions where the large-farmer class was numerically strong, townsmen made up a much smaller proportion of the officeholders. In County Limerick, for example, eleven of the fifteen tenant officers were farmers. Similarly, farmers predominated in Tipperary, where they occupied eleven of thirteen tenant offices; in Wexford (nine of nine); in Kilkenny (ten of twelve) in Westmeath (six of nine); in Meath (ten of ten); in Cork (eighteen of twenty-three). Cork, the largest and most economically diversified of the counties, was a good example of the weak-farmer strong-shopkeeper principle in operation. The five Cork townsmen were in four unions (Youghal, Fermoy, Dunmanway, and Skull) contiguous to the

Protestant region along the southern coast. The officers in the cattle-grazing unions of Kanturk, Millstreet, and Mitchelstown were all farmers. Mallow, the only conservative union in the group, was an exceptional case for which we can offer no explanation. In general, the rule applied that wherever the Catholic large-farmer class was strong, the guardians tended to elect farmers as chairmen.

In Chapter 2 I argued that the large farmers constituted a social and political elite in the Irish rural localities. This conclusion was based on the finding (drawn admittedly from a small sample of twelve officeholders plus fifteen farmers on the Castlebar and Westport boards of guardians) that all but three of the officeholders and three of the Castlebar and Westport guardians were farmers who occupied land valued at £50 or more. This was despite the fact that theoretically, because of the low property qualifications for holding the office of poor law guardian, farmers rated as low as £20, or even £8 in some unions, could have been elected to the boards and the offices. A random sample of the landholdings of thirty farmers who held offices in 1886 suggests that the same large-farmer bias was evident among that group.

Land Valuations	Number of Farmers
£4 to £19	2
£20 to £49	9
£50 to £99	7
£100 to £149	6
£150 to £199	1
£200 or more	5

It should be mentioned that these were minimum landholdings representing only the lots on which the guardians resided. Other holdings elsewhere in the union or outside it, if they existed, were not included. The largest single group were the nine in the £20–49 category. There were also two in the £4–19 category. Taken together the two groups made up 37 percent of the sample. In the 1877 sample (see Chapter 2) the under-£50 groups made up 20 percent, when only the officers are counted, and 22 percent, when the entire group including the Castlebar and Westport farmers are counted. There was, therefore, an added 15 to 17 percent in the smaller farmer categories in 1886.

These figures coincide with Conor Cruise O'Brien's similar finding about changes that occurred in the composition of the parliamentary party between

1880 and 1885. O'Brien did not analyze changes within the farmer class per se (there were only two farmers in the Home Rule party in 1880), but he analyzed changes within a number of general occupational categories and discovered an important shift in the party's social composition from landowners, larger businessmen, and persons in higher professions, to shopkeepers, farmers, and lower professionals. This "democratization," or shift downward from the higher social elements, occurred also in the boards of guardians' leadership between 1877 and 1886. However, the democratization of the tenant board officers should not be overemphasized. In 1886 nineteen (about two-thirds) of the thirty farmers sampled occupied farms of more than £50 valuation, and twelve (more than one-third) were above a hundred pounds. Thus the transfer represented in one sense a democratization of the offices, and in another sense the replacement of the old landlord elite with a new tenant elite.

The Landowning Officers of 1886

In spite of the large influx of farmers and shopkeepers, landowners managed to retain a good number of offices in Ulster and parts of the south. Their grip was the strongest in the office of chairman and weakest in the office of deputy vice-chairman, as a comparison of the three offices in 1877 and 1886 indicates:

	Landowning Officers	
	1877	*1886*
Chairmen	98.8%	66.7%
Vice-chairmen	93.3%	50.9%
Deputy vice-chairmen	71.8%	33.6%

Landowners were reduced by about one-third in the chairmanships, just under one-half in the vice-chairmanships, and just over one-half in the deputy vice-chairmanships. This pattern, furthermore, was not restricted to Ulster. In almost every union in the south where there was one landowner in office, the landowner was the chairman. It is understandable that poor law guardians, who were mostly farmers, should choose other farmers to act as their officers when given the opportunity to do so. But why, in an age when the cry "down with landlordism" fueled the fires of three movements that constituted the land war, should so many of the boards in the south have chosen landowners to fill the highest local public position it was in their power to bestow? Was there something about landowning officers of 1886 that made them different and more acceptable to the tenants than those of 1877?

This question is addressed in Table 21, which gives the median valuations of the holdings of landowning officers, by office, in 1877 and 1886. Once again, for the sake of contrast, Ulster is shown separately from the three southern provinces. As the table reveals, a reduction of land sizes occurred between 1877 and 1886 in both regions and in all offices except the Ulster chairmanships, where the median valuation rose from £2,036 in 1877 to £3,474 in 1886. The valuations in the other two offices began higher in Ulster and remained higher at the end in Ulster, but the differences between Ulster and the rest of Ireland in these two office categories were not great. It should be kept in mind, however, that landowners held a higher proportion of the vice-chairmanships and deputy vice-chairmanships in Ulster, so that they were proportionately more numerous as well as proportionately more landed. On the whole, the occupants of the two lower offices in all provinces in 1886 were small and middling landowners of a somewhat lower cut than their counterparts in 1877. The top level, in other words, had been sheared off.

The most significant changes in the north and the south took place in the office of chairman. The Ulster valuations increased by about 75 percent between 1877 and 1886, while the valuations in the other provinces declined by about 35 percent. In the south, therefore, not only were there about half as many landowning chairmen in 1886, but those who remained were not as well landed. In Ulster, on the other hand, a retrenchment of sorts appears to have taken place among the landowners, for only about

TABLE 21

Median Valuations of the Holdings of Landowning Officers in Ulster and the Other Provinces in 1877 and 1886

	Ulster		Other Provinces	
	1877	1886	1877	1886
Chairmen	£2,036	£3,474	£1,953	£1,262
Vice-chairmen	869	474	547	410
Deputy vice-chairmen	305	164	172	130

Note: The number in the sample for each group was as follows: Ulster—Chairmen: (1877) 40, (1886) 35; V.C.: (1877) 32, (1886) 23; D.V.C.: (1877) 22, (1886) 15. Other provinces—Chairmen: (1877) 105, (1886) 48; V.C.: (1877) 83, (1886) 29; D.V.C.: (1877) 57, (1886) 17.

10 percent of the landowning chairmen had been removed, while the wealth of the remaining group had increased by almost double. The removals in the southern chairmanships had occurred at the top of the scale; those in the north had occurred at the bottom.

The implications of these patterns in the north and south are broader than they would appear to be on the surface. An explanation for the differences involves an understanding of the symbolic nature of the office of chairman (as opposed to vice-chairman and deputy vice-chairman), and of the basis of the term "landlordism." In practice, landlordism was a vaguely-defined political term used by members of the popular party to denote any and all of the evils connected with the one-sided land tenure system in Ireland and the economic, social, and political privileges that the landlords gained from it. It included three categories of grievances: (1) those having to do with economic arrangements such as the monopolization of the land by the Ascendancy and the insecurity of land tenure; (2) those having to do with the social irresponsibility of the landed class, particularly the supposed indifference with which landlords evicted tenants from their holdings; and (3) those having to do with the political framework that enabled the landlords to monopolize the judicial benches and administrative offices and thus to dictate the conditions of their ascendancy. When these tests were applied to particular landlords, the one group that invited condemnation on all three counts was the absentee landowners—the great aristocrats and landed gentry who owned most of the land in Ireland (and therefore had most of the tenants); who rackrented the tenants through land agents while they resided in England or on the Continent; and who exercised through their offices in Parliament and the government a decisive influence over the daily lives of the Irish tenantry. Most of these landowners, moreover, were Anglo-Saxon Protestants. For an Irishman claiming to be a patriot and a champion of the people's cause to elect such an individual to the highest office on the board of guardians was, to his contemporaries, more than inexcusable; it was "flunkeyism" and false patriotism.

This was not always the case with the smaller landlords: the country squires and smaller landowners. Because they were small, they had fewer tenants and were also more vulnerable to the pressures placed on them to reduce rents and treat the tenantry more fairly. Many also exhibited features considered positive by the tenants but which were lacking in the aristocratic class. The small landlords resided on their holdings and dealt with the local tenantry directly. They often worked their own land and took an interest in the agriculture of the community, which included lending out their animal stock to their neighbors for breeding purposes. The small squires were not in a position to flee to more temperate climates whenever the political environment in Ireland grew torrid; they stuck to their estates and performed their social and political functions often in the face of great personal danger or discomfort. No doubt the more fanatical popular leaders regarded them with the same kind of contempt that they held for the great absentee landowners. But the bulk of the tenantry, who tended to be more moderate and more closely tied to the traditional social values, found it difficult to place these men in the same mental category with the faceless, unapproachable grandees who owned the great estates, or to rebuff them with the same force of conviction.

It is significant in this respect that the greatest changes in the chairmanships both in Ulster and the rest of Ireland occurred among the aristocrats. In Ulster in 1877 eleven men bearing titles held the high office. They accounted for 25 percent of the chairmanships in the province. By 1886 their number had risen to thirteen (30 percent). In the southern provinces, on the other hand, the number of titled chairmen declined between 1877 and 1886 from thirty-four (26 percent) to thirteen (10 percent). In Ulster, in other words, where landowners as a group were 10 percent fewer in 1886, aristocrats were 20 percent more numerous; in the south, where landowners as a group were about 50 percent fewer, aristocrats were almost two-thirds *less* numerous. As was to be expected, the aristocrats in the south persisted in office most assiduously in the region where most of the boards continued to elect three landowners to the offices—the conservative counties of the midlands and east coast. The two most formidable landowners, the Duke of Leinster and the Earl Fitzwilliam, continued to hold sway in their unions of Celbridge (Kildare) and Shillelagh (Wicklow), while six others held chairs in Parsonstown in Kings County (Earl of Rosse), Abbeyleix and Donaghmore in Queens County (Viscount de Vesci and Lord Castletown), Rathdown in Dublin County (Viscount Powerscourt), Carlow (Sir Thomas P. Butler), and Gorey, County Wexford (Earl of Courtown). The remaining five unions were Kilkenny (Marquess of Ormonde), Bandon (Earl of Bandon), Ballinasloe (Earl of Clancarty), Ballina (Sir Charles Knox-Gore), and Killala (also Sir Charles Knox-Gore). The last two unions named illustrate how firmly the Gore family controlled the politics of northeast Mayo.

Because the chairmanship of the board of guardians was the highest political honor that the people of a locality could bestow on an individual, it became a matter of principle among the tenantry to deny the honor to that other class, the absentee landowners, who most completely symbolized the old social system. But precisely *because* the aristocrats symbolized the status quo, the guardians of conservative Ulster made it a point to retain them in office and even install aristocrats where they had not held office before. This is the most likely explanation for the changes in the chairmanships observed in Table 21. It would be erroneous, however, to attribute the entire change in the south to the preference of the tenants alone. The landowners had to have a hand in the removal of the aristocrats and large landowning gentry, for this reason: in the two-part system under which the boards operated, each party—that is to say the ex-officios and elected guardians—nominated a slate of candidates for the offices, which they presented for the corporate consideration of the board. Nominations were arrived at either through a mutual understanding among the party members—for example, that the same person who held the office the previous year would be nominated—or by a caucus of the party members held before the election. Instances were extremely rare in which candidates were selected spontaneously at the time of the meeting.[6]

Under the nominating procedures, the decision to run a smaller landowner in place of a greater one resided not with the elected guardians, but with the ex-officios. Most probably, when an aristocrat was involved, the aristocrat's decision *not* to run preceded the ex-officios' decision to run a lower-ranking candidate. Probably not many magistrates would remove a noble officeholder from the slate without his own consent, or, for that matter, without his initiating the action. But regardless of who made the first move, the motivation and end result were the same. Over time, as the nationalists' strength on the boards increased and ex-officios in growing numbers lost their offices at the boards, practical considerations made it necessary for the ex-officios to reconsider their position. If they persisted in offering up candidates who were offensive to the elected guardians, they were bound eventually to meet the same fate as their colleagues on so many other boards and completely lose their voice in the administration of the poor law. They therefore nominated men who were more likely to be accepted—men who were respected by the tenants in their communities, who, like R. H. Borrowes of Naas, were less rigid in the application of the older conservative standards, and above all (from the ex-officios' standpoint), who attended every meeting and represented their views at the board. In some cases the new candidates were acceptable to the elected guardians, in others not, depending on how willing the elected guardians were to compromise.

Politics and Social Change

We can now attempt to sort out the various facts uncovered in the statistical analyses in this chapter and explore their implications for social and political change in Ireland. It is clear that the movement was strongest and most thorough in its effects in those parts of the country where large farms predominated and where Catholicism was the religion of practically the entire population. One might hypothesize from these facts that board nationalization received its strongest support from large Catholic farmers, and this hypothesis is further supported by the finding that outside of Connaught—which was clearly an exceptional case—the new guardians who took office were mostly large farmers whose property valuations were above £50. Reviewing the analysis of the political maps of 1877 and 1886, we can see that the changes in board offices occurred unevenly over time and within different regions, but that the changeover had begun to occur in the large-farm counties of Munster and Leinster even before the Land League. By 1877 most of the boards of guardians in the Limerick-Clare-Tipperary region and the Meath-Westmeath region had at least one tenant among its three officers, while in the rest of the country landlords tended to occupy all three offices. This additional fact enables us to advance the hypothesis one step further, and to say that the large farmers had already begun to make their political move before the opening of active hostilities in 1879, and that the Land League and Parnellite movements helped to speed up a process already in progress.

Most of the large farmers, who moved into the board offices both before and after 1877, were the cattle graziers discussed in Chapter 2, where, it will be recalled, they were described as a rural social elite who, by virtue of their growing wealth, economic independence of the landlord, and unique position among farmers—which brought them into contact with both urban and small-farmer classes—became also a political elite. Their early political activities in the Tenant-Right societies and on the boards of guardians, though far from radical by later standards, proved that they had begun to develop into an important political class by as early as the 1850s. As an elite class they dominated the political posts that were occupied by the tenantry, but restrictive property qualifications and a system of values that placed the highest premium on landownership kept them out of the most desirable and politically important posts in local government. These were the seats on the grand juries and the offices on the boards of guardians. The grand juries were out of their reach because of the aristocratically biased property qualifications and the screening processes of county government. But the only thing that stood between them and the fulfillment of their political aspirations at the boards of guardians was the conservative majority that dominated almost every board. Political power was within their grasp if only the majority could be turned to their side, and such a development was facilitated by the high rate of absenteeism among the ex-officios, and by the dependence of the elected conservatives on the votes of the ratepayers.

The first changes occurred in regions where Catholic cattle graziers were preponderant—north Munster and Leinster. There, the ratepaying electorate were most similar to the guardians themselves and consequently the guardians had the least difficulty in getting the support of the voters to obtain their majorities or near-majorities. Next came the Land League movement—a crucial development—which helped to broaden the landlord-tenant struggle to include the small-farmer electorate. Coercion exacerbated the process and Parnell completed it. After 1880 the poor law electorate began sending nationalists to the boards in increasing numbers, and it is probable that by 1886 there were nationalist majorities on every board outside Ulster. Then came the second stage of nationalization—the attack on the offices. Here, however, the expected transition in all areas of the south failed to occur. It was completed only in the regions where the antagonism toward landlords was greatest and the impulse to wrest political power from their hands was strongest—the cattle-grazing regions of Munster and Leinster. In the counties bordering Dublin to the south and west, also a cattle-grazing area, a minor attempt was made by the elected guardians to take over the offices in 1882 and 1883, but the movement was weakened by the existence of a strong Protestant farmer class and, perhaps, by a more moderate political tradition derived from centuries of political contact between Catholic and Protestant farmers. The arrangement struck between the nationalist-elected guardians and the ex-officios of Naas suggests that the Catholic farmers of the old English Pale counties had long before made peace with the landlords and were more interested in maintaining amicable relations than in creating new hostility by usurping the landlords' political power.

However, in the conservative midlands, as in the other unions in the south where the landlords for whatever reason remained strong, the elected guardians were in fundamental agreement on one point: the aristocracy—that symbol of landlord oppression and British rule—had to go. The landlords themselves, recognizing that their grip on the offices was weakening and would collapse altogether if they insisted on maintaining a rigid position, jettisoned the burden of their social obligations and put forth men whom the tenants in some regions found more acceptable. They compromised in the allocation of offices by admitting elected guardians into one or both of the lower offices. But the crucial difference between conditions in 1877 and 1886 was that in the earlier period the terms were dictated by the preferences of the landlords, whereas later they were dictated by the preferences of the tenants. Thus, in ways that were not revealed by the patterns in the maps at the beginning of this discussion, a transfer of power took place from landlord to tenant that had as many implications for the values of landed society as for those of tenant society. The test case for this thesis is Ulster. There, conditions remained essentially as they had been before: large landowners continued to hold the board offices, and the offices were assigned by the dictates of social protocol, that is to say, aristocrats in the chairmanships and smaller owners in the other offices, arranged in the order of their landholdings. This was in sharp contrast to the southern provinces, where the values of landed society were almost entirely abandoned. Where ex-officios were elected to office they tended to hold the higher offices, but few of them were aristocrats, and most were chosen not merely because they were landowners but because they satisfied a particular political qualification. In the south, in other words, a breakdown of older social values had even begun to take place within landed society; conformity to rigid social rules had begun to be replaced by a system of political choice. This change in attitude salvaged for the landowners some of their power and ensured for them a small but prominent place in the counsels of local government, a place they still retain today.

The apparent exception to the theory of the large-farmer class as a political elite was Connaught and the northwest. Clark's thesis, that there was indeed an elite but that this elite was a town rather than a country elite, certainly holds true for Mayo, Sligo, Roscommon, and Donegal. Why this particular characteristic should have appeared most strongly in the west is difficult to say. Perhaps it was because Michael Davitt settled on Mayo as his point of departure for the land war, and that being a Fenian he enlisted the support of the Fenians in the area, mostly townsmen, who held on to their elite positions thereafter. Historical accidents such as these often do account for inexplicable political developments. However, there are also signs that the cattle graziers of this area were not inactive, and that some of the important political leaders had economic and social connections with cattle graziers. James Daly, the journalist, John Louden, the barrister, and Charles O'Malley, the solicitor, are three examples. All three were occupiers of large farms, and at least two—Daly and Louden—were farmers' sons. (Daly's brother Charles was a cattle farmer and auctioneer and his uncle Patrick was an occupier of numerous large farms in different parts of the Castlebar union.) All three were Land Leaguers who eventually became chairmen of their boards of guardians. These three men were all townsmen in the sense that they lived and carried on their professions in a town, but who is to say that they were not conditioned for their part in politics by their farming background and experience? If any general statement is to be made about political leadership that would satisfy both Clark's findings and my own, it probably would go as follows.

In the three decades following the Great Famine there grew up in Ireland both a town and a country bourgeoisie—the first represented by a socially aspiring shopkeeper and publican class, the second by a socially aspiring cattle-grazier class. In 1879 these two classes allied, for their own respective reasons, in a general attack on both the British government and the landlords. They were congenial allies, for each came into contact with the other frequently in the course of ordinary trading, both were relatively free of dependence on the landlord, and both had an interest in improving the condition of the lesser farmer as well as achieving independence for Ireland. They therefore worked together to organize the farmers. In regions where the cattle graziers were numerically powerful (Munster and Leinster), they did not need the assistance of the shopkeepers and were able to wage the battle on their own. But in other places where they were numerically weak and were therefore unable to organize themselves effectively, the shopkeepers stepped into the void and became the dominant element. This may have occurred in Mayo, and might explain why there were more townsmen in the Mayo offices than elsewhere. This, of course, is a hypothesis that needs to be explored. The final answer will not come forth until a great deal more is known about the structure of local politics in rural Ireland.

✿✿ Epilogue

AFTER THE FAILURE of the Home Rule bill, the focus of Irish politics shifted again to the land question. During the summer of 1886 agricultural distress caused by continually declining prices brought new demands for rent reductions below the levels fixed by the land courts. In response to the demands, a few members of the Irish party—John Dillon and William O'Brien among others—established the "Plan of Campaign," a program sanctioned but never publicly endorsed by Parnell, in which tenants on selected estates were called on to offer the landlord a predetermined reduction in rent, and should the landlord refuse to make the abatement, to pay the proffered rent into a fund for the benefit of the evicted. The plan was instituted on the estates of eighty-four large landowners. In at least sixty instances the landlords prudently gave way and agreed to the tenants' terms. Abatements averaged about 25 percent. In twenty-four of these instances landlords put up a token resistance before agreeing to the terms. In the case of seventeen estates, where the landlords resisted the tenants' demand, evictions took place, with the result that hundreds of thousands of pounds were lost by both landlords and tenants, and also by the state through the employment of military forces and litigations.[1] But the plan was on the whole successful, and the ease with which the tenants gained their abatements proved how seriously the power of the landlords to resist had been impaired by the conflict of the seven preceding years. What we observed of the political aspects of landlord-tenant relations, the Plan of Campaign revealed of the economic aspects: by 1886 landlordism in all of its forms had been all but destroyed in the predominantly Catholic districts.

Unlike the land agitation of 1879–81, that of 1886–90 did not generate new conflict on the boards of guardians. Outside a few unions in the middle

227

or on the periphery of areas where landlords had already been removed from the board offices, such as Kilkenny in 1887, the balance between landlords and tenants in the board offices remained stable after 1886. Looking through *Thom's Directory* in 1890, one finds the same or similar names connected with the same offices as in 1886. In the Ulster chairmanships the ex-officios continued to dominate: John M. Sharpe, J.P., in Ballycastle; William A. Young, J.P., in Ballymena; Sir David Taylor, J.P., in Belfast; Sir J. Calvert Stronge, Bart., in Armagh; the Earl of Castlestuart in Cookstown; and the Duke of Abercorn in Strabane, to name a few. Similarly, in the midland and coastal counties of Leinster, one finds such names as Sir Thomas Butler, Bart. (Carlow), Viscount Powerscourt (Rathdown), Col. Charles G. Tottenham, D.L., J.P. (Rathdrum), the Earl Fitzwilliam (Shillelagh), the Right Hon. Viscount de Vesci (Abbeyleix), the Right Hon. Earl of Rosse (Parsonstown). Interestingly, the Duke of Leinster, who had been chairman of the Celbridge board in Kildare from the time of the board's establishment, was no longer chairman in 1890. He had been replaced by a smaller landowner, probably a Catholic, Robert Kennedy, Esq. Again, in Cork in 1890, the Earl of Bandon continued to retain the chairmanship of the Bandon union as he had in years past, and in Mallow and Kinsale—two other unions that had had ex-officio chairmen in 1886—Harmer D. Spratt, J.P., and William R. Meade, J.P., the same ex-officios, continued to hold sway.

Another sign that the tenant movement had reached its limits is found in a report in the *Leinster Express* of the 1889 poor law elections in the Kildare-Queens region. The report reveals that in those counties the old compromises reached between the ex-officios and elected guardians during the early part of the decade were still in effect, and even where antagonisms existed, as at Mountmellick, the elected guardians had not been able to bring about any change. The only difference was in the labeling of the two parties: the tenant element were still referred to as nationalists, but the landlords were now unionists instead of conservatives.

> The results of the poor law contests [in 1889], which, it is hardly necessary to say, are fought on political grounds, have been satisfactory to the Unionist Party. In none of our local unions has any change taken place calculated to reverse the old order of things. The marked indifference exhibited by Unionists in some unions is notorious. For instance, in the Naas union they do not care about coming forward, but, perhaps, this may be owing to the fact that the business is, so far, in no way mis-managed. In Abbeyleix Union the Unionists have lost two seats, which they had gained last year, but, as

their majority is large, this cannot effect any material change. Two Unionist victories have to be recorded in Mountmellick Union, but even with these, parties will be nearly evenly balanced.[2]

In Mountmellick, where the nationalists had unseated Colonel William D. Carden temporarily in 1882–83, only to lose the chairmanship back to him in 1884, Carden was again elected chairman in 1889.[3] Carden was still chairman in 1898, and he might have continued to be chairman afterward had the Local Government Act of 1898 not abolished the ex-officio membership when it converted the boards of guardians into committees of the newly-created rural and urban district councils.

Unions that had been nationalized continued to be governed by nationalists after 1886, but the character of the membership began to change toward the end of the century as younger men with newer ideas won seats on the boards and began to challenge the old-guard nationalists for their leadership positions. In the Westport union John Louden, the old Land Leaguer, who had returned to the board of guardians after being rejected by the Parnellites in the national movement, took over the board chairmanship when Lord John Browne resigned the office in 1886. Already by that summer his leadership was being challenged by another faction on the board—a group of Parnellites—who charged Louden with being "antinational." The Parnellite group missed unseating Louden by a few votes in 1887; in 1888 they succeeded, and replaced Louden with their own leader, John P. Ward, a Westport shopkeeper. In 1889 Louden's career as a poor law guardian came to an end when he failed to win a seat on the Westport board.[4] In the following decade, after Parnell's fall in 1890, republicanism began to reemerge, as Fenians—disillusioned with Parnell's failure to get results and dissatisfied with the squabbling, ineffectual parliamentary party divided, after Parnell's fall and death, into "Parnellites" and "anti-Parnellites"—began again to demand a more forceful national policy. This was the body of opinion that Arthur Griffith began by the end of the century to form into the new nationalist movement that eventually came to be known as *Sinn Fein* ("ourselves alone"). The new nationalists, a younger breed than the middle-aged nationalists who had first challenged the landlords' right to govern, began finding their way on to the boards and using the same kind of obstructive tactics against the older leaders as they had used in their time against the landlords.

Perhaps the most ironic incident of the kind was one that occurred at the Roscommon board at the end of the century, involving a group of the new nationalists and the board chairman, Thomas A. P. Mapother, the hero of 1872, who had been chairman in each successive year after 1881. The incident was described by Michael J. F. McCarthy in his bitterly anticlerical study of Ireland at the turn of the twentieth century, *Priests and People in Ireland*. The quote is McCarthy's; the date is not given.

> The Roscommon Guardians are assembled in meeting, Mr. T. A. P. Mapother, D.L., in the chair. Mr. McGreavy, a member of Bishop Clancy's flock, exclaims:—I observe the envelopes used this week in sending notices to the guardians had the letters 'O.H.M.S.' [On Her Majesty's Service] printed on the outside, and, seeing that these letters are emblematic of our subjugation to a barbarous race, let it be put down on the minutes that the clerk be ordered to cease ordering any more of these envelopes with any such degrading letters printed or written thereon; and for the future, that envelopes with some national emblem or lettering, such as 'On the People's Service' be substituted.
>
> The Chairman [Mapother] said they could not abolish any ancient practice without notice.
>
> Mr. McGreavy: I know Conservatives do not like to bring this change, but we are Progressives.
>
> The Chairman: If you mean to insinuate that I am a Conservative you are mistaken. I am not.
>
> Mr. McGreavy said he was glad to see the Chairman backing the Republicans. He thought such a practice should be abolished, as it was emblematic of their subjugation.[5]

Such was the pace of political change in Ireland in the last quarter of the nineteenth century that the heroic "descendant of the old Kings of Ireland" in 1872 was nothing more than a "Conservative" by 1900.

Another incident, which occurred in Castlebar in 1907, might have been just as ironic were it not for the fact that the leading character, James Daly, had actually grown increasingly conservative in his later years. Daly, one of the earliest and most devoted advocates of board nationalization, who had urged the expulsion of the landlords from board offices long before it became fashionable for the nationalist press to do so, had been vice-chairman of the Castlebar board from 1881 till 1882, then its chairman from 1892 till 1898, and an elected member of the Castlebar Urban District Council from 1898 till 1908. During the early years he remained a devoted follower of Parnell until the celebrated divorce court scandal and the deposition of Parnell as party leader in late 1890; thereafter, he grew more disillusioned and became an anti-Parnellite and critic of the entire leadership of the Home Rule movement, as he had been of the Land League leadership ten years earlier.[6] By 1907 he was seventy-one years old, almost a pauper as a result of some ill-advised land speculations during the late 1880s, and no longer the publisher of the *Connaught Telegraph*, having lost the paper in 1892 at the time of his financial disasters.[7] In 1908 Daly and a few other old nationalists on the Urban District Council formed a faction which the publisher of the *Telegraph* referred to as the "Conservative Party."[8] They may have founded the party as a counterweight to a wave of radical republicanism that had begun to arise in Castlebar politics and that found a number of advocates on the Castlebar District Council. At a meeting of the council in February 1908, Daly clashed with one of the young republicans over a matter concerning board business. The dispute led to an exchange of harsh words between the two men, and finally the republican pointed his finger at Daly and charged him with being not only an anti-nationalist who "casts abuse on the national leaders," but also, in his younger days, a "bum-bailiff." Daly rose to his feet, shook his walking stick at the offender, and declared, "I was the first man in Ireland in 1879 for proclaiming the policy 'the land for the people and he who tills the soil must own it,' and again in '81. My principles then are my principles today!" Then he threatened to thrash the offender within an inch of his life, and might have done so, had he not been subdued by a number of the other guardians.[9] In this turbulent fashion, power passed out of the hands of the first-generation nationalists to the second generation, just as it had done from the landlords to the tenants in Daly's own day.

The completion of the political cycle brings to an end this narration of the struggle for the poor law boards. It is now time to assess its significance for Irish history and for the interpretation of Irish history. It is fair enough to say that this study has raised more questions than it has answered. The fact that many of the conclusions have been posed as hypotheses rather than conclusive explanations derives in large measure from the extensiveness and diversity of the topics, and the obscurity of most of the participants, which limits the sources of evidence to what can be inferred from newspaper reports, incomplete sets of minute books, and general facts about the landholdings of individual participants. While a great deal of information can be culled from these sources, the difficulty in applying them to a study of 163 groups of men in the hope of deriving valid generalizations about the body as a whole must be discouraging for the most valiant of researchers. Not until much more is known about specific cases will it be possible to make concrete statements about Irish local politics with assurance. Nevertheless, certain facts revealed in the analyses can be interpreted with assurance from the evidence presented here.

The most concrete fact to emerge is the revolution itself. Between 1872 and 1886 (the exact beginning and ending dates might be disputed), about half the boards of guardians in the three southern provinces gradually removed all the landowners occupying offices and replaced them with tenant-occupiers; an additional portion removed only large landowners. This much is fact; now, how does this square with existing interpretations of Irish history? One might say first of all—and with the greatest certainty—that the revolution must force a reinterpretation of our current ideas about the development of local self-government in Ireland. The current view, which has not been challenged in sixty years, is that local self-government in Ireland dates from the Local Government or County Councils Act of 1898. At least this would be true for government in the counties; representative government in the cities and towns, it has been generally recognized, dates back to the municipal corporations acts of 1835 and 1841. For the "traditional" view of local government in rural Ireland we can go back to the 1917 appraisal of Ernest Barker's, that "in 1898 the squirearchy was dethroned, and local self-government through elective county councils which the Local Government Act created took its place. The Irish peasant, as he took over the possession of his holding from his landlords, also took over from the same hands the government of his county and rural district."[10] For the lack of any presentation of evidence to the contrary, this interpretation has stood to the present time.

If, by local self-government, we mean the abolition of the landlord-controlled grand juries and their replacement by county councils, the traditional view would be difficult to refute (although it is possible that a careful study of the grand juries prior to 1898 might also cast doubt on this aspect of the interpretation). However, it would be difficult to sustain an argument that held that the grand juries were synonymous with local government before 1898. By 1890, indeed by 1872, most of the grand juries' powers had slipped away to other agencies: boards of guardians, municipal corporations, town councils, the board of works, harbor boards, and numerous other specialized agencies that were responsible to the Local Government Board, not the grand juries. The administration of almost every new program or service established by Parliament after the Great Famine was given over to those newer agencies. The grand juries' principal concern throughout the last half of the nineteenth century involved local public works projects—road construction and maintenance, bridge repair, and the like, and to a lesser extent the maintenance of lunatic asylums and prisons, registration, the constabulary, and others. However, by 1890 the total revenues collected and disbursed by grand juries were only about one-third of the total local government expenditure. The second third was accounted for by the boards of guardians and the final third by municipal and town government.[11]

Because the municipalities and towns were administered by elective bodies containing no appointed element, one could assume that they would come under the definition of locally self-governing bodies. Therefore local self-government could be said to exist in the urban districts at least a half-century before the County Councils Act created the urban district councils. The boards of guardians did contain an elected element, but the existence of an appointive ex-officio membership might make it disputable whether they should equally be considered as representative bodies. However, if it could be demonstrated—as it has been in this study—that the boards of guardians, or a substantial portion of them, were in fact if not in theory governed by the elected element and that the ex-officios had little or no voice in their proceedings, then clearly that portion deserve to be counted among the truly representative bodies. Because of the gradations of tenant control that were exhibited on the boards after 1886, and the fact that many of the boards with landowning officers were in fact controlled by tenants, it would be difficult to assign a numerical proportion that would accurately indicate the extent of tenant control in Ireland. But if one made a conservative estimate—say, one-half of the boards in the four provinces controlled de facto by the tenantry—then it is clear that by 1898 half the poor law administration and all the municipal administration was governed locally by the tenantry. The abolition of the grand juries, therefore, simply completed a process that had been going on for some time and which, in the poor law administration, had begun to occur without any change in the law.

From a historical standpoint, the development of local self-government in Ireland must be viewed as the product of a combination of forces and events of which the Irish County Councils Act was only one. Even more significant than the County Councils Act for its political implications was the Poor Relief Act of 1838, which introduced the Irish countryman to representative local government for the first time and established the conditions whereby the Irish farmer could become involved in state politics either as a poor law guardian or as a voter. Without the boards of guardians there would have been few, if any, outlets for farmers to express themselves politically within the established governmental framework. Their participation would have been restricted to the occasional visit to the polls for a parliamentary election, or to providing some other kinds of support for their party's candidates either as individual campaigners or as members of an extraparliamentary political association like the Home Rule Association or the National League. What the boards of guardians provided was the opportunity for regular and continual exposure to the political process *within* the political system. Although it would be difficult to measure the overall impact that sixty years of such exposure might have had on the political habits and attitudes of the Irish people, it would not be too presumptuous to say that the educational experience itself helped to prepare the people—at least those above the poorest classes—for their eventual assumption of power in the new county government. When, therefore, the County Councils Act was enacted, the Irish people were already fully aware of the administrative and political processes of local government, and their awareness must be attributed in great measure to their experience in the poor law administration.

One of the questions with which historians have had to deal in Irish history is why the Irish people, after centuries of British rule in which violence and rebellion against the authority of the state was a common fact—why, when they had the opportunity to create their own government in the Free State, did they choose a parliamentary and democratic form of government that did not degenerate into a dictatorship? Without attempting to go into the entire question, which would require a book in its own right, we might address ourselves to one explanation based on events within the period of this study—the argument that constitutionalism in Ireland may have been a product of the Parnellite experience. Conor Cruise O'Brien, for example, acknowledges that Parnell himself, while a parliamentarian, was more inclined—in his style of leadership and in the principles on which his leadership was based—more toward dictatorship than democracy. For O'Brien, the decisive influence was the Irish Parliamentary party. Thus: "For the adherence of Ireland to parliamentary democracy, we have to thank not the principles of Parnell, but the example and conduct of the party which he formed. . . . They were upright and consistent, faithful to their pledges, disciplined in action, and courageous in defence of the principles on which they were elected. They served Ireland well, and might have served her better if they had not—mainly through [Parnell's] own fault—lost their leader."[12]

No doubt the example of the party helped to influence the Irish people's attitudes favorably toward representative government—although one would be hard-pressed to find ways of establishing a cause-and-effect relationship. But can we be certain that the party's influence—which declined after Parnell's fall—was durable, or more durable than other past experiences such as O'Connell's Repeal party or "Grattan's Parliament," or that the example of Parnell himself did not far outweigh the example of his party? The significance of Parnell for the future of Irish politics resided more in the myth than in the man himself or the principles for which he stood. The myth was not of a man bravely maintaining his constitutional stand against rebellious forces in Ireland, but rather, as J. C. Beckett has put it, of the " 'lost leader' who had turned his back on British party politics, and had tried in vain to rescue the nation from the fatal entanglement of the liberal alliance." Beckett adds, "The Parnellite movement, which was far more widespread than its meagre representation in parliament would suggest, bred a suspicion of clerical influence, a contempt for majority opinion, a distaste for political manoeuvre, that helped to create an atmosphere congenial to the growth of a more radical nationalism than the Home Rulers ever dreamt of."[13] Who was more influential, the man or the party? It is a question that will probably never be answered.

If we move, however, on to more concrete ground—the ground of practical experience—we can try to imagine the effect on constitutional and democratic attitudes that might have resulted from sixty years of experience with representative government in the poor law administration—experience that was not limited to a handful of Irish M.P.'s but that included more than 3,000 representatives sitting in continual session. One hardly meets an Irishperson today who is not able to mention at least one ancestor who sat on a board of guardians. The business discussed by the boards was trivial compared to the momentous matters taken up by Parliament, but once the boards became politicized the stakes were as high for the localities as the parliamentary stakes were for the country as a whole. Thus the boards were, as contemporary conservatives liked to refer to them pejoratively, "small parliaments," in which local politicians practiced their skills of debate and political maneuver and learned a respect for the uses of political power, while the tenant electorate learned to express their hostilities on the ballot, rather than in the streets. In attempting to estimate the practical importance of the boards for the development of constitutional attitudes, one need only consider that according to the biographies in *Dod's Parliamentary Companion*, at least seven of the Parnellites who were in the party after 1885 had come up through the ranks of the boards of guardians.[14] This figure does not include others, like T. P. O'Connor, who had been a member of the Tipperary board but who chose not to mention it in *Dod's*, or still others, like Timothy and Edward Harrington, who, though never guardians, gained early political experience in the local government struggle. Thus in the boards of guardians the Irish people found a practical and attainable school in which to develop the virtues necessary for a successful parliamentary democracy.

An additional fact to emerge from the analysis is that most of the leaders of the tenant movement, indeed, most of the poor law guardians, were large farmers. This was in spite of a poor law franchise and a set of property qualifications that would have enabled middling and even small farmers to hold elected seats. When this fact is combined with the findings of Arensberg and Kimball—that Irish rural society in the early twentieth century was made up of a small farmer class and a large farmer, or cattle grazier, class, each having a separate value system and each operating under different social and economic conditions—and when it is placed against the background of a post-Famine economic boom that involved the conversion of much of the land in Ireland from arable to pasture, it is possible to deduce the existence during the last half of the nineteenth century of a rising class of cattle graziers who formed a rural social, economic, and political elite. Contemporaries recognized a distinction between small and large farmers, often using the term "hundred-acre farmer" to describe the latter, but historians have not attempted to explore the implications of the distinction for political developments of the period. In Chapter 2 we saw evidence of a deep involvement of cattle graziers not only in the poor law administration but also in the political clubs of the pre-Land League period. These impressions are supported by Clark's investigations of these clubs. It is clear that many of the large farmers who led the attack on the ex-officios from within the boards of guardians were also leaders of the political organizations outside.

If indeed the large farmers composed a rural elite, then it may be necessary to reexamine the movements of the eighties keeping in mind the possibility that these movements might have reflected the interests and aspirations of the large farmers more than those of the tenantry as a whole, which is the current approach. One contemporary author who investigated the Plan of Campaign, T. W. Russell, for example, claimed that after interviewing tenants on a number of Plan of Campaign estates, he came away with the distinct impression that the plan insisted "on well-to-do men getting absurd reductions [in rent] that operate against a settlement suitable to the poorer tenants." All tenants agreed, under threat of reprisal (or so Russell believed), that none should settle until all agreed to settle. Thus, though some smaller farmers were offered good terms by their landlords, they were unable to accept the terms and were ultimately evicted from their holdings. In one typical case a tenant was willing to pay his landlord, Colonel Vandeleur, £20, which was less than 25 percent of the arrears on his holding, and although Vandeleur offered to settle for even less, £19 9*s*, the farmer refused because "he had been warned to stop the parley."[15] It would be interesting, indeed, to know what happened to the evicted farmer's holding after he vacated it. Did it pass over to another small farmer, or was it converted to pasture for the use of some expanding cattle grazier? And what of the holdings of the thousands of small farmers who were evicted during the Land League agitation? These questions open up the possibility of a divergence of interest—perhaps even class exploitation—within the tenant class. This pessimistic view need not be the only way of interpreting the events; it is only one of many possibilities that could arise from a reinvestigation of the period along the lines suggested.

We have used the existence of an agrarian elite to explain a further fact to come to light in the analysis—the variations of political radicalism within the three southern provinces. It is common knowledge among students of Irish history that extremism was most prevalent in Munster and along the western coast, and indeed Clark's discovery that most of the Land League arrests occurred in these areas simply adds statistical proof to an already well-known fact. But apart from this general knowledge, little is known about differences of attitude or gradations of extremism from one locality to the next. Such knowledge is important to have if for no other reason than to identify the social classes who were most active in the political agitation, but it can have other uses as well. It could be that social class and religion were not, as the analysis in Chapter 6 suggested, the only factors that determined local political complexion. Political tradition undoubtedly played a large part in some areas, such as in Munster and south Leinster, where nonpolitical agitation dated back over generations and resistance to governmental authority had become, by 1880, a matter of habit. So also might political tradition account for the conservatism of the Pale counties along the east central coast, where old, established Catholic families who had been accustomed to dealing with the Ascendancy for generations dominated the popular political movements. Their nationalism was no less fervent, but their political style might have been modified and their attitudes toward Protestants and landowners softened by the experience.

The influence of the Roman Catholic Church is another factor to be taken into account. It is probably not coincidental that the largest region of radicalism on the boards of guardians was the area of Munster that fell within the archdiocese of Cashel, governed by T. W. Croke, the "Land League archbishop." Croke, an unswerving nationalist and advocate of land reform, exerted a powerful influence on national politics and played a major part in helping, as William O'Brien put it, "to broaden the [land] issue from one that affected the famine-stricken to one that enlisted the interest of every man in the nation, and to rouse the major portion of the Bishops and priests into an ardent participation in the infant agitation, which they had at the outset regarded with suspicion and dislike."[16] It would be difficult to believe that Croke's indelible influence on national politics was not also felt in local politics either through direct instructions to his flock or by the example he set for them and for his priests. I have uncovered no evidence of Croke's involvement in the board nationalization movement, but I have found many examples of priests' participating in nominations and campaigns through league branches. The exact role of the clergy in the local movements has never been clearly defined, but they were certainly a factor to be taken into account, and the preferences of the bishops and priests in different regions might help to explain some of the patterns that were revealed in the political maps in Chapter 6. Some detailed studies of politics in particular localities would help to provide some of the answers, and the political maps produced in this study could serve as a starting point.

What, finally, can be said of the significance of the board nationalization movement for its own time? Did it contribute in any way toward molding the character of the period or should it be regarded simply as a consequence of external events that would have occurred regardless of the existence of any boards of guardians? It is possible to cite a number of positive contributions of the movement toward the political agitation in general. There was, first of all, the financial contribution, which helped to promote and maintain the land agitation. The fact that landlords paid about five-eighths and the tenants only three-eighths of the poor rates meant that for every pound expended to relieve an evicted tenant or the family of a suspect, about twelve-and-a-half shillings was paid by the landlord. The nationalist guardians took advantage of this imbalance in the rating system by granting maximum payments, in the form of outdoor relief, to tenants who had been victimized as a result of their participation in the land agitation. Thus the guardians not only encouraged tenants to keep up their resistance, but they forced the landlords to pay most of the bill for it. And, as Robert Staples pointed out, had the guardians not provided this relief, the payments would have had to come out of the Land League's and National

League's evicted tenants' funds. Therefore, to the extent that the rates were used for political purposes, they represented a cash contribution to the national movement.

A second contribution was in the publicity gained by the national movement from the poor law campaigns, board resolutions, and boards' proceedings. Poor law activities were covered extensively in both the nationalist and conservative press. Usually the reports went beyond the events themselves and drew conclusions about their significance for the broader political issues. Each nationalist victory at the poor law polls was viewed as a victory for the tenantry against landlordism and colonialism (or, for the conservatives, a victory of "demagoguery" over "good government"). The passing of a political resolution was viewed as a conquest for free speech or self-government, or as a show of support for "Mr. Parnell, the leader of the Irish people." The contests over the offices were seen as but another phase in the continuing struggle for national and land rights. For the reading public these events must have possessed an immediate and tangible quality that even the events in Parliament did not have; the participants were their own sons and neighbors, the vanquished ex-officios their own landlords and rent collectors. While there were always other political events to capture public attention and keep up interest in the struggle, the continual publicization of the issues at the annual elections and weekly meetings of the guardians must have had some impact on opinion in the localities. Such, at any rate, was the belief of William O'Brien, who thought that every boardroom in the country could be the focus of public opinion, and who rarely missed any opportunity in *United Ireland* to use an event at a board of guardians' meeting to teach his readers a lesson in patriotism and independence. And on the other side of the coin, the landowners and conservatives were no doubt spurred on to even greater heights of opposition by the indignities suffered by the ex-officios at the hands of bold and arrogant nationalists. The boards were, after all, the local arena in which the great conflicts of the day were fought.

It is possible too that the board nationalization movement helped to lend continuity to the Home Rule movement by providing the local league branches with a positive political function during periods when the national movement was inactive. From 1882 to 1885 there would have been little to occupy the branches were it not for the poor law elections. The need to organize nominating conventions, hold caucuses, and conduct campaigns in the localities helped not only to prepare the branch members for their role in the general election of 1885, but also to provide them with an identity and a raison d'être separate from that assigned to them, in vague terms, by the National League. What was the function of the local branch in the Home Rule movement? In theory its function was supportive: to raise revenues, to organize opinion behind the national movement, to supply delegates for the party's nominating conventions. Yet Parnell distrusted the branches. He never established the executive council that was to be elected by the branch members and that was to determine policies for the entire movement; he gave them almost no voice in nominating national candidates, though the league's charter stated that the candidates were to be chosen by delegates of the local branches. And he assigned the conduct of parliamentary electoral campaigns to special hand-picked committees, rather than to the branches. For Parnell, who needed to strike a balance between the need, on the one hand, for public support and on the other, for tight control over the organization, the appearance of democracy was more important than its substance. It was therefore in local government that the branches found an outlet for their energies and a means of contributing directly to the political agitation. The benefits derived by the national movement from this situation are inestimable but they must have been substantial.

But perhaps to emphasize connections between the national and local movements is to obscure one of the important points that I have tried to make in this study, namely, that the board nationalization movement was really a separate, self-sustaining movement carried on by local politicians who were moved by forces that transcended the powerful influences of Parnell and Davitt and the movements they led. It was rooted in the social structure of Ireland—a structure that had been made obsolescent by the changing economic and social conditions of post-Famine Ireland. The process began with the clearing away of the marginal farmers and the reconstruction of the Irish economy around a thriving export cattle trade. It then accelerated with the construction of the railways, the rise of important market centers, and the improvement of communications—including a rising literacy rate—which produced an independent and aspiring class of farmers and townsmen. This process, which social scientists often call "modernization," ultimately took its toll on the old social system which placed a higher value on birthright than attained status.

In the new Ireland there was less room in government for the landed aristocrat or country gentleman who laid claim to a seat of power on the sole justification that his father held it, or that that was the way it had always been. Neither was there validity to the old argument that the

owners of the soil—by the simple virtue of the fact that their land ownership gave them the greatest stake in the community—would naturally
be the best administrators. These notions, on which the original poor law
had been founded, had already, by 1872, been undermined by the boards
of guardians because of the existence of a class of educated, attentive, and
business-like administrators—successful farmers and shopkeepers who believed they had earned the right to exercise power but who were denied
that right by the existing value system. These were the same men who
argued outside the boards that "he who tills the soil must own it," and
they soon began to apply the same principle to their dealings with landlords
in local government. The resulting revolution became caught up in the
nationalist and land reform movements, so that within a few years it was
impossible to identify the motives of the participants. The right to exercise
power was certainly one of the stakes in the struggle, as was the right to
own land. But underlying these was the third issue, never openly voiced
but nonetheless as compelling as the other two: that every man should
have the right to receive honors commensurate with his station in life. It
was human dignity, perhaps more than any other social issue, over which
the battle between the aristocrats and the farmers was fought.

❦❦ Methodological Appendix

THERE ARE no doubt others who, like me, have come to the study of Irish society and politics, well intentioned and with a methodological plan already designed, only to discover that the hoped-for sources of information were simply nonexistent. This is certainly true of Irish local studies in the last half of the nineteenth century, for the historian soon discovers that the census manuscripts of 1860–1900, which contained a great deal of vital information about the religions, occupations, family sizes, and landholdings of the great mass of the population, were casually destroyed by some unthinking and insensitive bureaucrats at the beginning of the twentieth century. Invaluable local government documents—not just a few but all of them prior to 1916—were likewise destroyed in the Custom House fire of 1921 by partisans hoping to immobilize the British administration in Ireland. Gone also are the poor law election poll books with their record of names and votes—invaluable guides to the extent of politicization at different times—which might have been made to yield information not only about partisan support in the localities but also about voter apathy and participation. The destruction of the poor law rate books, which contained an exact record of the address, valuation, acreage, and rent of each owner and occupier of land—the only such record in Ireland—was the result not of the act of any single group of men, but of the careless record-keeping of all local government officials from the rent-collectors and guardians to the Local Government Board. The haphazard treatment of these books caused one historian in 1908 to observe distressfully to his colleagues: "In at least some of the Irish unions, the rate-books are not forthcoming. . . . In one case with which I am acquainted, the discovery was made that they were sold as waste paper with a whole mass of possibly useless union rubbish."[1]

242

The wide gaps that currently exist in our knowledge of nineteenth-century Irish society and local politics may be attributed not to researchers' lack of interest in the subject, but rather to the paucity of documentation which makes the application of quantitative methods extremely difficult, if not, in many cases, impossible. Yet the situation is not entirely hopeless. Documents do exist through which essential data about individuals can be acquired directly or indirectly. Some of the sources employed in this study might prove useful to other researchers embarking on similar studies. In most cases, some shred of knowledge is needed about the individual in question other than his name—an address, a townland, an occupation. From these bits of information other information can be gained through the skillful use of the sources in combination to create a profile of the individual which, though not precise, would fall within acceptable limits of probability. In this study, for example, I have made extensive use of five general sources: (1) *Thom's Irish Almanac and Official Directory* (published annually after 1830); (2) the 1876 parliamentary paper known as the Domesday Book, formally entitled "Return of Owners of Land, of One Acre and Upwards in the Several Counties, Counties of Cities, and Counties of Towns in Ireland"; (3) the valuation manuscripts in the General Valuation Office in Dublin (the records for the six counties that Northern Ireland comprises are in the Public Record Office in Belfast); (4) newspapers; and (5) a number of periodically issued commercial directories.

The names of the boards of guardians' officers were obtained from *Thom's Directory*. The annual issues of the directory contain an abundance of information about Ireland and the United Kingdom—economic and fiscal statistics, population statistics, names of directors of the civil service and the magistracy, the members of the bar, the churches, the military, and the Irish administration at all levels, and numerous other listings including, at the end, a Dublin-and-suburbs trade directory of every place of business in Dublin and environs, with its owner and address. Also included are lists of the nobility and gentry of Ireland, and of the 500 largest landowners with their acreage and valuations. A section entitled the "County Directory" lists, by county, population, and land statistics, the names of all appointed county officials, magistrates presiding in the county, minor local government officials, and the principal officials in each poor law union in the county. The boards of guardians' officers are found in the latter sections, which, unfortunately, do not list the nonofficeholding guardians. *Thom's Directory*, therefore, is an invaluable guide to people in government, in the professions, and in high society. But its usefulness for social history is limited. Its directories do not cover trades and professions outside Dublin, nor do they include occupiers and smaller landowners, or elected officials of local government.

For occupational data on persons in the provinces, the most useful sources are the commercial directories, of which there are several for this period in the National Library of Ireland. The most generally useful is *Slater's Royal National Commercial Directory of Ireland*, which was published in three editions in 1870, 1881, and 1894. The directory covers all of Ireland, listing—within sections arranged first by county, then within the county by town or village—the various trades and professions carried on in the towns and the names and addresses of the tradesmen and professionals. It also lists county and union officials, but, like *Thom's Directory*, omits guardians who were not officeholders. The advantage of *Slater's* over other directories is that it covers almost every town in Ireland; its disadvantage is that it sacrifices in depth what it gains in scope: traders in small villages are either not listed or included with those of nearby towns, making it difficult for the researcher to identify them, and farmers are almost omitted altogether. These defects are not as evident in the more localized directories, which confine their listings to counties or specific regions. By far the best of these is *Guy's Directory of Munster* (1886),[2] a voluminous collection of resident gentry, business men, and farmers in every community in Munster. Townsmen are listed by their address, farmers by townland, making it easy to identify the occupations of persons for whom addresses or townlands are known. Persons wishing to study local politics in the south Leinster area during the Parnellite period will find invaluable aids in the *Kilkenny City and County Guide and Directory* (1884)[3] and the *Nationalist and Leinster Times District Directory* (Carlow: 1888).[4] The former gives, in addition to the usual commercial information, the names of all members of boards of guardians and town councils in County Kilkenny in 1883; the latter gives the same information for Kildare, Queens, and Carlow for 1887, and also includes lists of the members of National League branches in those counties. The existence in one directory of both the occupations and the political affiliations of the people in an entire locality is naturally priceless to the historian. Other local directories are listed in the Bibliography.

Additional information about individuals can be culled from the local newspapers. This would include not only direct references to individuals that might have appeared in the reports of events and organization meetings, but also information revealed in advertisements. If, for example, it were ascertained through a commercial directory that a particular poor law guardian or National Leaguer was a "grocer," that information in itself might be significant. But if the researcher wished to know more about the individual, such as how large a grocer he was or whether he carried on other business activities outside his principal occupation, this information might be revealed in newspaper advertisements. To name just one example, Robert McCowan, who contested a board of guardians' seat for Tralee in the election of 1881 (see Chapter 4), was listed in *Slater's* (1881) as a grocer and Lloyds agent. But an advertisement for Robert McCowan & Co. in the *Kerry Sentinel* revealed that he was also a land agent, shipping agent, seed merchant, and hardware merchant; the size of the advertisement, which covered a half-page in the *Sentinel*, suggested that he was an eminently successful businessman. It thus became obvious that he was much more than just a grocer and Lloyds agent: he was probably the owner of Tralee's version of today's department store. The newspapers, therefore, can be an excellent source of supplemental data. Their main deficiency, of course, is that the evidence is haphazard, and—because advertisements were relatively costly—biased toward the more prosperous businessmen.

By far the most useful sources employed in this study were the Domesday Book and the valuation records. The Domesday Book, published in 1876, has long been recognized and exploited by historians as the authoritative source of information about the holdings of landowners during the 1860s, '70s, and '80s. The book lists both the total acreage and total valuation of the land held in fee by owners of more than one acre of land, and gives the name and principal address of each owner, first for all holdings in Ireland, then for those within the various counties. Thus the researcher who has only the name and approximate address (say, the poor law union or county) of an individual can ascertain three facts about him: (1) whether he was a landowner; (2) if he is a landowner, his address; and (3) the size and relative value of his landholdings. If the individual does not appear in the Domesday Book, it may be deduced that he was a tenant-occupier or renter, in which case the valuation records come into play.

The valuation records, which have been utilized to great advantage by genealogists and legal researchers, have been—it would not be an exaggeration to say—virtually untapped as a source of social history. Much of this neglect, I am sure, derives from the difficulty of handling and understanding the documents. The original valuation by Richard Griffith was performed at the end of the 1850s, and no general re-evaluation was performed until the founding of the Free State. The original entries gave the lot numbers, in order, within each townland, and next to each lot number the name of the occupier or occupiers (if the lot was divided or held in common), the immediate lessor (not the holder in fee), the acreage, and the valuation. The valuations were broken down into a portion representing buildings and a portion representing land. The townlands were then grouped into electoral divisions, which were bound in separate volumes, and the volumes were collected, alphabetically, into poor law unions and filed together with other unions in the same county. Subsequently, whenever a particular holding changed hands or was revalued, the correction was recorded by crossing out the old name or amount in colored ink, and entering above that the new name or amount in the same color ink. A different color was used for each year, so that an entry made in a particular color indicated the year in which the transaction occurred.

Needless to say, the union clerks, who kept the books, soon found that they had not enough space to enter all the changes that occurred over time, so they established the practice of periodically (about every two to five years) recopying the current information on new sheets and starting afresh with their crossings-out and re-entries. These new ledgers were stacked up on the older ledgers, and when the volumes became too cumbersome (after seven, ten, or twenty years, depending on the size of the electoral division and the number of transactions), a new volume was begun. What the researcher finds when entering the General Valuation Office, therefore, is an enormous number of books, grouped by county, then by poor law union, and then by electoral division. The electoral division books contain sets of ledgers of townlands, arranged chronologically with inclusive dates often poorly marked. In these ledgers are listings of names of individuals, with no other identifying marks, and the acres and valuations of the properties they leased out or occupied. If the same name appears next to two lots, whether adjacent or separate, there is no way of knowing whether the occupiers were the same person or different men with the same name. It would appear that such an arrangement would be of little value to the social historian, whose conclusions are only as valid as the accuracy of his information. Yet these few facts divulged in the valuation records can be made to yield a good deal of data, not only about the landholdings but also about the occupations of the tenants in question.

I used the valuation records as follows. If an officer of a board of guardians did not appear in the Domesday Book, his address was ascertained through *Thom's Directory* and he was located in the appropriate electoral division in the valuation records. If he appeared in the valuation records as an occupier but not a lessor, his status as a tenant was considered confirmed. If he was listed in one of the commercial directories as occupying a shop or an office at the same address, the occupation stated in the directory was taken as his occupation. But if he did not appear in the directory, and if the valuation records showed that the bulk of the valuation of his holdings was on the building rather than on the land he occupied, he was classified as a shopkeeper. Conversely, if the bulk of the valuation was on the land and only a small portion on the building, he was classified as a farmer. As inexact as this method might appear, there were very few cases in which an identification of either shopkeeper or farmer was difficult to make. Because the valuations were based on the annual income that a holding might be expected to bring, a high valuation on a building and a low valuation on the land around a building must certainly suggest that the principal income from the holding was derived from the building rather than the land. Conversely, a higher valuation on the land suggests that the land was the producer of the income rather than the building. In my experience there were very few cases in which the valuation was evenly divided; in most cases it was either 90 percent on the land or 90 percent on the building.

In most of the analyses in this study, the landholdings that appeared in the valuation records at the address given as the tenant's residence were treated as though they were the tenant's entire holdings. This may not have been the case for many of the farmers in the samples, because large farmers, particularly cattle graziers, often occupied farms in different locations in their communities. For this reason I was careful to state that the valuations and acres shown for the farmers represented not a total but a minimum valuation and acreage. This distinction did not detract from the value of the findings but on the contrary enhanced their credibility, since the argument being made—that the guardians were large farmers—can only become more convincing with the knowledge that the valuations may not have represented the full extent of their holdings.

In one analysis—that of the farmers on the Castlebar and Westport boards in 1877 (see Chapter 2)—I stated that the given valuations were not minimums but were the total extent of the farmers' holdings in the entire union. An explanation for that assertion is in order, given the statement just made that there is no way of knowing whether the same name appearing next to two or more holdings meant that one and the same man occupied the holdings. I will qualify that: there would be no way of knowing whether two tracts of land bearing the same name were occupied by the same man if there were no clues with which to link the two names together. But if it could be shown with reasonable certainty that the names shown in the valuation records belonged to the same person, it could be safely assumed that that person was the occupier of both tracts. Fortunately, it is possible to establish such a connection within the valuation records themselves, independent of outside sources. If it is found that the two or more holdings that had the same name were later vacated on the same date, and that the holdings were passed on to the same person, a simple deduction would lead one to conclude that the occupier was one person, that he had either died or liquidated his holdings, and that the holdings had gone over to a common receivership. It is highly improbable that two men with the same name would have died in the same year and left their holdings to the same heir. This at any rate was the assumption on which I based my Castlebar and Westport research.

❧❧ Notes

Prologue

1. Most of the material for this Prologue was pieced together from articles and editorials published in the *Roscommon Journal* between April 6 and June 8, 1872. The board meeting of May 18 was reported at length in the issue of May 25. Statements made here about the attendance of particular board members or groups are based on a ten-week sample of board meetings reported in the *Journal* between March 4 and May 11, 1872. During that period, the average attendance at meetings of the board was 8.3 guardians per meeting, of which 1.8 was accounted for by ex-officios and 6.5 by elected guardians.

2. Edward Henry Churchill (Crofton), Baron of Mote; Gentleman of the Bedchamber to the Lord Lieutenant of Ireland, 1867–68; Representative Peer (Conservative), February 1873.

3. *Roscommon Journal*, May 4, 1872.

4. Ibid., May 25, 1872.

5. Ibid., June 8, 1872.

6. Ibid., May 25, 1872.

7. Ibid., April 6, 1872.

8. C. Raleigh Chichester, letter to the editor, *Roscommon Journal*, May 25, 1872. The letter to the *Roscommon Messenger* is referred to in this letter.

9. *Roscommon Journal*, May 25, 1872.

10. Ibid.

11. Ibid.

12. *Roscommon Messenger*, June 1, 1872.

13. *Roscommon Journal*, June 8, 1872.

14. Ibid., November 1, 1873.

15. Ibid., June 1, 1872.

16. Ibid.

17. Ibid.

Chapter 1

1. Michael Davitt, *The Fall of Feudalism in Ireland* (London: Harper & Bros., 1904), p. 120.

2. The great difficulties experienced by the boards of guardians during the Great Famine are given forceful treatment in C. Woodham-Smith's *The Great Hunger* (New York: Harper & Row, 1962), with the use of workhouse records and guardians' minute books uncovered by Woodham-Smith in the Castlebar union in County Mayo. Another study that

deals briefly with the guardians' administrative role is T. P. O'Neill's essay, "The Organization and Administration of Relief," in *The Great Famine*, ed. R. D. Edwards and T. D. Williams (Dublin: Browne & Nolan, 1956).

3. Richard O'Shaughnessy, "Local Government and Taxation in Ireland," in *Local Government and Taxation in the United Kingdom*, ed. J. W. Probyn (London: Cassell Potter, Galpin & Co., 1882), pp. 328–331. See also William F. Bailey, *Local and Centralised Government in Ireland* (London: Cassell & Co., 1888), p. 30.

4. Thomas W. Grimshaw, "A Statistical Survey of Ireland, 1840–1880," *Journal of the Statistical and Social Inquiry Society of Ireland* 68 (November 1888), Summaries of Statistics, parts 5 and 6.

5. Bailey, *Local and Centralised Government*, pp. 14–18, supplies a useful synopsis of the compositional procedures governing the county authorities.

6. O'Shaughnessy, "Local Government," p. 323.

7. George Nicholls, *A History of the Irish Poor Law* (London: John Murray, 1856), p. 178.

8. O'Shaughnessy, "Local Government," p. 326.

9. The names of unions, counties where located, and numbers of electoral divisions are given in *Unions and those electoral divisions in Ireland which extend into two or more counties* H.C. 1872 (705), 60:827. The paper also contains a useful map of unions and workhouse locations.

10. No precise proportion was ever calculated, but five-eighths was generally acknowledged by the government and others to be the landlords' share. See, for example, Robert Staples, "Local Government in Ireland," *Fortnightly Review* (July 1886): 108; also speech by B. M. Bagot at the meeting of the Roscommon board of guardians, *Roscommon Journal*, June 8, 1872.

11. The county cess was a tax levied by the grand jury of a county on the occupiers of land in the various baronies composing the county.

12. O'Shaughnessy, "Local Government," p. 328.

13. Nicholls, *Irish Poor Law*, p. 207.

14. Bailey, *Local and Centralised Government*, pp. 29–30.

15. Nicholls, *Irish Poor Law*, p. 207.

16. Ibid.

17. Ibid., p. 267.

18. For the numbers of ex-officio and elected guardians on each board during the period covered by this study, see Table 2.

19. Nicholls, *Irish Poor Law*, p. 208.

20. Lord Clements, *The Present Poverty of Ireland* (London: Charles Knight & Co., 1838), p. 136.

21. After 1843 (6 & 7 Vic. C. 92) ex-officio guardians could be elected if a vacancy occurred during the year as a result of death or removal.

22. Nicholls, *Irish Poor Law*, pp. 173–174, 208.

23. Ibid., pp. 290, 291.

24. Ibid., p. 208.

25. These percentages were calculated by comparing the names of office-holders in 1867 and 1877. The percentages do not reflect multiple changes which may have occurred in particular offices during the intervening years. Thus if the name of an officer on a board was different from the name associated with that office during the earlier year, this was counted as one change, even though the office may have changed hands several times in the interim. Therefore the percentages reflect a *minimum* turnover rate probably considerably below the actual rate.

26. *Thom's Irish Almanac and Official Directory* (Dublin: Alexander Thom, 1844). This annual publication provides a wealth of official and statistical information including names of public officials and of persons licensed to practice in the professions, and annual statistics of all kinds relating to both Britain and Ireland but emphasizing Ireland. It is an indispensable research tool and often, as in the case of boards of guardians' officers, the only extant source for information about obscure persons in public service in Irish local government.

27. Parliament. *Parliamentary Papers*, 1876, vol. 80, "Return of the Owners of Land, of One Acre and Upwards in the Several Counties, Counties of Cities, and Counties of Towns in Ireland," pp. 61ff.

28. Ireland, General Valuation Office, *Valuation Records* (hereafter *V.R.*). A guide to the use of these records is provided in the Methodological Appendix.

29. Further justification of this classification, citing internally developed evidence, is offered in the Methodological Appendix.

30. The ratio of mean valuation to mean acreage was in 1881 £53 (valuation) to fifty-nine acres in Meath, £8 (valuation) to thirty (acres) in Mayo, or a difference of about 350 percent.

31. Hodson's valuation was £1,186; Emly's was £2,169.

32. Finlay Dun, *Landlords and Tenants in Ireland* (London: Longmans & Co., 1881), p. 231. Dun toured Ireland in 1880 as a reporter for the *Times* and recorded his impressions of a large number of landowners based on interviews with owners and their tenants.

33. Clements, *Poverty of Ireland*, p. 136.

34. Parliament, *Parliamentary Papers*, 1878, vol. 17 (*Reports*), "Report on System under which Guardians and members of local boards in England and Ireland . . . are elected . . . with Proceedings, Evidence, Appendix and Index," p. 263.

35. Ibid., p. 559.

36. Ibid., p. 501.

37. The six unions were Ballina, Castlebar, Claremorris, Killala, Swinford, and Westport. The sample was compiled from the first ten meetings of the boards following the annual poor law elections in 1877, as reported in their minute books. In three cases (Killala, Westport, and Swinford) the minute books covering that ten-week period have not survived, so the sample was taken from the ten meetings nearest in time for which minute books exist. The books and periods used for the various unions were the boards of guardians minute books (*National Library*) Ms. 12369 (Ballina), March 31–June 9, 1877; Ms. 12407 (Castlebar), April 7–June 9, 1877; Ms. 12501 (Claremorris), March 28–June 20, 1877; Ms. 12565 (Killala), March 28–July 18, 1874; Ms. 12582 (Swinford), September 17–November 19, 1878; Ms. 12613 (Westport), January 6–March 9, 1876.

38. *Leinster Express*, March 28–June 13, 1877.

39. *Limerick Reporter*, April 6–June 15, 1877.

40. Parliament. *Parliamentary Papers*, 1884, vol. 68 (*Accounts and Papers*) "Return of the number of attendances of poor law guardians at the board meetings of each poor law union in Ireland, in the year ended 25th March 1884," pp. 55–59.

41. The ratio of elected guardians to ex-officios at meetings at which an election formed a part of the boards' business was on average 4.5 (elected) to 2.0 (ex-officio). The ratio at other meetings (at which no election took place) was about 4.0 (elected) to 1.0 (ex-officio).

42. A Guardian of the Poor, *The Irish Peasant: A Sociological Study* (London: Swan Sonnenschein & Co., 1892), pp. 89–90.

43. *Nation*, November 13, 1869.

44. Parliament, "Report on System under which Guardians . . . are elected," p. 559.

45. Minute books, mss. 12407–12408 (Castlebar), April 5–November 29, 1877.

46. Dun, *Landlords and Tenants*, p. 231.

47. Minute books, mss. 12613–12614 (Westport), January 6–July 10, 1876.

48. Nicholls, *Irish Poor Law*, p. 208.

49. The use of this tactic is extremely difficult to document, but one of the witnesses who came before the select committee in 1878 cited the South Dublin union as one in which it was utilized extensively: "It was quite common for the landlord who assigned his proxy not to know for whom the proxy was cast. It was even common for him not to know the person to whom the proxy was assigned. An agent for the one party or the other would come up to a landlord and say 'I am come from the Conservative or Liberal Party' as the case may be, and the gentleman would generally give over the proxy unquestioned. . . . In the South Dublin union in 1876 one proxy holder held 48 proxies, and in 1877 another held 88.

Throughout the South Dublin Union the largest proxy holders in each division could cast a total of 209 votes." Parliament, "Report on System under which Guardians . . . are elected," pp. 583, 623.

50. Ibid., p. 209.

51. Parliament, *Parliamentary Papers*, 1884–85, vol. 10 (*Reports*), "Report of the Select Committee of the House of Lords on Poor Law Guardians (Ireland) Bill, with Proceedings, Evidence, and Index," p. 306.

52. Ibid., (Richard Bourke), p. 333.

53. Dun, *Landlords and Tenants*, p. 231.

54. Parliament, "Report on System under which Guardians . . . are elected," p. 270.

55. *Hansard Parliamentary Debates*, 3d series, vol. 239 (1878), p. 68.

56. Ibid., pp. 68–69.

57. Ibid., pp. 87–88.

58. See, for example, the testimony of John Mulligan, Parliament, "Report on System under which Guardians . . . are elected," p. 582; also speech by E. Dwyer Gray, *Hansard*, p. 68.

59. Peter Walsh, a magistrate and ex-officio guardian of the Carrick-on-Suir union, told the House of Lords in 1884 that "the people look to the ex-officios as protectors, although there is such a terror inflicted on them by the [Land] Leaguers that they would vote against their own interest." Parliament, "Report of the Select Committee of the House of Lords on the Poor Law Guardians . . . ," p. 473.

60. J. H. Whyte, "Landlord Influence at Elections in Ireland, 1760–1885," *English Historical Review* (October 1965): 755.

61. Davitt, *Fall of Feudalism*, pp. 164–165.

Chapter 2

1. Grimshaw, "A Statistical Survey," Table 1.

2. Davitt, *Fall of Feudalism*, p. 155.

3. Thomas N. Brown, "Nationalism and the Irish Peasant, 1800–1848," *The Review of Politics* 15 (October 1953): 423–433.

4. Ibid., pp. 403–411.

5. William E. H. Lecky, *Leaders of Public Opinion in Ireland*, 2d ed. (London: Longmans, Green & Co., 1871), p. 298.

6. Brown, "Nationalism," pp. 443–444.

7. J. H. Whyte, *The Independent Irish Party, 1850–59* (Oxford: Oxford University Press, 1958), p. 9.

8. Whyte, "Landlord Influence at Elections."

9. Whyte, *Independent Irish Party*, p. 6.

10. The position of the church hierarchy with regard to nationalist politics is discussed in Emmet Larkin, *The Making of the Roman Catholic Church in Ireland, 1850–1860* (Chapel Hill, N.C.: University of North Carolina Press, 1981). See also E. R. Norman, *The Catholic Church in Ireland in the Age of Rebellion, 1859–1873* (Ithaca, N.Y.: Cornell University Press, 1965).

11. J. C. Conroy, *A History of Railways in Ireland* (London: Longmans Green & Co., 1928), pp. 18–38.

12. Rory Oge, "Getting On in Ireland," *Dublin University Magazine* 41 (April 1853): 472–474.

13. Parliament. *Parliamentary Papers*, 1854–55, vol. 11 (*Reports*), "Report from the Select Committee on Postal Arrangements . . . ," p. 257.

14. Parliament. *Parliamentary Papers*, 1867–68, vol. 41 (*Accounts and Papers, no. 416*), "Return of the Names of All Railway Companies in the United Kingdom which Construct or Use Electric Telegraphs," p. 34.

15. Newspapers were granted special discount rates for telegraph. The cost of transmitting a hundred-word news report between any two points in the United Kingdom

was ls., or the newspaper could hire a private line for £500 annually. Parliament. *Parliamentary Papers*, 1876, vol. 13 (*Reports*, no. 357), "Report from the Select Committee on Post Office (Telegraphic Department)," pp. 185–186.

16. S. N. Elrington, "The Press—As It Was and Is," *The Irish Builder* 9 (March 1, 1867): 65–66.

17. Brown, "Nationalism," p. 422.

18. For facts concerning economic conditions in Ireland during the last half of the nineteenth century, I have drawn heavily upon the findings of the excellent study by Barbara Lewis Solow, *The Land Question and the Irish Economy, 1870–1903* (Cambridge, Mass.: Harvard University Press, 1971). Conditions prior to 1876 are discussed in chapters I–IV.

19. Ibid., chapters I–IV.

20. J. Lee, "The Railways and the Irish Economy," in *The Formation of the Irish Economy*, ed. L. M. Cullen (Cork: Mercier Press, 1968), p. 79.

21. John Long, *The Proposed Great Munster Fair in Limerick* (Limerick, 1851), pp. 4–7.

22. *Limerick Chronicle*, April 27, 1853.

23. Solow, *Land Question and Irish Economy*, pp. 101ff.

24. Grimshaw, "A Statistical Survey," Table 1.

25. Conrad M. Arensberg and Solon T. Kimball, *Family and Community in Ireland* (Cambridge, Mass.: Harvard University Press, 1940).

26. The information contained in the next three paragraphs is taken from Chapter I of the Arensberg and Kimball study.

27. Clements, *Poverty of Ireland*, p. 154.

28. This occurred under the Medical Charities Act of 1851 (14 & 15 Vic. C. 47).

29. *Clare Advertiser*, March 3, 1883.

30. The mean farm size in Sligo in 1880 was twenty-six acres, and in Leitrim, twenty-four acres. The mean valuations were, respectively, £13 and £19. Grimshaw, "A Statistical Survey," Table 1.

31. Louden's own testimony during the Parnell Commission hearings. Parliament, *Parliamentary Papers*, 1890, vol. 27. "Report of the Reprint of the Shorthand Notes of the Speeches, Proceedings and Evidence before the Commissioners . . . under the Special Commission Act, 1888," vol. 9, p. 540.

32. Whyte, *Independent Irish Party*, p. 6n.

33. Conor Cruise O'Brien, *Parnell and His Party, 1880–90* (Oxford: Clarendon Press, 1957), pp. 125–126.

34. Samuel D. Clark, *Social Origins of the Irish Land War* (Princeton, N.J.: Princeton University Press, 1979), p. 214.

35. Whyte, *Independent Irish Party*, p. 6n.

36. Parliament, *Parliamentary Papers*, 1881, vol. 96 (*Reports*), C. 2931, "Census of Ireland, 1881: Preliminary Report," p. 12.

37. Ibid.

38. Davitt, *Fall of Feudalism*, p. 77.

39. Anonymous, "A New Leaf Turned Over, A.D. 1861," *Dublin University Magazine* 58 (October 1861): 511.

40. *Newspaper Press Directory* (London: C. Mitchell & Co., 1870), p. 115.

41. Lawrence J. McCaffrey emphasizes this aspect of Butt's character in his "Irish Federalism in the 1870s: A Study in Conservative Nationalism," *Transactions of the American Philosophical Society* n.s., 52, part 6 (1962).

42. J. C. Beckett, *The Making of Modern Ireland, 1603–1923* (London: Faber & Faber, 1966), p. 377.

43. McCaffrey, "Irish Federalism," pp. 9–10.

44. McCaffrey, "Irish Federalism," p. 13.

45. Ibid., passim.

46. Ibid., pp. 39–45.

47. Davitt, *Fall of Feudalism*, p. 79.

48. The Edenderry Home Rule Club's members were about evenly divided over obstruction. When in 1877 a member introduced a motion calling for a discussion of the

language of Sir P. O'Brien, M.P. for Kings, who attacked Parnell in Commons for his use of obstructive practices, the motion was defeated by a vote of 10–8, indicating that a narrow majority of the members supported O'Brien's attack. *Nation*, September 1, 1877.

49. *Leinster Express*, February 3, 1877.
50. McCaffrey, "Irish Federalism," p. 36.
51. *Nation*, October 21, 1871.
52. *Roscommon Journal*, May 25, 1872.
53. *Limerick Chronicle*, April 6, 1872.
54. Ibid.
55. Ibid.
56. *Roscommon Messenger*, March 8, 1873.
57. *Nation*, March 15, 1873.
58. *Roscommon Journal*, November 1, 1873.
59. *Nation*, August 15, 1874.
60. "Report on System under which Guardians . . . are elected," p. 209.
61. Fenelon's farm, located in Kilgowan, Kildare, was 106 acres and had a valuation of £77. He had four tenants, probably his farm laborers, who rented small quarter-acre holdings from him. *Slater's Royal National Commercial Directory of Ireland* (Manchester: Isaac Slater, 1881), p. 469; *V. R.*, Naas: Usk (1883), pp. 10–11.
62. *Leinster Express*, March 31, 1877; April 14, 1877.
63. Ibid., April 6, 1878.
64. *Nation*, April 7, 1877.
65. Ibid., February 17, 1877.
66. *Waterford Mail*, October 9, 1877.
67. Solow, *Land Question and Irish Economy*, pp. 119–120.

Chapter 3

1. Discussions on gombeen men and money-lending practices in nineteenth-century Ireland may be found in T. A. Finlay, "The Usurer in Ireland," *New Ireland Review* (June 1894): 304–316; Dun, *Landlords and Tenants*, p. 227; and A Guardian of the Poor, *The Irish Peasant*, pp. 41–42.
2. Parliament. *Parliamentary Papers*, 1881, vol. 16 (Bessborough Commission), "Royal Commission on Agriculture: Preliminary Report of the Assistant Commissioners for Ireland," p. 116.
3. Parliament. *Parliamentary Papers*, 1883, vol. 77, (*Accounts and Papers*), C. 3808, "Criminal and Judicial Statistics: Ireland, 1882–1883," p. 101.
4. T. W. Moody, "The New Departure in Irish Politics, 1878–79," *Essays in British and Irish History in Honor of James Eadie Todd*, ed. H. A. Cronne, T. W. Moody, and D. B. Quinn (London: Frederick Muller Ltd., 1949), pp. 303–333.
5. Ibid., p. 320.
6. Davitt, *The Fall of Feudalism*, p. 133.
7. Ibid., pp. 145–146.
8. Ibid.
9. This information and other facts about the personal life of James Daly were supplied by several of Daly's descendants and other members of his family, particularly his daughter-in-law, Honaria Daly, his granddaughters, Shiela Daly and Mrs. Evelyn Cahalane, his grandson by marriage, William Mongey, who has since passed away, and his grandniece, Angela Garavan and her family. All those mentioned went to extraordinary lengths to clear up certain murky details about Daly's life, background, and familial ties—for which I am deeply grateful.
10. *V. R.*: Castlebar union; Brea.
11. Mentioned at a meeting of the Castlebar Urban Council, *Connaught Telegraph*, May 30, 1908.
12. *V. R.*: Castlebar union; Buncarn East, Buncarn West E.D.'s (1858–73), pp. 151, 152.

13. *Nation*, December 18, 1875.
14. *Connaught Telegraph*, June 14, 1879.
15. Ibid.
16. Ibid., April 14, 1877.
17. Davitt, *Fall of Feudalism*, pp. 146–147, erroneously gives the date of April 19. The meeting actually took place on April 20.
18. Ibid.
19. Samuel Clark, "The Social Composition of the Land League," *Irish Historical Studies* 17, 4 (September 1971): 459.
20. Moody, "The New Departure," p. 304.
21. John Devoy, *Recollections of an Irish Rebel* (New York: Charles D. Young, 1929), p. 314.
22. *Connaught Telegraph*, June 14, 1879.
23. See Chapter 2, especially Table 2.
24. Parliament. *Parliamentary Papers*, 1890, vol. 27 (*Reports*), "Report of the Special Commission, 1888 . . . " (Parnell Commission), p. 539.
25. King's Inn *Register* (1856).
26. Parliament, "Report of Special Commission" (Parnell Commission), p. 539.
27. Westport union minute books (1876), April 1, 1876.
28. Parliament, "Report of Special Commission" (Parnell Commission), pp. 539–540.
29. Ibid., p. 540.
30. *Connaught Telegraph*, June 14, 1879.
31. Davitt, *Fall of Feudalism*, p. 166, claimed that "it was extremely difficult to obtain a chairman or the proposer of a resolution at the earlier meetings, owing to fears of landlord resentment."
32. Ibid., p. 164.
33. Norman Dunbar Palmer, *The Irish National Land League Crisis* (New Haven: Yale University Press, 1940), p. 141.
34. Davitt, *Fall of Feudalism*, pp. 162–163; Parliament, "Report of Special Commission" (Parnell Commission), p. 547.
35. William O'Brien, *Recollections* (London: Macmillan & Co., 1905), p. 224.
36. Davitt, *Fall of Feudalism*, p. 177.
37. Ibid., pp. 181–192.
38. Ibid., p. 163.
39. C. Cruise O'Brien, *Parnell and His Party*, p. 8.
40. Ibid., pp. 11–35.
41. All together thirty newspapers were surveyed, including (in alphabetical order) *Ballinrobe Chronicle, Belfast Newsletter, Clare Independent, Clare Journal, Connaught Telegraph, Cork Constitution, Cork Examiner, Drogheda Argus, Freeman's Journal, Galway Vindicator, Irish Times, Kerry Sentinel, Kildare Observer, Kilkenny Journal, Leinster Express, Limerick Chronicle, Meath Herald,* and *Cavan Advertiser, Nation, Newry Standard, The People* (Wexford), *Roscommon Journal, Sligo Champion, Tipperary Advocate, Tipperary People, Ulster Gazette, Waterford Mail, Waterford News, West Cork Eagle.* Not all these newspapers were published or available for both years.
42. *Connaught Telegraph*, March 6, 1880.
43. *Freeman's Journal*, April 12, 1880.
44. *Connaught Telegraph*, April 10, 1880. The division of Belcarra was contested between an uncle of James Daly's, Patrick Daly, who had held the seat for years, and Thomas Reilly, a Land Leaguer. Daly won by a substantial margin, 81 to 51. A second contest, that of the Straide division, was fought between Patrick White, a Land Leaguer, and Andrew Walsh, the bailiff of Sir Roger Palmer. As one might expect in this division, which was the birthplace of Michael Davitt, the Leaguer won by a large margin, 112 to 56. Contests three and four pitted two Conservatives, Myles Jordan, a J.P., and Francis Carty, the bailiff of J. F. B. Tardy, against, in both cases, Patrick W. Nally, a Land Leaguer and the son of a tenant-farmer, William Nally, who was already a member of the board. Nally was beaten badly in both contests, 94 to 24 and 58 to 22. His father kept his seat without a contest. In

the fifth contest, Joseph W. Walsh, along with James Daly, the leading agitator in Castlebar at the time, won a place on the board against a Conservative incumbent, Arthur C. O'Donnell, by the close vote of 47 to 42. The sixth contest was fought between two brothers apparently on nonpolitical grounds.

45. C. Cruise O'Brien, *Parnell and His Party*, pp. 40–41.

46. Samuel Clark has shown in his recent study "The Social Composition of the Land League" that during the organizational phase townsmen in general and shopkeepers, publicans, and professional men in particular, as well as farmers, were overrepresented in the movement in terms of their proportions within society. This indicated a middle-class social base for the movement.

47. Ibid., p. 462.

48. *Limerick Reporter*, March 1, 1881.

49. C. Cruise O'Brien, *Parnell and His Party*, pp. 121–122, 127, 133.

50. Ibid., p. 133.

51. Ibid., p. 50.

52. Ibid., p. 51.

53. Ibid., pp. 55–57.

54. Davitt, *Fall of Feudalism*, p. 302; C. Cruise O'Brien, *Parnell and His Party*, p. 60.

55. *Freeman's Journal*, February 15, 1881.

56. *Irish Times*, December 22, 1880.

57. Ibid., February 24, 1881.

58. *Freeman's Journal*, March 1, 1881.

59. *Irish Times*, March 3, 1881.

60. Ibid., March 25, 1881.

61. *Clare Independent*, March 18, 1881.

62. *Clare Advertiser*, March 26, 1881.

63. *Freeman's Journal*, March 24, 1881.

64. *Roscommon Journal*, February 19, 1881, *Drogheda Argus*, March 26, 1881; *Freeman's Journal*, March 14, March 24, 1881.

65. "Several" divisions did not hold meetings and were therefore not represented at the convention. *Roscommon Journal*, February 12, 1881.

66. *Nation*, March 4, 1881.

67. *Cork Examiner*, quoted in the *Nation*, March 26, 1881.

68. Instances are cited in the *Connaught Telegraph*, February 26, March 12, 1881.

69. Ms. PC660, *Land League Papers*, letter from O'Neill to Brennan, March 4, 1881.

70. *Clare Independent*, April 2, 1881.

71. *Irish Times*, March 12, 1881.

72. *Freeman's Journal*, March 19, 1881.

73. *Kerry Sentinel*, April 1, 1881. Another case of landlord intimidation, in County Sligo, is reported in the *Sligo Champion*, March 12, 1881.

74. *Leinster Express*, April 2, 1881.

75. *Clare Advertiser*, March 26, 1881.

76. *Belfast Newsletter*, March 29, 1881.

77. *Kerry Sentinel*, March 25, 1881.

78. *Irish Times*, March 24, March 25, and March 26, 1881.

79. Ibid., March 25, 1881.

80. *Nation*, April 2, 1881.

Chapter 4

1. The names of the other eight were: David Finlay, J.P., Bawnboy; Lt. Gen. Ed. Roche, Midleton; Capt. Somerville, Skull; A. J. Cooke, J.P., Listowel; Richard Hale, J.P., Dromore West; Nicholas P. O'Shea, J.P., Kilmacthomas; H. Villiers Stuart, M.P., Dungarvan; and W.H. O'Sullivan, M.P., Kilmallock. The last named was a Home Rule

M.P. who was an elected guardian. He was not defeated in a contest as the others were but simply retired as chairman.

2. *Limerick Reporter*, March 5, 1881. Five new Land Leaguers were elected to the board, but the former board officers were all reelected without a contest. Ibid., April 1, 1881.

3. Harrington claimed credit for the officer turnover in Listowel. "I worked for some time to tear down among the elected guardians of Listowel the notion that they could not govern the board independently." *Kerry Sentinel*, April 8, 1881.

4. Paul Bew, *Land and the National Question in Ireland, 1858–82* (Atlantic Highlands, N.J.: Humanities Press, 1979), pp. 104, 124, 127.

5. See Sean O'Luing, "Aspects of the Fenian Rising in Kerry, 1867," *Journal of the Kerry Archaeological and Historical Society* 3 (1970): 131–153, passim.

6. Rowland P. Blennerhassett, returned in an 1872 by-election.

7. Samuel B. Hussey, *The Reminiscences of an Irish Land Agent*, comp. by Home Gordon et al. (London: Duckworth & Co., 1904), p. 93.

8. *Kerry Sentinel*, March 15, 1881.

9. Ibid.

10. Ibid.

11. Kelly, also a town commissioner, was a close friend of Harrington's, and when Harrington went to Dublin to join the National League, he took Kelly with him and gave him the post of a paid field agitator. S.P.O.: Criminal Law and Proceduure Act, 1887, Prosecutions IX, p. 63. The listing gives his name as Thomas Kelly, arrested and sentenced to six months imprisonment on February 12, 1889, for taking part in a criminal conspiracy in Dungloe, Co. Donegal. In the appeal, the name was corrected to John Kelly, "a paid organizer of the National League." Prosecutions X, p. 38.

12. *Kerry Sentinel*, March 22, 1881.

13. *Kerry Sentinel*, April 1, 1881.

14. Reports in the *Sentinel* prior to the election estimated the number of Land Leaguers already on the board at seven. Just after the election the *Nation* reported that the League had won thirteen new seats in the Tralee union. These additions brought the League's total to twenty. But at a party caucus following the election there were twenty-five league guardians present, and one other who was absent because he had been arrested during the intervening week should be counted. Hence, there were six more league guardians at the time of the caucus than were numbered in the election reports. Unless the election reports were erroneous, the six additional members converted to the league side after the election.

15. *Kerry Sentinel*, April 1, 1881. The account of the election of officers that follows was reported in the same edition.

16. The fourth uncommitted guardian abstained in the voting.

17. *Kerry Sentinel*, April 8, 1881.

18. *Kerry Sentinel*, May 6, 1881.

19. Ibid., March 30, 1883.

20. Ibid., March 29, 1881.

21. Landowners were identified through "Return of the Names of Proprietors, and the Area of Valuation of All Properties, in the Several Counties in Ireland," Parliament, *Parliamentary Papers*, 1876, vol. 88 (*Accounts and Papers*), p. 395. Occupations of nonlandowners were identified through *Slater's Royal National Director of Ireland* (Manchester, 1881). And the valuations of holdings were ascertained from the General Valuation Office, *V.R.* (1881), Tralee union, Tralee electoral division.

22. The shopkeeper category is an eclectic one, including retailers of all kinds, such as bakers, grocers, drapers, spirit merchants, butter merchants, and so forth; it also comprises publicans, innkeepers and other persons who do not fit reasonably into any other category. A few artisans who were on the list were included in the shopkeeper category because they all had shops in the town. Persons who appeared in the sources as both farmers and members of a town occupation are counted in the town occupation, for it was thought best to consider as farmers only those voters who earned their livelihood almost entirely from agriculture. The classification system therefore contains a slight bias toward the town oc-

cupations and, within the town occupations, toward the shopkeeper class. But the number who appeared in two or more occupational categories was small and insufficient to distort the overall results of the survey.

23. Bew, *Land and National Question*, especially chapters 5 and 8.

24. F. S. L. Lyons, *Ireland Since the Famine*, (Glasgow: Fontana/Collins, 1973), pp. 216–217.

25. In the absence of the census manuscripts and other sources giving religious denominations of individuals during this period, living natives of the region who are familiar with family names are still the best source for this kind of information.

26. A discussion of the historical background of this policy may be found in L. P. Curtis, Jr., *Coercion and Conciliation in Ireland, 1880–1892* (Princeton, N.J.: Princeton University Press, 1963), pp. 1–3. The remainder of the book is devoted to an examination of the policy during the Parnellite years.

27. John E. Pomfret, *The Struggle for Land in Ireland, 1800–1923* (Princeton, N.J.: Princeton University Press, 1930), pp. 196–219.

28. C. Cruise O'Brien, *Parnell and His Party*, pp. 65–67.

29. Clark, "Social Composition of the Land League," pp. 451–457. The only clergyman arrested under the Protection of Person and Property Act was the famous Father Eugene Sheehy of Kilmallock.

30. *Limerick Reporter*, March 5, 1881.

31. C. Cruise O'Brien, *Parnell and His Party*, pp. 73–74.

32. Ibid., p. 80.

33. *Limerick Reporter*, March 5, 1881.

34. National Library of Ireland, *National Land League Papers*, PC. 660. Letter from Walsh to Brennan, August 2, 1880. This collection contains the only surviving official papers of the Land League. Almost all of the hundreds of documents are reports from local branches giving data concerning branch finances, and in many cases requesting legal or financial aid. Often, interesting bits of information concerning the state of the agitation or the relationships of the members are also included. Although they are a potentially valuable source of information on local politics, this unsorted collection of documents has been tapped by few historians.

35. *Connaught Telegraph*, January 18, 1881.

36. Farmer's sons and agricultural and other laborers committed a much higher proportion of violent crimes than did farmers, traders, businessmen, professional men, innkeepers, and publicans. These latter groups made up the greater portion of the Land League membership. See Clark, "Social Composition of the Land League," passim.

37. *Connaught Telegraph*, June 14, 1879.

38. "The majority of boycotting carried on is at the instance of irresponsible parties who, to satisfy a private spleen, ape the position of the leaders, and recommend a system that must ultimately, if persisted in, succeed in undoing all the good that has been achieved by the land agitation." Editorial in the *Connaught Telegraph*, January 8, 1881.

39. Davitt, *Fall of Feudalism*, p. 239.

40. See Chapter 3.

41. *Connaught Telegraph*, April 2, 1881.

42. Ibid., April 16, 1881.

43. Ibid., May 14, 1881.

44. Ibid., August 13, 1881.

45. Ibid., October 1, 1881; *Freeman's Journal*, September 27, 1881.

46. *Connaught Telegraph*, October 1, 1881.

47. Ibid., November 5, 1881.

48. Ibid., October 28, 1881.

49. Ibid., March 18, 1882.

50. Letter to the editor from Thomas Cunningham, *Connaught Telegraph*, October 28, 1882.

51. *Connaught Telegraph*, October 28, 1882.

52. Ibid.

53. Ibid.
54. Ibid., March 11, 1882.
55. C. Cruise O'Brien, *Parnell and His Party*, p. 131.
56. *Limerick Reporter*, March 8, 1882.
57. *Kerry Sentinel*, March 24, 1882.
58. See Chapter 2.
59. C. Cruise O'Brien, *Parnell and His Party*, p. 69.
60. *United Ireland*, February 4, 1882.
61. *Roscommon Herald*, March 18, 1882. The *Clare Independent*, March 18, 1882, published a similar note, depicting the electoral struggle in that region as one against coercion and "landocracy."
62. *Roscommon Herald*, March 25, 1882.
63. Ibid., April 8, 1882.
64. Ibid.
65. *Limerick Reporter*, March 31, 1882. According to the *Reporter*, the guardians had no objection to Lord Emly or to Robert McDonnell, the former vice-chairman, who was also unseated by a nationalist tenant, "but the strong sense of wrong felt by the people in the present state of things . . . stimulated them to sacrifice every other sentiment except that of exhibiting their resentment consequent on arbitrary arrests without bail or manprise." (A search of the *Oxford English Dictionary* and several well-known law dictionaries turned up no definition for the term "manprise." Apparently the reporter used the word erroneously, perhaps meaning to say "reprieve.")
66. *Limerick Chronicle*, April 25, April 29, 1882.
67. Ibid., June 8, 1882.
68. *Leinster Leader*, March 28, 1882; *Connaught Telegraph*, March 25, 1882; *Limerick Reporter*, March 27, 1882; *United Ireland*, April 8, 1882. The case of P. W. Nally of Balla illustrates clearly the change that had come over the electorate between the poor law elections of 1881 and 1882. Nally was one of the first three men to be arrested under the coercion act, his arrest occurring at the beginning of March 1881, just before the poor law elections. He contested seats in two divisions of the Castlebar union in absentia in 1881 and lost both contests by wide vote margins. In 1882 he contested one of the divisions again and won.
69. *United Ireland*, April 8, 1882.
70. William O'Brien, *Recollections*, p. 412.

Chapter 5

1. The best treatment of this period—especially of Parnell and the Home Rule movement—is found in C. Cruise O'Brien, *Parnell and His Party*. The narrative of events of 1882–86 are in chapter III, pp. 80–118; the party and political machine are examined in chapters V and VI, pp. 119–158.
2. *Times*, October 18, 1882, p. 7.
3. C. Cruise O'Brien, *Parnell and His Party*, pp. 127–128.
4. Ibid., pp. 128–132.
5. *Annual Register* (1883).
6. A detailed examination of the activities of the Roman Catholic hierarchy in Ireland and their conversion to Home Rule is in Emmet Larkin, *The Roman Catholic Church and the Creation of the Modern Irish State, 1878–1886*. This volume is the first in a projected series by Larkin, entitled *A History of the Roman Catholic Church in Ireland in the Nineteenth Century*.
7. Beckett, *Making of Modern Ireland*, p. 394. The effect of the franchise act on the fortunes of the Parnellite party has been greatly disputed. C. Cruise O'Brien has concluded that the importance of the act on the results of the general election of 1885 has been overemphasized. C. Cruise O'Brien, *Parnell and His Party*, p. 87.
8. C. Cruise O'Brien, *Parnell and His Party*, p. 133.
9. Ibid., p 133.

10. A map of Ireland showing the areas won by Parnellites and Conservatives can be found in the *Pall Mall Gazette*, December 18, 1885, p. 1. Vote margins are discussed in the *Annual Register* (1885), and C. Cruise O'Brien, *Parnell and His Party*, pp. 150–151.

11. C. Cruise O'Brien, *Parnell and His Party*, p. 153.

12. *Kilkenny Journal*, April 1, 1885.

13. The proceedings were reported in the *Irish Times*, February 1, 1883. The delegates who attended were Thomas Gaffikin and Robert Stuart (Belfast); Robert Alexander, J.P., and John Dornan (Larne); Thomas McElderry, John Megaw, and Thomas McAfee (Ballymoney); Col. Thomas Waring, D.L., J.P., and William Anderson (Lurgan); James Patrick, J.P. (Ballymena). This may not have been a complete list.

14. *Freeman's Journal*, March 5, 1883.

15. Eighteen delegates were reported as attending the second meeting, of whom six had attended the first meeting. *Morning News* (Belfast), March 3, 1883.

16. *Freeman's Journal*, March 5, 1883.

17. *Limerick Reporter*, April 2, 1886.

18. It dissolved the Waterford branch during the election campaign of 1885 by the simple method of sending a telegram: "Branch dissolved by order." *Freeman's Journal*, October 21, 1885.

19. The years, subjects, and disposition of the bills introduced were as follows:

1880	Certain clergymen to be added to ex-officios.	Not proceeded with.
1881	Secret ballot in poor law elections.	Not proceeded with.
1882	Election of guardians (general reform).	Not proceeded with.
1883	Election of guardians.	Not proceeded with.
1884	Election of guardians (abolition of ex-officios).	Killed by Lords.
1885	Election of guardians (abolition of ex-officios).	Killed by Lords' amendment.
1886	Election of guardians.	Withdrawn.
1887	Election of guardians.	Not proceeded with.
1888	Election of guardians.	Not proceeded with.
1890	Election of guardians.	Not proceeded with.

20. *Times*, October 18, 1882.

21. The Queen told Parliament in her opening address that year that representative local government would serve the Irish people in two ways: by "confirming popular control over expenditures and supplying a yet more serious want by extending the formation of habits of self-government."

22. O'Shaughnessy, "Local Government."

23. William O'Connor Morris, "Irish Local Government," *Macmillan's Magazine* (August 1883): 286–292.

24. For a complete discussion of the central board scheme and Parnell's and Chamberlain's parts in it, see C. H. D. Howard, "Documents Relating to the Irish 'Central Board' Scheme, 1884–85," *Irish Historical Studies* 8 (1952–53): 237–263. See also C. Cruise O'Brien, *Parnell and His Party*, pp. 90–100, and Curtis, *Coercion and Conciliation*, pp. 17–19.

25. Howard, " 'Central Board' Scheme," pp. 240–241.

26. John Redmond, who was eventually to succeed Parnell as chairman after Parnell's death in October, 1891, stated this point of view explicitly in 1892 when discussing a comprehensive local government reform measure that was before Parliament: "The attitude of the Irish Nationalists towards local Gov't is essentially different from their attitude towards Home Rule. On the latter subject we do not believe in accepting half a loaf in preference to no bread. . . . Not so, however, in the question of Local Government. On this subject our attitude is entirely different. It is plainly a matter for compromise, for taking what we can get . . . and seizing the first opportunity afterwards to strengthen and improve our position." John E. Redmond, "The Irish Local Government Bill," *Fortnightly Review* (May 1, 1892): 622.

27. *United Ireland*, March 14, 1885.

28. C. Cruise O'Brien, *Parnell and His Party*, passim.

29. Clark, *Irish Land War*.

30. Nicholls, *Irish Poor Law*, p. 331.

31. The amendment was incorporated in the Protection of Person and Property (Ireland) Act, 1881.

32. Staples, "Local Government in Ireland," p. 107. John Redmond in 1892 freely admitted the use of outdoor relief for political purposes. Discussing boards of guardians which had been dissolved by the Local Government board in recent years, he wrote: "These [dissolutions] have simply been incidents in the political and agrarian war. . . . In almost all cases the boards have been dissolved because of granting outdoor relief to evicted tenants when they had no authority in the law for doing so." Redmond, "Irish Local Government Bill," p. 630.

33. Sir Henry A. Robinson, *Memories Wise and Otherwise* (London: Cassell & Co., 1923), pp. 131–132. Robinson spent his entire public career in the local government administration in Ireland, as poor law inspector (1879–87), local government commissioner (1887–98), and vice-president of the Local Government Board (1898–1921). See P. J. Meghen, "Irish Local Government and the Robinson family," *Administration* 9 (Winter 1961–62): 291–308.

34. *Limerick Chronicle*, February 24, 1883.

35. *Independent* (Clare), March 14, 1885. Apparently Forster considered Clune dangerous enough to be handled with special security precautions. Under Forster's direct orders, Clune was imprisoned for an entire year in 1881–82, which was an extraordinarily long internment for suspects. Clune served most of his time in Naas jail and was then transferred to Kilmainham. Ibid., April 7, 1883.

36. From March 1881 to March 1883 no ex-officios attended any regular meetings of the board, although a few did appear for the officers' elections of 1882 and 1883. *Independent* (Clare), April 7, 1883. The Poor Law Attendances Report of 1884 showed three attendances for ex-officios at regular board meetings from March 1883 to March 1884.

37. *Independent* (Clare), December 8, 1883.

38. Ibid.

39. The Tulla board followed the orthodox nationalist line on the emigration question. They believed that to assist paupers to emigrate was to play into the hands of the landlords and British authorities by helping them rid the country of the potentially troublesome element. Therefore they refused even to consider applications from paupers wishing to emigrate. See, for example, the board meeting reported in the *Independent* (Clare), March 29, 1884.

40. The deputy vice-chairman of the board, George Bingham, held a small farm valued at £37 in fee. But he was an elected guardian, and he probably had no tenants on his holding. Therefore he could not be considered a landlord or a representative of the landlord class.

41. *Limerick Reporter*, April 2, 1886.

42. Ibid.

43. See the *Kilkenny Journal*, March 28, 1885, and April 3, 1886.

44. Ibid., February 12, 1887.

45. Ibid.

46. Ibid., March 30, 1887.

47. Ibid.

48. The Mountmellick nationalists succeeded in turning out the ex-officio officers in 1882, apparently because three ex-officios had arrived at the election meeting too late to participate in the election proceedings. The next year and for the rest of the decade the ex-officios arrived punctually and won all three offices. *Leinster Express*, April 15, 1882; April 7, 1883; April 10, 1886; and April 6, 1889. The chairman of the Mountmellick board, Col. Henry D. Carden of Knightstown, was an arch-conservative who founded the "Loyal and Patriotic," a Conservative party club in Queens County. *Leinster Leader*, May 8, 1886.

49. Dun, *Landlords and Tenants*, p. 19.

50. See Chapter 2.

51. For Fenelon see *Slater's* (1881), p. 469, and *V.R.: Naas; Usk* (1883), pp. 10, 11. For Driver see Domesday Book under Kildare.

52. *Leinster Express*, March 31, 1877; April 2, 1881.

53. Ibid., April 2, 1881.
54. Ibid., April 1, 1882.
55. Parliament, "Report of the Select Committee of the House of Lords on the Poor Law Guardians . . .," pp. 512–513.
56. *Leinster Express,* May 15, 1881; September 28, 1881.
57. Ibid., May 22, 1886.
58. *Connaught Telegraph,* January 27, 1912; October 28, 1928.
59. A Guardian of the Poor, *The Irish Peasant,* p. 90.
60. *Connaught Telegraph,* November 25, 1882; January 25, 1908. For additional information about the young Lord Lucan and his popularity with the tenant-occupiers of Mayo, see Smith, *The Reason Why.*
61. The chairman of the Lismore board was J. Douglas Pyne, M.P.; the chairman of Waterford was P. J. Power, M.P. Pyne won his seat for Waterford county in the general election of 1885; Power won his seat in a by-election in 1886.

Chapter 6

1. The city of Cork was 85 percent Catholic in 1871. The two conservative unions (in 1886) to the north and south of the city had even smaller Catholic populations: Mallow, 78 percent, and Kinsale, 75 percent. Bandon, just to the east of Cork, was 82 percent Catholic. Of the unions around Cork city, only Midleton was more than 90 percent Catholic (94 percent). Bantry and Skibbereen, the two other conservative unions in 1886, were both strongly Catholic (94 percent and 91 percent), but the farms in these West Riding unions were exceedingly small. Parliament, *Parliamentary Papers,* 1871, vol. 72 (*Reports*) C. 873, "Census of Ireland, 1871," pt. 1, 2, no. 2, p. 352–356.
2. Five members of these two landowning families were ex-officio members of the board. The officers' election meeting of 1886 was attended by only seven members, of whom four, Major Ernest Knox (chairman), William R. Kirkwood (vice-chairman), Joseph Kirkwood, and Captain Robert Kirkwood, were of the families mentioned. James Knox Gore (deputy vice-chairman) was not a regular attender, but all the others were, and there was rarely a meeting of the board at which at least two, if not all five, of the men mentioned were not present. See Killala minute books (1886), ms. 12569, N.L.I.
3. Clark, "Social Composition of the Land League," pp. 447–469.
4. Clark, *Irish Land War.*
5. The rate of non-identification was high in Galway. Of the fifteen tenant-officers in the county in 1886, the occupations of only eight were identified—three as farmers through *Slater's* (1881 and 1894), and five as farmers through the valuation records.
6. In the one such case that I came across in my research, the guardians of the Dungarvan union in Waterford in 1881 offered the chair to a J.P., Henry A. Fitzgerald, a hard-working member who assumed the tedious chore of making up all the relief lists for the board. A majority of nationalists were present at the meeting and were determined to eject the old board chairman, H. Stuart Villiers, M.P., and replace him with Fitzgerald, who was not a nationalist. They apparently did not consult Fitzgerald before making their decision, for when the nationalist leader, John Wall, offered him the chairmanship saying, "You are here wet and dry days at this board, and you ought to be chairman," Fitzgerald declined, saying that he would rather cut off his right hand than oppose the present chairman and vice-chairman, although he would gratefully accept the deputy-vice-chairmanship if the board deigned to offer it to him. The nationalists then proceeded to elect two elected guardians to the high and middle offices and to nominate Fitzgerald for the low office. But Fitzgerald, a gentleman to the end, decided that under the circumstances it would be an affront to Villiers to accept the office, and he gratefully declined.

Epilogue

    1. Davitt, *Fall of Feudalism*, p. 520.

    2. *Leinster Express*, March 30, 1889.

    3. Ibid.

    4. *Connaught Telegraph*, September 11, 1886; January 22, 1887; April 2, 1887; April 7, 1888; March 9, 1889.

    5. Michael J. F. McCarthy, *Priests and People in Ireland* (Dublin: Hodges, Figgis & Co., 1903), pp. 157–158.

    6. Although Daly's editorials supported Parnell as late as December 1889, by December 1890, less than a month after the party meeting at which Parnell was deposed as party chairman, Daly was referring to him as a "discrowned dictator." *Connaught Telegraph*, December 27, 1890. In the *Telegraph* of June 18, 1892, the last issue published under Daly's ownership, Daly bemoaned the fact that Parnell might have "achieved an almost incalculable amount of good for Ireland and her people," but only left her with "a pitiable record of depravity, selfishness, immorality and disunion."

    7. The valuation records show a number of farms in the Castlebar area being taken over by a James Daly during the last two years of the 1880s. By 1891 all these farms had been transferred to other occupiers. In the first issue of the *Telegraph* under the new ownership, the new editor wrote that Daly had had to relinquish control of the newspaper in order to "devote himself to the pursuit of other concerns which had begun to press upon him heavily." *Connaught Telegraph*, June 25, 1892. It is probable that Daly became involved in land speculations, that he lost a great deal of money in the speculations, and that he had to sell the newspaper to recover some of the losses.

    8. Ibid., January 25, 1908.

    9. Ibid., May 30, 1908.

    10. Ernest Barker, *Ireland in the Last Fifty Years, 1866–1916* (Oxford: Clarendon Press, 1917), p. 22.

    11. In 1890 the local government expenditure in Ireland was £3,559,000, which was divided as follows: grand jury cess, £1,110,430; town taxation, £826,899; and poor rates, £1,099,221. T. W. Grimshaw, *Facts and Figures about Ireland* (Dublin: Hodges, Figgis & Co., 1893), p. 49.

    12. C. Cruise O'Brien, *Parnell and His Party*, pp. 354–355.

    13. Beckett, *Making of Modern Ireland*, p. 404.

    14. The seven were William Abraham (Limerick union), John Deasy (Cork), John Finucane (Limerick), Patrick J. O'Brien (Nenagh), Thomas O'Hanlon (Newry), Patrick J. Power (Waterford), Jeremiah D. Sheehan (Killarney and Tralee).

    15. T. W. Russell, *Disturbed Ireland: The Plan of Campaign Estates* (London: Truslove & Shirley, 1889), pp. 11–20.

    16. William O'Brien, *Recollections*, p. 275.

Methodological Appendix

    1. Thomas Laffan, "A Note on Certain Public Records," *Journal of the Royal Society of Antiquaries in Ireland* 38 (September 30, 1908): 185–186.

    2. *Guy's Directory of Munster* (Cork: Francis Guy, 1886).

    3. George Henry Bassett, *Kilkenny City and County Guide and Directory* (Dublin: Sealy, Bryers & Walker, 1884).

    4. *Nationalist and Leinster Times District Directory* (Carlow: Nationalist and Leinster, Times, 1888).

❀ Bibliography

Manuscript Materials in Dublin

General Valuation Office. Valuation records.

King's Inn. Register of admission.

National Library of Ireland. Minutes of the meetings of the Castlebar board of guardians.

————. Minutes of the meetings of the Westport board of guardians.

————. National Land League papers.

Public Record Office. Calendar of all Grants of Probate and Letters of Administration.

————. Letters of Administration.

State Paper Office. Prosecutions under the Criminal Law and Procedure Act, 1887.

————. Registered papers of the Chief Secretary's Office.

Parliamentary Debates and Papers

United Kingdom. *Hansard Parliamentary Debates*, 3d series, vol. 239 (1878).

United Kingdom. Parliament. *Parliamentary Papers*, 1854–55, vol. 11 (*Reports*, no. 445). "Report from the Select Committee on Postal Arrangements in the City and County of Waterford, and Counties of Tipperary, Cork, and Limerick."

————. 1864, vol. 53 (*Accounts and Papers*, no. 377). "A Return of the Poor Law Unions in Ireland, Showing the Names of the Townlands in Each Union, and Specifying the Counties in which the Townlands are Situated."

————. 1867–68, vol. 41 (*Accounts and Papers*, no. 416). "Return of the Names of All Railway Companies in the United Kingdom which Construct or Use Electric Telegraphs."

————. 1871, vol. 72 (*Reports*). C. 873, "Census of Ireland, 1871," Parts I, II, no. 2.

————. 1872, vol. 51 (*Accounts and Papers*, no. 399). "Returns of Those Unions and of Those Electoral Divisions in Ireland which Extend into Two or More Counties (with a Map)."

———. 1873, vol. 29 (*Reports*). C. 794, "First Report of the Local Government Board for Ireland."

———. 1874, vol. 56 (*Accounts and Papers*, no. 253). "Return from Each Poor Law Union in Ireland, of the Number of Persons Entitled to Vote in Each such Union for Poor Law Guardians. . . ."

———. 1876, vol. 13 (*Reports*, no. 357). "Report from the Select Committee on Post Office (Telegraphic Department)."

———. 1876, vol. 80 (*Accounts and Papers*). "Return of the Names of Proprietors, and the Area and Valuation of All Properties, in the Several Counties in Ireland."

———. 1876, vol. 80 (*Accounts and Papers*), C. 1492, "Return of Owners of Land, of One Acre and Upwards in the Several Counties, Counties of Cities, and Counties of Towns in Ireland."

———. 1876, vol. 72 (*Accounts and Papers*). C. 1377, "Census of Ireland, 1871, Part III, General Report."

———. 1878, vol. 17 (*Reports*). "Report on System under which Guardians and members of local boards in England and Ireland . . . are elected . . . with Proceedings, Evidence, Appendix, and Index."

———. 1881, vol. 16 (Bessborough Commission). "Royal Commission on Agriculture: Preliminary Report of the Assistant Commissioners for Ireland."

———. 1881, vol. 18 (*Reports*). C. 2678, "Royal Commission on the Depressed Condition of the Agricultural Interest: Assistant Commissioners' Reports."

———. 1881, vol. 96 (*Reports*). C. 2931, "Census of Ireland, 1881: Preliminary Report."

———. 1882, vol. 55 (*Accounts and Papers*). "List of All Persons Detained in Prison under the Statute 44 Vic. c. 4 Intitled 'An Act for the Better Protection of Person and Property in Ireland.' "

———. 1882, vol. 55 (*Accounts and Papers*). "Return, as to Each County in Ireland, Stating the Name of the Lieutenant, and the Date of His Appointment as such; Names of the Local Magistracy, with Dates of Appointment . . . ."

———. 1882, vol. 75 (*Accounts and Papers*). C. 3332, "Agricultural Statistics of Ireland . . . 1881."

———. 1882, vol. 77 (*Reports*). C. 3204, "Census of Ireland, 1881: Ulster"; C. 3148, "Census of Ireland, 1881: Munster."

———. 1882, vol. 79 (*Reports*). C. 3268, "Census of Ireland, 1881: Connaught."

———. 1882, vol. 79 (*Accounts and Papers*). C. 3379, "Supplement to the Alphabetical Index of the Townlands and Towns of Ireland . . . in 1871."

———. 1882, vol. 97 (*Reports*). C. 3042, "Census of Ireland, 1881: Leinster."

———. 1883, vol. 77 (*Accounts and Papers*). C. 3808, "Criminal and Judicial Statistics: Ireland, 1882–1883."

———. 1884, vol. 68 (*Accounts and Papers*). "Return of the number of attendances of poor law guardians at the board meetings of each poor law union in Ireland, in the year ended 25th March 1884."

———. 1884–85, vol. 10 (*Reports*). "Report of the Select Committee of the House of Lords on Poor Law Guardians (Ireland) Bill, with Proceedings, Evidence, and Index."

———. 1887, vol. 28 (*Reports*). C. 5043, "Poor Relief (Ireland) Inquiry Commission, Report and Evidence with Appendices."

———. 1889, vol. 61 (*Accounts and Papers*). "Return of Cases in which Objections were Lodged Against Provisional Orders Issued by the Local Government Board of Ireland . . . ."

———. 1890, vol. 27 (*Reports*). C. 5891, "Report of the Special Commission, 1888 . . ." (Parnell Commission).

———. 1892, vol. 67 (*Accounts and Papers*, vol. 34—Sess. 1). "Return showing for each County in Ireland the Average County Cess, and for each Electoral Division, the Average Poor Rate for the Five Years Ended 1890 . . . ."

———. 1892, vol. 68 (*Accounts and Papers*, no. 298—Sess. 1). "Return of the Boards of Poor Law Guardians in Ireland Dissolved or Warned by the Local Government Board for Ireland, since 1880, with the Reason in each Case."

———. 1906, vol. 51 (*Reports*). C. 3202, "Report of the Viceregal Commission on Poor Law Return in Ireland: Vol. I, Report."

Directories

Bassett's Limerick Directory, 1879–80. Limerick: G. H. Bassett, 1880.

Bassett, George Henry. *The Book of Tipperary*. Dublin: Sealy, Bryers & Walker, 1889.

———. *Kilkenny City and County Guide and Directory*. Dublin: Sealy, Bryers & Walker, 1884.

———. *Louth County Guide and Directory*. Dublin: Sealy, Bryers & Walker, 1886.

———. *Wexford County Guide and Directory*. Dublin: Sealy, Bryers & Walker, 1885.

The Belfast and Province of Ulster Directory. Belfast, 1884.

Dod's Parliamentary Companion. London, 1886.

Egan, P. M. *History, Guide and Directory of County and City of Waterford*. Kilkenny: P. M. Egan, 1895.

Guy's Directory of Munster. Cork: Francis Guy, 1886.

Nationalist and Leinster Times District Directory (Carlow, Kildare, and Queens). Carlow: Nationalist and Leinster Times, 1888.

Newspaper Press Directory. London: C. Mitchell & Co., 1861.

The Official Traveling Guide. Dublin: Official Printing Co., 1880.

Slater's Royal National Commercial Directory of Ireland. Manchester: Isaac Slater, 1870, 1881, and 1894.

Thom's Irish Almanac and Official Directory. Dublin: Alexander Thom, 1844.

White, Geoffrey H. *The Complete Peerage*. London: St. Catherine Press, 1953.

Newspapers

Ballyshannon Herald
Bassett's Daily Chronicle (Limerick)
Belfast Newsletter

Clare Independent and Tipperary Catholic Times (Ennis)
Clare Advertiser and Kilrush Gazette
Connaught Telegraph (Castlebar)
(Cork) *Constitution*
Cork Examiner
Drogheda Argus
Freeman's Journal (Dublin)
Galway Vindicator
(Ennis) *Independent and Munster Advertiser*
Irish Times (Dublin)
Kerry Sentinel (Tralee)
Kilkenny Journal
Leinster Express (Naas, Athy, Maryborough)
Leinster Leader (Maryborough)
Limerick Chronicle
Limerick Reporter and Tipperary Vindicator (Limerick)
Londonderry Standard
Mayo Constitution (Castlebar)
Nation (Dublin)
Newry Telegraph
Northern Whig (Belfast)
Pall Mall Gazette (London)
Roscommon Herald (Boyle)
Roscommon Journal (Roscommon)
Roscommon Weekly Messenger (Roscommon)
Times
Tipperary People
United Ireland (Dublin)
Waterford Mail
Waterford News
West Cork Eagle (Skibbereen)

Contemporary Writings

Bailey, William F. *Local and Centralised Government in Ireland: A Sketch of the Existing Systems.* London: Cassell & Co., 1888.

Banks, Benjamin, ed. *Compendium of the Irish Poor Law.* Dublin: Alexander Thom, 1872.

Clements, Robert Bermingham, Viscount. *The Present Poverty of Ireland.* London: Charles Knight & Co., 1838.

D. B. "Irish Local Government." *Nation* (Dublin), January 17, 1884, pp. 51–53.

Davitt, Michael. *The Fall of Feudalism in Ireland.* London: Harper & Brothers, 1904.

Devoy, John. *Devoy's Post Bag, 1871–1928.* Edited by William O'Brien and Desmond Ryan. Dublin: C. J. Fallon, 1948.

———. *Recollections of an Irish Rebel.* New York: Charles D. Young, 1929.

Dun, Finlay. *Landlords and Tenants in Ireland.* London: Longmans & Co., 1881.

Egan, Patrick K. *Ballinasloe: A Historical Sketch.* Ballinasloe: Tostal Council, 1953.

Elrington, S. N. "The Press—As It Was and Is." *The Irish Builder* 9. (March 1867): 65–66.

Finlay, T. A. "The Usurer in Ireland." *New Ireland Review* (June 1894): 304–316.

Grimshaw, Thomas Wrigley. *Facts and Figures about Ireland.* Dublin: Hodges, Figgis & Co., 1893.

———. "A Statistical Survey of Ireland, 1840–1880." *Journal of the Statistical and Social Inquiry Society of Ireland* 68 (November 1888): 321–362.

A Guardian of the Poor. *The Irish Peasant: A Sociological Study.* London: Swan Sonnenschein & Co., 1892.

Hancock, W. Neilson. "On the Anomalous Differences in the Poor Laws of Ireland and of England." *Journal of the Statistical and Social Inquiry Society of Ireland* 8 (January 1881): 123–142.

Hussey, Samuel B. *The Reminiscences of an Irish Land Agent.* Compiled by Home Gordon et al. London: Duckworth & Co., 1904.

Laffan, Thomas. "A Note on Certain Public Records." *Journal of the Royal Society of Antiquaries in Ireland* 38 (September 30, 1908): 185–186.

Lecky, William E. H. *Leaders of Public Opinion in Ireland.* 2d ed. London: Longmans, Green & Co., 1871.

Lloyd, Clifford. *Ireland Under the Land League.* London: William Blackwood & Sons, 1892.

Long, John. *The Proposed Great Munster Fair in Limerick.* Limerick, 1851.

McCarthy, Michael J. F. *Priests and People in Ireland.* Dublin: Hodges, Figgis & Co., 1903.

Miller, Alexander E. "Local Self-Government in Ireland." *Monthly Review* (November 1902): 48–69.

Morris, William O'Connor. "Irish Local Government." *Macmillan's Magazine* (August 1883): 286–292.

"A New Leaf Turned Over, A.D. 1861." Dublin University Magazine 58 (October 1861): 503–512.

Nicholls, Sir George. *A History of the Irish Poor Law.* London: John Murray, 1856.

O'Brien, William. *Recollections.* London: Macmillan & Company, 1905.

Oge, Rory. "Getting on in Ireland." *Dublin University Magazine* 41 (April 1853): 472–478.

O'Shaughnessy, Richard. "Local Government and Taxation in Ireland." In *Local Government and Taxation in the United Kingdom,* edited by J. W. Probyn. London: Cassell Potter, Galpin & Co., 1882.

Redmond, John E. "The Irish Local Government Bill." *Fortnightly Review* (May 1, 1892): 621–633.

Robinson, Sir Henry A. *Further Memories of Irish Life.* London: Herbert Jenkins, 1925.

———. *Memories Wise and Otherwise.* London: Cassell & Co., 1923.

Russell, T. W. *Disturbed Ireland: The Plan of Campaign Estates.* London: Truslove & Shirley, 1889.

Staples, Robert. "Local Government in Ireland." *Fortnightly Review* (July 27, 1886): 105–113.

Writings in Irish Studies

Arensberg, C. M., and Kimball, S. T. *Family and Community in Ireland.* Cambridge, Mass.: Harvard University Press, 1940.

Barker, Ernest. *Ireland in the Last Fifty Years, 1866–1916.* Oxford: Clarendon Press, 1917.

Beckett, J. C. *The Making of Modern Ireland, 1603–1923.* London: Faber & Faber, 1966.

Bew, Paul. *Land and the National Question in Ireland, 1858–82.* Atlantic Highlands, N.J.: Humanities Press, 1979.

Bonn, Moritz J. *Modern Ireland and Her Agrarian Problem.* Translated by T. W. Rolleston. Dublin: Hodges, Figgis & Co., 1906.

Brown, Thomas N. "Nationalism and the Irish Peasant, 1800–1848." *Review of Politics* 15 (October 1953): 403–445.

Clark, Samuel D. "The Social Composition of the Land League." *Irish Historical Studies* 17, 4 (September 1971): 447–469.

————. *Social Origins of the Irish Land War.* Princeton, N.J.: Princeton University Press, 1979.

Conroy, J. C. *A History of Railways in Ireland.* London: Longmans, Green & Co., 1928.

Cullen, L. M. *Life in Ireland.* London: B. T. Batsford, 1968.

Curtis, L. P., Jr. *Coercion and Conciliation in Ireland, 1880–1892.* Princeton, N.J.: Princeton University Press, 1963.

Donnelly, James S., Jr. *The Land and People of Nineteenth-Century Cork: The Rural Economy and the Land Question.* London and Boston: Routledge and Kegan Paul, 1975.

Feingold, William L. "The Tenants' Movement to Capture the Irish Poor Law Boards, 1877–85." *Albion* 7, 3 (December 1975): 216–231.

Freeman, T. W. *Ireland: A General and Regional Geography.* London: Methuen & Co., 1969.

Howard, C. H. D. "Documents Relating to the Irish 'Central Board' Scheme, 1884–85." *Irish Historical Studies* 8 (1952–53): 237–263.

Lee, J. "The Railways and the Irish Economy." In *The Formation of the Irish Economy,* edited by L. M. Cullen. Cork: Mercier Press, 1968.

Lyons, F. S. L. *Ireland Since the Famine.* Glasgow: Fontana/Collins, 1973.

McCaffrey, Lawrence J. "Irish Federalism in the 1870's: A Study in Conservative Nationalism." *Transactions of the American Philosophical Society,* n.s. 52, pt. 6 (1962).

McDowell, R. B. *The Irish Administration, 1801–1914.* London: Routledge & Kegan Paul, 1964.

Meghen, P. J. "Irish Local Government and the Robinson Family." *Administration* 9 (Winter 1961–62): 291–308.

Moody, T. W. "The New Departure in Irish Politics, 1878–79." In *Essays in British and Irish History in Honor of James Eadie Todd,* edited by H. A. Cronne, T. W. Moody, and D. B. Quinn. London: Frederick Muller Ltd., 1949.

Norman, E. R. *The Catholic Church in Ireland in the Age of Rebellion, 1859–1873.* Ithaca, N.Y.: Cornell University Press, 1965.

O'Brien, Conor Cruise. *Parnell and His Party, 1880–90*. Oxford: Clarendon Press, 1957.

O'Luing, Sean. "Aspects of the Fenian Rising in Kerry, 1867." *Journal of the Kerry Archaeological and Historical Society* 3 (1970): 131–153.

O'Neill, Thomas P. "The Organization and Administration of Relief." In *The Great Famine: Studies in Irish History, 1845–52*, edited by R. Dudley Edwards and T. D. Williams. Dublin: Browne & Nolan, 1956.

Palmer, Norman Dunbar. *The Irish National Land League Crisis*. New Haven: Yale University Press, 1940.

Pomfret, John E. *The Struggle for Land in Ireland, 1800–1923*. Princeton, N.J.: Princeton University Press, 1930.

Solow, Barbara Lewis. *The Land Question and the Irish Economy, 1870–1903*. Cambridge, Mass.: Harvard University Press, 1971.

Whyte, J. H. *The Independent Irish Party, 1850–59*. Oxford: Oxford University Press, 1958.

———. "Landlord Influence at Elections in Ireland, 1760–1885." *English Historical Review* (October 1965): 740–760.

Woodham-Smith, Cecil. *The Great Hunger: Ireland 1845–1849*. New York: Harper & Row, 1962.

Index